CLASSICS

OF THE SILENT SCREEN

3.00

CLASSICS of the SILENT SCREEN

A Pictorial Treasury by

JOE FRANKLIN

THE CITADEL PRESS · *Secaucus, New Jersey*

Dedicated to my wife Lois and my son Brad—
without whose cooperation this book was written.

Sixth paperbound printing, 1972

Copyright © 1959 by Joe Franklin
Research Assistant: William K. Everson
Published by Citadel Press, Inc.
A subsidiary of Lyle Stuart, Inc.
120 Enterprise Ave., Secaucus, N.J. 07094
In Canada: George J. McLeod Limited
73 Bathurst St., Toronto 2B, Ontario
Manufactured in the United States of America

ISBN 0-8065-0181-2

Contents

PART THREE: APPENDIX

Foreword

This is an enthusiastic book. I love the silent screen and think that the film makers of those days did some magnificent things—some of them so magnificent that they have never been equalled. So you will find a lot of superlatives in this book, such as "masterpiece" and "genius," "great" and "superb." I haven't used these words lightly, and if they turn up with amazing regularity, it is because in this book we are dealing with the cream of the crop—seventy-five players selected from hundreds, fifty films selected from thousands!

They have all been chosen because, in one way or another, they are great. I have no patience with writers on the film who temper their respect for motion pictures with condescension, who use phrases like "commendable" and "not without interest" in place of the sincere and unrestrained praise so many of these grand films and performers so richly deserve.

In compiling a book of this sort, the biggest problem is not so much which films and players to include, but rather which ones to leave out. It is a tremendously difficult decision to make. I feel that Chaplin's *The Gold Rush* is a "must"—yet in its way his *Easy Street* is equally good, and perhaps even funnier. Harold Lloyd's *Safety Last* cannot possibly be omitted—but this does not mean that Buster Keaton's *Our Hospitality* is not just as good. Including the best of Lloyd and the best of Keaton seems only a partial solution to the dilemma. And what of all the other comedians —from cheerful, breezy little Billy Bevan to the underrated and brilliant Charlie Chase?

And the dramatic stars? It was a pity not to have been able to include more of the real pioneers, like Hobart Bosworth, Edward Earle and Lois Meredith; such box office stalwarts of the 20's as Antonio Moreno, Rod La Rocque, Monte Blue and Owen Moore; the legions of western idols including Ken Maynard, Buck Jones and Hoot Gibson; or such delightful flapper-age

heroines as Marceline Day, Jacqueline Logan, Sue Carol and Shannon Day.

I list these names not so much as an advance tip-off as to who *isn't* in the book (although of course many of them are represented via films), but to stress that there is a definite reason for every name and title that *is* included. Every one was weighed in terms of historical, box office, artistic or innovational importance. Milton Sills' *The Sea Hawk*, for example, was a dandy swashbuckler—but I selected in its stead *The Black Pirate*, which served to illustrate so many additional facets of the development of the movies.

Since this book is devoted exclusively to the American silent screen, perhaps I should stress that the foreign stars included—notably Greta Garbo (if one can justifiably call her a foreign star), Pola Negri and Emil Jannings—all achieved fame in Hollywood movies on a par with that of their American contemporaries. Werner Krauss, Ruth Weyher, Asta Nielsen and many other great European luminaries made no films in the United States at all, and the outstanding silent films of such fine directors as Fritz Lang, G. W. Pabst and René Clair could hardly be represented, since they made no films in this country until the sound era. However, you'll find, these few names excepted, all of the great directorial talents represented in this book—D. W. Griffith, James Cruze, Charles Chaplin, Herbert Brenon, William Wellman, King Vidor, the great Swedish director Victor Seastrom—and some of the lesser-known but no less worthy directors like William Beaudine, George Fitzmaurice and Albert Parker.

In short, this book is (or it is my fond hope that it is) two things. Firstly, and only indirectly, it is a rough history of the silent movies as seen through the films that were either the greatest artistic triumphs or the greatest box office triumphs. Secondly, and more importantly, it is a rich sampling of some of the highspots of the silent era—rich enough I hope to bring back happy memories to those of you who remember the films and players, and to stimulate interest and an eagerness to see them among those of you who are too young. It would have been easier by far to have included many more films and many more stars—and said far less. But that has been done before. In devoting more space to individual films and players it has been possible to pay a more comprehensive tribute to the silent films—not just to *say* that they were great, but to explain *why*—and by implication if not by name, to all the wonderful motion pictures and the fine actors and actresses who through no lack of merit on their part now find themselves on the editorial equivalent of the cutting room floor.

I should like to extend my warmest thanks to William K. Everson, my Research Assistant on this book, and to the following individuals and institutions who so generously supplied photographs for it: John E. Allen, Gerald D. McDonald, George Eastman House (Rochester, N. Y.), Sandra Everson, George J. Mitchell Jr., Marjorie Oplotka (of the Museum of Modern Art, New York), and Samuel M. Sherman.

JOE FRANKLIN

Part One
50 GREAT FILMS

The train robbers overpower the engineer and stop the train.

The Great Train Robbery, 1903

The engineer a captive, the robbers prepare to line the passengers up. At least a hundred people stream out of the coach—presumably a goodly portion of the citizens of Dover, New Jersey, having the times of their lives as actors!

New Jersey's scenery was to be a substitute for the West for a good many years after *The Great Train Robbery*. The westerns didn't really go West until 1910.

That *The Great Train Robbery* was almost accidentally a good film shouldn't be held against it; in fact, quite to the contrary, it has frequently been praised for things it just didn't do. It has been called the first story film (which it wasn't), the first "feature film" (at nine minutes it was hardly that!) and the first western, which, in a manner of speaking, it was. Certainly it was the first film to establish the basic "horse opera" pattern of crime, pursuit, and capture. It even foreshadowed the shape of much later westerns, such as *Jesse James*, by placing the stress on the outlaw rather than on the law; there was no individual hero in *The Great Train Robbery* at all. More accomplished films had undoubtedly been made before 1903, but to my knowledge no film had so successfully combined good story-telling with good direction and good technical work.

Produced for the Edison company, it was practically a one-man show. Edwin S. Porter wrote, produced (the word then covered directing as well), and photographed it. Porter was primarily a technician, and the film has some extremely able effects—superimposition, stop motion, and so on, as well as far more imaginative camerawork than was common at that date. The astonishing thing is, however, that Porter had stumbled on to the secret of film construction and editing without really knowing it; Porter put it together the way a good story-teller would, changing locale, building to an exciting climax, cutting from one scene to another. To Porter this must have seemed just common sense. Obviously he couldn't have understood the possibilities

of his work or have been capable of developing them further. Curiously, *The Great Train Robbery*, which earned him overnight fame, was to remain his best picture. In the following years, his pictures remained steadfastly on the same level; and what was new and inventive in 1903 was already old-hat by 1908. And by 1914, when Porter directed Mary Pickford in the feature *Tess of the Storm Country*, his technique hadn't progressed one iota, and the film was so outdated as to be beyond belief. But his failure to develop into a top director (perhaps *the* top director, since he'd had an edge of several years on both Griffith and Ince) didn't seem to worry him, and he went happily back to what he knew best—the purely mechanical side of the business.

For a short and simple little action film, *The Great Train Robbery* stills holds up surprisingly well. It keeps on the move. Its horseback chases, the robbery on the train, and the fight atop the coal tender, are still exciting if not completely convincing. In a realistic sense, the film was in any case rather defeated by the obviously inaccurate cowboy clothes, the painted interior sets, and the inadequacy of New Jersey (the film was shot around Dover, New Jersey) to represent the wild, untamed West. But until Griffith's *The Adventures of Dollie* in 1908 it remained probably the single most important motion picture made anywhere; and in retrospect, with the western going stronger than ever, it even overshadows that first directorial effort of Griffith's.

The Perils of Pauline

1914

The principal characters of *The Perils*—villain Koerner (Paul Panzer), heroine Pauline (Pearl White, of course), and hero Harry Marvin (Crane Wilbur).

The inclusion of Pearl White's famous serial in this section is something of a paradox, for if I were writing on the fifty *worst* movies of all time, it would also have to be included! However, no matter how stern—or how charitable—a view one takes of this work, the fact remains that it has to be regarded as one of the immortals. Not quite the first serial, having been preceded by *The Adventures of Kathlyn,* it was nevertheless the film that put serials on the map, that established Pearl White as a star, and that set up the basic ingredients that were to be the serial's stock in trade for years to come. The debit side of the ledger is far lengthier, but since audiences enjoyed the film so much back in 1914—and since obviously everybody who worked on the film had a grand time too—it seems unfair (and unnecessary) to go into detailed criticism. It is sufficient to say that the direction by Louis Gasnier was so appalling as to be beyond belief, and both photography and editing were crude and inept. And by 1914—indeed, by 1909—both expert photography and imaginative editing had been achieved by others. By far the worst (and most amusing) of this serial's crimes however were its fantasically illiterate subtitles, written without any basic knowledge of grammar, full of spelling errors, sentences that a mentally retarded child of five wouldn't use, and such howlers as using the word "immoral" when "immortal" was intended. And yet, who can argue with a box office success? Many great serials followed *The Perils of Pauline;* in the 20's especially, the serials of Pathé revealed genuine imagination and terrific excitement; yet when one thinks back to the serial era, it is always the title

The Perils of Pauline that springs to mind first.

It had only a very simple overall plot—that of villain Paul Panzer scheming to steal Pearl's inheritance, preferably by having Pearl killed off. Pearl—or Pauline—was a trusting soul, and despite the most damning evidence against Paul, she continued to regard him as one of her best friends—until the closing episode. Other than this connecting thread, there was no real plot, and for the most part, each episode contained a different adventure which was resolved within the chapter. The cliff-hanging endings came later. Thus Pearl battled redskins in one episode, was flung from a cliff high in the Rockies (New Jersey's Palisades provided a convenient location for this), won an international motor race, was kidnapped by gypsies, was blown up at sea by a mad old pirate, and so on. The acting from the lesser players was on the same level as the writing and direction, but Pearl White— a lovely girl, with an easy, assured acting style— managed to convince one that she was much too bright a girl to be mouthing such idiotic subtitles. Crane Wilbur made a rather stolid, but serious and likeable hero; later he became a prolific writer and director. And Paul Panzer's jovial villainy was either the hammiest ever, or a remarkable anticipation of the Noah Beery-Montague Love brand of skulduggery that came into its own with the swashbucklers of the 20's.

Crane Wilbur rescues Pearl from another predicament.

In an episode entitled "The Deadly Turning," Crane Wilbur tries to dissuade Pearl from entering a motor race.

Gypsies were invariably villains in early movies. Here they have plucky Pearl in their power in chapter 12.

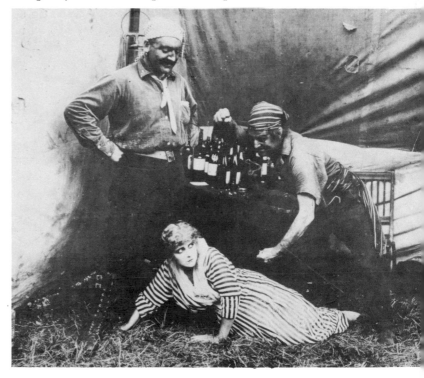

The Spoilers
1914

William Farnum, as Glennister, rides into town for the final showdown. The western town and streets were all realistic, unglamorous—and very muddy.

This first of the five film versions of Rex Beach's famous adventure novel of the Alaskan gold-rush might possibly seem a trifle over-rated to the casual viewer today, even were he lucky enough to see a good complete print. So much has been written, and told, about this early melodrama, and so few people have actually seen it in recent years, that legends about its merits, and tales about the savagery of its famous fight scene, have been enabled to grow without the counterbalance of critical analysis.

Frankly, today it is a film that needs a little patience —and perhaps a little kindness too. It was never a great film; nor did it pretend to be. It *was* an important film, and by many standards, an advanced one. Not advanced in technique perhaps; in structure and in editing, it seems quite primitive compared with the work of D. W. Griffith. It didn't have the polish and production know-how of the Thomas Ince productions. But it did have many other things to its credit. For one thing, 1914 was still fairly early in the history of the full-length feature film. Five-and six-reel features had been made since 1912, usually rather badly, and in a "stagey" fashion. *The Spoilers* wasn't stagey, and it didn't drag. Its background of the brawling goldfield town was remarkably vividly created and, whether by luck or design it is now difficult to tell, the very lack of production polish seemed to enhance the realism.

The subtitles, following the style of the newspaper cartoon rather than the motion picture, admittedly were unimaginative. The names of the characters speaking would be written on the title card, with their line of dialogue adjacent—somtimes two or three characters (and speeches) on the same card. It is a device that has the effect of taking the viewer out of

A highlight of the great climactic fight; in 1914 it was the screen's first big fistic battle. And it still packs a wallop today!

Glennister is victorious, triumphantly proclaiming "I broke him—with my hands." Alaska is cleared of the claim-jumpers headed by McNamara, and law and order returns.

the picture. But the straight narrative titles, often lifted bodily from Beach's original prose, were colorful and vivid.

Considering the Selig Polyscope Company's lack of experience with feature pictures (or even with good shorts) it was, in fact, a surprisingly good production. The story, of course, was an exciting one, and up to that time no such colorful adventure had been given the benefit of a seven-reel treatment. The story, with its many characters and interweaving sub-plots, moved along well, though in a rather straightforward fashion, climaxing of course in the famous fight between William Farnum and Tom Santschi.

So much has been written about the realism of this fight—of how Bill and Tom really clawed at each other's faces, and didn't pull their punches—that it inevitably disappoints a little today. But one shouldn't forget that a real fight often does look forced and clumsy. The slickly-staged outsize battle between John Wayne and Randolph Scott in a later re-make was certainly more exciting, thanks to sharp editing, use of breakaway furniture, innumerable doubles, and other elements of deception, but it was also quite an impossible battle, physically. The Farnum-Santschi set-to had no such trickery behind it, and in 1914, when screen fights had been largely limited to short scuffles and brief exchanges of blows, it created an understandable sensation.

Kathlyn Williams and Wheeler Oakman supported Farnum and Santschi; all became comparatively big names in the silent screen (and all continued in talkies too), but Farnum was the only one to achieve really top stardom. Within a few years he was one of Fox's most important players.

Directed by Colin Campbell, *The Spoilers* was certainly the best picture the generally unimaginative Selig company ever put out—and perhaps the only one that made a real contribution to screen history, eclipsing even DeMille's famous *The Squaw Man,* with William Farnum's brother, Dustin.

The Birth
of a Nation
1915

David Wark Griffith, creator of *The Birth of a Nation*.

Writing a few paragraphs on *The Birth of a Nation* and hoping to do it some kind of justice is like trying to condense the Bible, or all the plays of Shakespeare, into a short synopsis. The film warrants a complete volume, and one day possibly it will get one.

Undoubtedly, *The Birth of a Nation* is the most important single film in the evolution of the screen, although not necessarily the greatest. But it is the film from which all movie grammar derives, and most important of all, it is the film which overnight won worldwide respect for the motion picture medium, and raised it from a mere novelty entertainment to the status of an art.

A vignette of Sherman's march to the sea.

The first American film of any real size and scope, and certainly, at three hours, the longest up to that time (1915), *The Birth of a Nation* dramatizes the events leading up to, and following, the Civil War of 1861-65. Part One includes a prologue depicting the introduction of slavery into America in the seventeenth century, and the rise of the abolitionist movement. From there it goes into the outbreak of the Civil War, and finishes with Lee's surrender and the assassination of Lincoln. The second part of the film—the half that has always aroused so much controversy over its alleged anti-Negro bias—concerns the effects on the South of Lincoln's death, the exploitation of the newly-freed Negroes by unscrupulous Northern politicians and industrialists, and the rise of the Ku Klux Klan to save the old South from anarchy. It is essential to point out that the Klan of that period was vastly different, both in conception and activities, from the sheeted bigots of today. Whether or not the Klan of the post-Civil War period was justified is something that we'll leave to the historians, but it was essentially a patriotic and not a terrorist force.

Colonel Cameron (Henry B. Walthall) leads his troops out of Piedmont.

Griffith told of this tremendous, turbulent and unhappy period with a mixture of documentary and romanticist styles. It would be possible to eliminate the personal stories entirely, and be left with a vivid and accurate reconstruction of the times—the huge battle scenes, superlatively staged and photographed, like Mathew Brady stills come to life, the scenes in Lincoln's cabinet and field hospitals, the guerilla raid on Piedmont, the sacking of Atlanta, the surrender of Lee, the death of Lincoln, the reconstruction in the South, the new Southern "Parliament" dominated by Negroes, and the bloody clashes between Negro militia and the Klan. As Woodrow Wilson stated after seeing the film, "It is like writing history with lightning; my only regret is that it is all so terribly true."

The film's alleged anti-Negro bias has provoked controversy ever since the film's release, and further comment here would certainly solve nothing. Let me just say that basically the film *is* historically accurate—but that, naturally, it is an accuracy from a Southern viewpoint, and at times emotionalism may outweigh discretion in certain respects. Griffith certainly did not set out to make a biased film, and indeed most of the incessant storm that has continued ever since has been whipped up and sustained not by Negro interests but by political interests—ironically, the same sort of circumstance which caused the unrest in the South in the first place!

It is certainly easy to see however, why the film excited so much feeling at the time. Audiences were not accustomed to films which manipulated their feelings and worked on their emotions. The cutting, the dovetailing of sequences, the ideas implanted, all of these things and more had tremendous impact on a film audience which as yet had no inkling of the power of the film for suggesting thought. It was, and still is, political dynamite. It is also a job of film-making of the first magnitude. Since it is still a film to take one's breath away today, one can imagine the effect it must have had in 1915, and not only for its sheer spectacle. Some of its best moments were quiet and delicately underplayed scenes, with thoughts and emotions suggested by the merest trembling of the lips, or sudden look of pain in the eyes. The subtle performances Griffith achieved in a period when pantomime was more prevalent than genuine acting were not lost on

These massive battle scenes were staged on the site of what is now the Universal Studio in California.

A dramatic moment of trench-fighting, superbly and realistically recreated.

The assassination of Lincoln at Ford's Theatre. Inset, Joseph Henaberry as Lincoln.

movie audiences, and most of the players in *The Birth of a Nation* soon become top-ranking "names"—especially, of course, the leads, Lillian Gish, Mae Marsh (a particularly fine performance as the tragic "Little Sister") and Henry B. Walthall as "The Little Colonel" and leader of the Klan—perhaps the most moving of his many fine screen performances. There were other notable performances too, from Wallace Reid as an athletic young blacksmith, Walter Long as a renegade Negro, George Siegman, one of Griffith's favorite villains, Ralph Lewis, playing the counterpart of the real-life Thaddeus Stevens, Joseph Henaberry (as Lincoln), Raoul Walsh (as John Wilkes Booth), Donald Crisp as General Grant, Miriam Cooper,

The Reconstruction period: The Ku Klux Klan raids the Negro militia in Piedmont.

The triumphant march of the Klan, with Lillian Gish and Miriam Cooper at its head.

Bobby Harron, Spottiswoode Aitken, Elmer Clifton and so many others—down to mere extras like Bessie Love and Erich von Stroheim.

But, of course, it is the spectacle for which *The Birth of a Nation* is best remembered—great vast panoramas of action, many of them masked by Griffith into "panel shots" of exactly the same proportions as today's Cinemascope screens.

The Birth of a Nation is my nomination for the most dramatic movie *title* of all time, and the picture itself cannot help but be in the "Top Five" list of any responsible movie critic or historian.

The greatest set of all time, from what may be the greatest movie of all time. Griffith's fantastic Babylon set, of which this is only a portion, still takes one's breath away. The Ruth St. Denis dancers are on the steps in the foreground.

Intolerance, 1916

In characterizing it as "the greatest film of all time" and "the only film fugue," the late Professor Theodore Huff, one of the world's leading film historians, went on to say that *Intolerance* was perhaps the only film entitled to take its place as an individual work of art alongside Beethoven's Fifth Symphony, the works of Michelangelo, and so on.

These are big statements—but statements not made without a great deal of thought. Is it possible to single out any one film, and say "This is the greatest"? Frankly I don't know. But if I were asked, "What film is greater than *Intolerance*?" I couldn't provide an answer.

Intolerance never was, and probably never will be, a popular box office film. It was way ahead of its time in 1916. It's still ahead of its time today. And certainly no director exists today with the genius and vision of

D. W. Griffith, who conceived and directed *Intolerance*. Even if one did, it is unlikely that any studio would back him up and give him a really free hand. It has been reliably estimated that to remake *Intolerance* today just the way it was made in 1916, but with the addition of a sound track, would cost in excess of thirty million dollars!

In this mighty thirteen-reel film (cut down from many times that length) Griffith attacked intolerance and bigotry through the ages. He did so via four separate stories. A modern story, based on an actual case of labor troubles and the problems of a young couple (Mae Marsh and Robert Harron) came to its climax with the husband condemned to death for a murder he didn't commit. A biblical story concerned the betrayal and crucifixion of Christ. France in the Middle Ages provided the setting for a third story

In the Babylonian sequence, George Siegmann, one of Griffith's favorite villains and also one of his most reliable assistants, played Cyrus the Persian, who ultimately overthrew Babylon. In the background is the revolving Sun Image, an important part of the Persians' religious rites.

Alfred Paget as Belshazzar and Seena Owen as the Princess Beloved.

(starring Marguery Wilson and Eugene Pallette) of religious intolerance under the regime of Catherine De Medici. And the fourth and foremost story was concerned with the enmity of Belshazzar of Babylon and Cyrus the Persian, and culminates in the Fall of Babylon. Constance Talmadge, Seena Owen, Elmo Lincoln, Wallace Reid, Elmer Clifton, Alfred Paget, Tully Marshall and many other big-stars-to-be were featured in this episode.

Griffith didn't tell his stories episodically, one by one, but told them simultaneously, in parallel action. He began by devoting long stretches of film to each story, to establish the period and the characters. Then as the film progressed, he cut more rapidly from story to story to emphasize the injustices common to all eras. And as all four stories reached their climaxes, he cut with fantastic fluidity from one story to another from Cyrus' chariots racing to destroy Babylon to Catherine's troops about to massacre the Huguenots, and back to the modern story with the condemned boy starting his walk to the gallows. Not only was the idea vast in conception, but it was magnificent in execution, each cut almost mathematically planned—long shot of one story to long shot of another, close-up to close-up, and so on. The rhythm and tempo increased until, in the words of Iris Barry, it was "like watching history pour across the screen like a cataract."

Intolerance was, and is, the most advanced example of film technique. Almost every device you see on the screen today came from, or was perfected in, this picture. But as entertainment it baffled and exhausted its audiences, which were not only unused to social indictments, but just couldn't grasp the meaning of it all. Today's audiences are better able to understand it, but they are no less exhausted by it.

In terms of purely popular entertainment, its Babylonian sequence came off best. The sheer massiveness of the sets have never been equalled. Griffith almost built a full-scale replica of old Babylon!

The big battle scenes remain the most enormous, and the most expertly directed, in all movie history. Despite a screen full of huge scaling towers and thousands of battling extras, Griffith so unerringly composed his shots that the eye of the spectator was automatically concentrated on the detail he wanted noticed. The excitement and realism of these scenes have never been surpassed—from overall grandeur to individual vignettes, such as those horribly convincing medium shots of heads being lopped off in the course of battle!

Intolerance had a profound influence on film-making everywhere. The Russians, for instance, invited Griffith to come over and take charge of their entire movie industry. And, though he declined, the film was used as a sort of textbook to instruct their top directors—Eisenstein, Pudovkin, etc.—all of whom showed quite evidently in their films how much they had been influenced by Griffith, and indeed, admitted that influence quite openly.

Many of the men who worked on the film as Griffith's assistants—W. S. Van Dyke, Erich von Stroheim, and

Constance Talmadge as the Mountain Girl.

others—went on to become top directors, while almost all of its players subsequently became top-ranking stars. Mae Marsh's performance in it, beautifully and sensitively underplayed, remains one of the supreme performances of the silent screen. Everybody in it, from Walter Long and Miriam Cooper, to Lillian Gish (seen only as a woman rocking a cradle, in the symbolic scenes linking the separate stories), was just right, but, next to Mae Marsh, the biggest hit was Constance Talmadge. As the rowdy mountain girl in the Babylonian sequence, she displayed the wonderful, almost Fairbanksian, sense of fun that was soon to make her one of the screen's top comediennes. In fact, everybody benefitted from *Intolerance* but its creator, Griffith. The enormous production costs ate up all his profits from *The Birth of a Nation,* and most of his other resources as well. And it was such a resounding box office flop that he spent years paying off every nickel of the debts it incurred. Its failure would have stopped a lesser man dead in his tracks—but Griffith went right on making movies, good commercial ones to make money and the occasional film made for art alone (such as the unusual and sensitive *Isn't Life Wonderful?*) which lost it all again.

Griffith had a colorful, if checkered, career ahead of him, and many more great films. But he was never again to make a film of the stature and magnitude of *Intolerance.*

Nor, for that matter, was anyone else.

Robert Harron and Mae Marsh as the young married couple in the modern story. Tom Wilson is the friendly policeman. This interesting scene was edited out of the final release version.

Blaze Tracey (Hart) learns of the minister's arrival in town.

Hart usually treated any woman as "a lady" in his films, but made a rare exception here. He manhandles the saloon girl Poppy (Louise Glaum) when he finds the drink-sodden minister (Jack Standing) in her rooms.

Hell's Hinges, 1916

To many William S. Hart is merely the prototype of the "strong, silent hero," now outdated and quaint. This illusion is no doubt furthered by the fact that Hart's features are almost never shown these days and current generations know him chiefly by chopped-up and gagged-up excerpts á la "Flicker Flashbacks." On Hart's great and sincere love of the West, and of his efforts to translate this love to the screen, both as actor and director, I have dwelled at some length elsewhere in this book. I will just reiterate here, by way of introduction, that Hart's rugged, austere, poetic westerns were the first "adult" westerns (what a hackneyed phrase that has become!), and that the best of them stand up wonderfully well today, not only as westerns, but also as films.

Hell's Hinges is classic of its kind. Together with the simpler *The Toll Gate* and the more actionful *The Narrow Trail*, it is one of the best of Hart's pictures. To dismiss it casually as a western would be a mistake, for it more closely resembles the Swedish *The Atonement of Gosta Berling* or Somerset Maugham's *Rain* than it does the traditional western, such as *Riders of the Purple Sage*.

Hell's Hinges has elements quite alien to the standard western—including the systematic seduction of a minister by the town trollop, and the minister's subsequent drunken madness and savagery, going so far as to burn down his own church. ("To Hell with the Church—let's burn it down!" reads his subtitle!)

Hart has been accused of being too sentimental a director, which at times he undoubtedly was. But there was always real power behind that sentiment. It is astounding that his tremendous talent as a director has gone unrecognized for so long. The camera placement in *Hell's Hinges*, the simple yet effective symbolism, and the flair for spectacle, as in the brilliantly handled mob scenes in which all of Inceville goes up in flames, the real "feel" of the old, dusty, unglamorized West, all should have earned Hart a reputation as one of the great directors. Certainly Hart, on the strength of his directorial performance here, is entitled to rate as one of the leaders among the rivals to Griffith, lower down on the artistic scale though they were.

For the most part, *Hell's Hinges* offers high-powered drama rather than straightforward western action. It is the story of a minister, weak-willed, and with no belief in his calling, who comes West to assume the spiritual leadership of a frontier community. His sister, knowing of his weakness, hopes it will make a man of him. Hart plays Blaze Tracey, an outlaw, feared yet respected, and having his own curious code of honor. He and Silk Miller (Alfred Hollingsworth) decide to run the minister out of town before religion can take root in Hell's Hinges. But Hart, although he sees

The church destroyed, the minister dead, Hart leaves the heroine (Clara Williams) sobbing by the body of her brother while he squares accounts.

This scene from the climax of *Hell's Hinges*, as Bill squares off for a showdown, can be found duplicated in most of the Hart westerns. Behind a pair of six-shooters, Hart was the most deadly-looking western star of them all!

through the minister's facade right away, is impressed by the sincerity of the man's sister. Because of her, he champions the minister's cause, stands up against the lawless elements, and helps in the building of a church.

But Silk Miller has no intention of giving up so easily. He has the town's trollop, Louise Glaum, seduce the minister the night before he is to open the new church. Disgraced before his flock, the minister launches into a wild orgy of drinking and, while Hart is out of town, leads the saloon element in an attack on the church. Despite fierce opposition by the God-fearing townspeople, the church is burned, and the decent citizens put to rout. The minister is shot and killed in the melee.

Returning to town, Hart finds the girl he now loves by the body of her dead brother—and in fury marches on the saloon-stronghold of Silk Miller's gang in this Sodom of the West. In a rugged climax, he kills Miller in a duel, and sets fire to the saloon. The whole town burns to the ground, and Bill and the heroine set out to find a new life together somewhere "over the mountains."

Apart from a single blow, there are no fisticuffs, and only one short riding sequence. Hart reserves his action for the final two reels of mob fighting and the blazing town, withdrawing all restraints to slam over one of the most powerful and spectacular action sequences that he ever created. Fine camerawork, utilizing long panoramic shots and beautiful lighting, excellent editing, and a sure control over the masses of extras,

fuse these scenes into an episode of astonishing vigor. Hart, his assistant, Cliff Smith, his writer, C. Gardner Sullivan, and cameraman Joe August (who later did such fine work for John Ford) were one of the sturdiest (and least recognized) teams of craftsmen the cinema ever produced. Sullivan was one of the finest of early screen-writers, and one of his most interesting plot-lines was the one he developed here in *Hell's Hinges*—the contrasting of Hart's reformation ("a man wholly evil," as an early subtitle tells us) with the parallel degeneration of the minister.

But *Moving Picture World*, leading trade paper of the day, while enthusiastic about the film, and referring to "the genius of direction," tended to be critical of Hart's screen character, and remarked: "Good enough actor not to require a perpetual repetition of the Western badman reformed through the sweet and humanizing influence of a pure-minded girl, Hart should try himself out in some other role . . . . Hart is a fine type and capable of picturing imperfect man as he really is and long has been, a composite being, the riddle of the world."

But good old Bill took no notice of the Easterners who were trying to tell him how to make westerns. He went on making them *his* way. Ten years later, those same criticisms levelled at *Tumbleweed*, on which he had again refused to compromise, finally put him out of business. But what a grand actor and film-maker he was—with twelve years of picture-making that will surely some day be acclaimed as they deserve to be!

Broken Blossoms

1919

Richard Barthelmess played "The Yellow Man." Arriving in London from China to preach his religion, he encounters a British minister just leaving for China to "convert the heathen!"

The greatness of *Broken Blossoms* is almost as fragile as its sensitive title. It is a film very easily shattered both by insensitive audiences, and by the inadequate presentation it is often given today. An exquisite little romance, ending in tragedy, and asking eloquently (and pitifully) for understanding between different races and different beliefs, it provided a marked contrast with the gigantic spectacles and melodramatic romances that its director, D. W. Griffith, had hitherto been mainly concerned with. Richard Barthelmess plays a young Chinese who comes to London's Limehouse section, hoping to bring with him the peace of Eastern religious beliefs. His hopes are soon crushed, and his only joy is in the silent adoration of a winsome street waif, superlatively played by Lillian Gish. She is constantly beaten by her brute of a father, a sadistic boxer, played by Donald Crisp. After a particularly savage beating, she runs away, and the worshipping Barthelmess takes her in, treating her only as something to be cherished, without revealing the depths of his love. Her father is informed of what has happened, and his parental "feelings" are suddenly aroused. He "rescues" his child during the Chinese boy's temporary absence, and in a fit of drunken rage, beats her to death. Barthelmess, arriving too late, kills the brute, and then, taking the body of his beloved back to his room—the only place where she had ever known peace —he kneels by her side and kills himself.

For all its tenderness, it was an ugly story, demanding as much sensitivity and understanding as its audiences could give it. More than that, it needed the very special visual treatment that Griffith gave it. Photographically it was superb, with its striking sets beautifully lit. Moreover, its tinting and toning were an integral part of the whole; gentle rose hues, savage reds, rich blues for the night scenes, and other tones

25

Lillian Gish gave an unforgettable performance as the waif of the slums who found in the Chinese boy her only true friend.

matching every mood and nuance. Audiences that see this film in its rare public viewing today almost invariably see a black-and-white print, which is tantamount to seeing but a pale shadow of what the film originally was. In black and white the tenderness and beauty fade, the ugliness and sheer melodrama are strengthened. The film's whole balance is thus shifted.

But in its original form the film still weaves that same magic spell that Griffith—and Lillian Gish—gave it in 1919.

Doug Fairbanks strikes a jaunty pose in his jauntiest movie. The girl entering so much into the right spirit of things is Kathleen Clifford.

Till the Clouds Roll By, 1919

Made in late 1919, *Till the Clouds Roll By* was Doug Fairbanks' second film for United Artists, in which he was a partner with Mary Pickford, D. W. Griffith, and Charles Chaplin. It was almost the last of the old-style Doug (only *The Mollycoddle* and *The Nut* lay ahead before a complete switch to swashbucklers) and it was easily the best. Bursting with energy and good humor, it zipped along at a fantastic pace, with Doug hardly still for a minute, hanging by his feet as he proposes to his girl, clinging to the side of a door and swinging himself back and forth gleefully as she accepts, bounding out of windows, and clambering over an entire building to avoid having a black cat cross his path.

The film was a neat satire on psychiatry too, with some incredibly elaborate dream sequences containing trick effects that are as baffling today as they were in 1919. It's typical of Doug that the psychiatrist who motivates the whole plot turns out to be an escaped lunatic. "To blazes with worrying about *why* things happen," was Doug's philosophy, "just make the best of everything, face life with a smile, and above all, don't take anything too seriously."

It was a philosophy that Doug had propounded in all of his earlier pictures too, but it never seemed to make more sense than here. What a pity that Doug lost so much of this joyful spirit in his later swash-bucklers. It's interesting that there's a moment in *Till the Clouds Roll By* when Doug's girl has walked out on him, and he's so depressed that he contemplates suicide. It takes him but a few minutes to snap out of it, and bound after her. Just four years later, there was an almost identical situation in *The Thief of Bagdad*. But *there* it took Doug almost four reels to recover his zest for living—and, incidentally, to put some life back into the picture. Doug's acrobatics really come to the fore in the closing reel of *Till the Clouds Roll By* as he performs some greased-lightning stunts aboard the Lackawanna Ferry, atop speeding railroad cars and in the deluge of a full-scale flood. The flood was brought about by a dam breaking—all very spectacular stuff, matched in with some expert minia-tures—and all for the sake of good comedy! Kathleen Clifford was the girl, Frank Campeau the seedy villain, and Victor Fleming (of *Gone With the Wind*) directed, but it was Doug's show all the way, and no one else really mattered much!

27

Dr. Jekyll and Mr. Hyde
1920

John Barrymore as the good Dr. Jekyll, in the clinic for the poor maintained at his own expense.

In 1920, years before Hollywood had created a real horror cycle, and before Lon Chaney had established himself as a master of the macabre, no fewer than two versions of Robert Louis Stevenson's classic thriller were put into production. One was a minor "quickie" (with a happy ending showing the whole thing to be a dream), produced by Louis B. Mayer. It even shifted the locale of the story to New York. This one was soon forgotten!

But Paramount's version, filmed at their Long Island studios, with John Barrymore as the hapless doctor who succeeded all too well in separating the good and evil personalities in man, was quite another matter. A fine Grand Guignol thriller in its day, it remains a powerful and effective film even now, despite several ambitious later versions with, among others, Conrad Veidt, Fredric March and Spencer Tracy.

The thirteenth of Barrymore's films, it was the first to present him in a bizarre role calling for horrific makeup. That Barrymore thoroughly enjoyed himself in the romp is proved not only by the astounding zest with which he throws himself into the more gruesome moments (his change-over scenes, his apparition-appearance as a giant spider, the savage murder sequence) but also by the increasing frequency with which he injected himself into similarly bizarre situations, even in films which did not particularly call for them! In *Don Juan* he has a scene directly deriving from his change-over scene in *Dr. Jekyll and Mr. Hyde*, and in *The Sea Beast* (the first of his two versions of *Moby Dick*) he quite inappropriately (but effectively!) repeated his Hyde makeup in the role of the tortured Capt. Ahab!

Barrymore's Jekyll and Hyde might not have pleased Stevenson too well. Nita Naldi, as a sexy dancer in a London dive, displayed some incredible cleavage in a role not even referred to in the original story. And doubtless feeling that they were off on a real literary binge, the adaptors changed the motivation of the story completely by "borrowing" the character of Lord Henry from Oscar Wilde's *The Picture of Dorian Gray* and making him, in the person of Brandon Hurst (and with an assist from lifted Oscar Wilde lines) Dr. Jekyll's evil mentor. Stevenson might have complained, but audiences in 1920 didn't. Apart from literally *two* John Barrymores, and lovely Nita Naldi, they also had the charming Martha Mansfield, and the less charming (but no less popular) Louis Wolheim to rivet their eyes to the screen.

The evil Hyde attacks the woman that as Jekyll he loves and reveres more than life itself. Millicent is played by Martha Mansfield.

When Sir George Carewe (Brandon Hurst) discovers the secret of his dual identity, Barrymore, as Hyde, clubs him to death.

Way Down East

1920

Lillian Gish as Anna.

Way Down East, undoubtedly one of the most commercially successful of all the D.W. Griffith films, was also one of the strangest. An old stage melodrama, *Way Down East* was outdated already in 1920, at least in story content. It was the tale of Anna, a poor and honest country girl tricked into marriage (a fake marriage of course) by a callous city playboy. After a few days of (for her) deliriously happy wedded life, he begins to neglect her. Then, when she announces that they are to have a baby, he tells her the truth about their "marriage" and deserts her. Anna has her baby shortly afterwards, and it dies.

Ostracized by the community, she takes to the road, and finally finds refuge as a serving girl at the home of fairly prosperous but somewhat puritanical farmers, from whom she conceals her past. She finds herself falling in love with the son, but refuses to admit it to him. Then her former "husband" reappears as the local Squire, and ultimately her secret is revealed. For the play's climax, she was driven out into the snow, only to be rescued by the son after he had squared accounts with the Squire in a fistic battle.

Nobody could quite understand why Griffith paid $175,000 for the film rights to this hoary old tale, but as usual, the old maestro knew just what he was doing. Probably out of misguided reverence for the original, and not wanting to have audiences find the expected ingredients missing, Griffith retained rather too much of the play's "cornball" comedy content. Comedy was never a Griffith strong point, and the yokel comedy here was the film's weakest single ingredient. But in other respects the material seemed surprisingly fresh, due largely to Griffith's imaginative direction and Lillian Gish's flawless performance, and also to an unusually good cast and some breathtakingly beautiful camerawork. And, of course, Griffith's traditional "last-minute-rescue," a sequence devised entirely by Griffith, and not to be found in the original at all.

Griffith's "Simple Story of Plain People," as the film's subtitle put it, was set in New England of the 20's—but actually Griffith deliberately gave it a timeless quality, and overcame much of the Victorianism of the story by using that story as an attack on bigotry and prejudice. In his hands, the characters became much more three-dimensional than they had been on the stage. Even Lowell Sherman's wonderfully lecherous villain wasn't too bad really; just before the seduction scene, he has a twinge of conscience which *almost* holds him back. And in the end he does, belatedly, offer to marry Anna.

As for Lillian Gish, her performance is so moving and dynamic (it prompted John Barrymore to remark that she quite surpassed Duse and Bernhardt) that any thoughts of stereotype in her role are instantly dispelled. As the fluttering, happy country girl in the early scenes, pleasantly bemused by the wonders of the big city, as the ecstatically rapturous wife, and then as the suddenly matured, tragically bereaved mother,

Lowell Sherman as Lennox Sanderson, the big city playboy who loves Anna in his fashion—but not enough to resist the temptation to seduce her via a sham marriage ceremony.

Richard Barthelmess plays David Bartlett, the honest farm boy who really loves Anna, and finally wins her.

she gives one of her very best and most moving performances. In a purely visual sense, she gets a great deal of help from Griffith's two ace cameramen, Hendrik Sartov and G. W. Bitzer. Sartov, who was Miss Gish's favorite cameraman, contrives some wonderful shots of her—wandering, forlorn, Chaplin-like, down a long country road, or standing by a well at twilight, a white dove nestling against her cheek.

Richard Barthelmess, with comparatively little to do until the second half of the film, gives a pleasing, virile performance as the hero, and there is an exceptionally good performance in a supporting role by Mary Hay (who was Barthelmess' wife). Burr McIntosh and Kate Bruce made a fine farming couple, and most of the none-too-original comedy relief fell to Creighton Hale.

Despite its fine acting and lyric photography, the film is best remembered today for its great climax—Lillian rushing, distraught, into the blizzard, collapsing on the frozen river, and then being trapped on an ice-floe as the ice breaks and rushes towards the falls. Despite its serial-like melodrama, it was so expertly (and convincingly) handled by Griffith that even today it has audiences on the edges of their seats, bursting into enthusiastic (and relieved) applause when the rescue is finally effected. Barthelmess, in pursuit, runs across the treacherous ice-packed river, jumping from floe to floe, reaching Lillian ultimately at the very brink

The son (Richard Barthelmess) rebels against the puritanical bigotry of his father (Burr McIntosh). Mother, intervening, is Kate Bruce, Griffith's perennial "mother" from his Biograph days.

On location for the big climactic scene: Griffith stands by the camera at the right, with Lillian Gish in the right foreground. G. W. Bitzer, Griffith's ace cameraman, is at the camera in the center.

of the falls, picking her up and beginning the dash back to safety even as the floe on which they are standing begins to plummet over to destruction.

This sequence thrills because so much of it is obviously *real*. Griffith, then with studios at Mamaroneck in New York, shot many of the blizzard and ice-floe scenes along the Connecticut river, with Lillian lying freezing on the ice, thinly clad, and being revived periodically with cups of steaming tea. So expertly were these scenes cut in with one or two later studio shots, and with scenes of Niagara Falls, that is was well nigh impossible to tell the studio from the actual. In any event, it was one whale of a sequence.

Way Down East was a much-needed goldmine for Griffith. Its profits enabled him to keep going on his own, and to finance other massive films—*Orphans of the Storm* among them. But it was the last real financial blockbuster that Griffith was to have, and only five years later he was to be forced to surrender his independence, and go to work as a contract director for Paramount.

Griffith and his great cameraman Billy Bitzer shooting the climactic scenes. It's incredible that a picture of such scope and beauty could emerge from such a crude-looking camera.

Barthelmess in a scene from the film's climax.

33

Douglas Fairbanks as the foppish Don Diego listens in mock alarm as Garcia (Noah Beery, extreme right) tells what will happen to Zorro when he catches him.

The Mark of Zorro, 1920

When Douglas Fairbanks made *The Mark of Zorro* in 1920, he was not at all sure of how the public would react to it. He was attracted to Johnston McCulley's story, "The Curse of Capistrano," because it was a lively yarn that provided ample—and logical—scope for both comedy and action. It was also, in essence, a western—and some of his most successful films to date had been westerns. But it was also a flamboyant costume drama, with a hero who wore a cloak instead of a rangeland shirt, and used a duelling rapier instead of a six-shooter. This represented very much of a change-of-pace from Doug's typical role of the go-getting American playboy; so much so that Doug figured that the film might well please as a novelty, but could not possibly constitute a radical change in the form of his movies yet to come. In fact, as soon as it was finished, he reverted to type with a peppy comedy called *The Nut*. But when that one was completed *The Mark of Zorro* had already gone into release, and its tremendous popularity with both critics and public convinced Doug that from now on he should stick to swashbucklers.

The Mark of Zorro remains one of the best of Doug's cloak-and-sword adventures because it is essentially a product of the *old* Doug. It has the zip and pace of his early films, is fairly short (only seven reels), and doesn't allow spectacle and décor to swamp the action. It's a fairly small-scale film. It probably cost only a quarter as much as its sequel, *Don Q, Son of Zorro,* and it's several times as good.

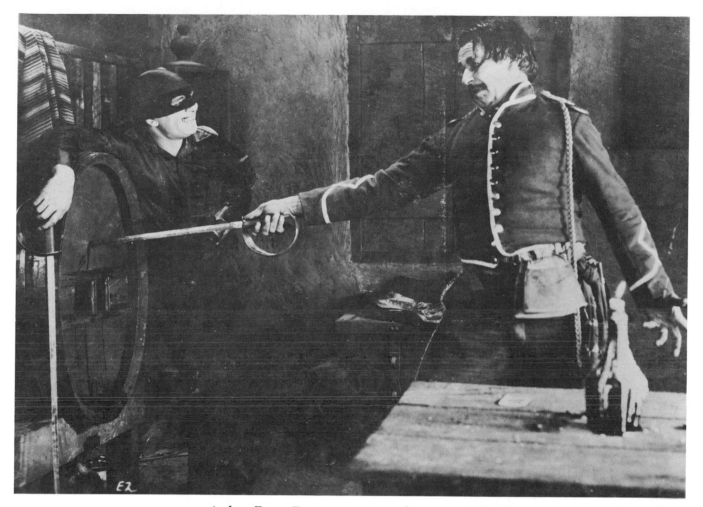

And as Zorro, Doug proves more than a match for Garcia every time the two cross swords.

As the famous Mexican Robin Hood, Doug had a chance to masquerade as a fop, with many delightful comedy touches of his own—touches quite missing from Tyrone Power's stylish but stolid remake—and to spring into frequent action as Zorro, crusader for the rights of the oppressed Mexicans. There are a couple of fine duel sequences, and a wonderful chase towards the end, in which Doug eludes his pursuers with some fantastic acrobatics. Marguerite de la Motte, one of Doug's favorite leading ladies, was in the unenviable position of despising Doug the fop (whom her parents want her to marry), loving Doug the daredevil (not knowing that Zorro and Don Diego are one and the same) and being loved by slimy Robert McKim, who doesn't object to marrying her, but is determined to get her *any* way he can. McKim, fine old Ince villain, was about the only player in *The Mark of Zorro*, who took any of it seriously. Certainly the film's No. 1 villain, Noah Beery, didn't; indeed, after being continually bested by the intrepid Zorro, he threw down his sword at the end and jovially decided to be friends with the masked hero.

Richard Barthelmess as David, with Lassie. Director Henry King shot the film on locations near his own home, which may account for the complete "rightness" of every exterior scene.

Tol'able David, 1921

Tol'able David is one of those timeless pictures that seems every bit as great today as when it was made. A piece of Americana as authentic as the best of Mark Twain, it will doubtless still be shown a hundred years from now as an example of part of the changing American scene. Indeed, even today the particular milieu that it depicts has already become a thing of the past, so the film has an added cultural and historical significance that it didn't have on its original release.

Based on a novel by Joseph Hergesheimer, it is a simple tale of mountain folk, focussing on the youngest son of a large family who yearns to drive the mail, a position of honor and trust held by his elder brother.

The story takes a melodramatic turn when the community is plagued by the arrival of three outlaws, escaping from a sheriff's posse in the neighboring state. One of them, a moron, savagely beats the elder brother (well played by Warner Richmond) and cripples him for life. The father, knowing that his action will mean his own death, but determined not to falter from the path of honor, takes down his gun and goes seeking justice—only to be shot down.

Young David (Richard Barthelmess), now the man of the family, is determined in his headstrong fashion to rush out and right this wrong. But his distraught mother dissuades him, and he reluctantly settles down

A moment from the great fight scene, in which young David (Richard Barthelmess) battles it out with the murderous Hatburn clan.

to earn money to support his bereaved family, by working in a grocery store. Eventually, it happens that he is entrusted with the mail for one trip. He runs afoul of the sadistic trio, who attempt to steal the mail and kill him. But after one of the most savage and painfully realistic fights the screen has given us, young David, shot and beaten, wins out and returns to town—less proud of his victory over the Hatburns than his of the fact that he brought the mail in and didn't betray the trust placed in him.

In synopsis form, it may sound unduly melodramatic. And certainly it has its melodramatic elements, particularly with scene-stealing Ernest Torrence playing the lecherous and feeble-minded leader of the Hatburns. But, apart from the closing reels, it is not a savage or even particularly eventful film. It tells its tale leisurely, sketching in the countryside, the people and the way of life quite admirably. Movingly played and beautifully photographed (lovely long panoramic shots of the countryside, fascinating vignettes of individual detail), it was dominated by the moving and forceful performance of Richard Barthelmess, who managed to look a good deal younger than he was. It remains his most famous role and his best performance.

Initially, the story had been owned by Griffith, who saw no immediate likelihood of filming it—especially after the not dissimilar *Way Down East*. Barthelmess, then wanting to set up his own company, took the property off Griffith's hands, and with director Henry

King formed Inspiration Pictures, for release through First National.

The choice of King to direct *Tol'able David* was a particularly happy one. Prior to 1921, King, a former actor, had always been a competent director, but never a brilliant one. And to a large degree, that categorization still stands. He is a good organizer, will take huge crews to locations all over the world, turn out "big" pictures and "big" moneymakers, like *The Snows of Kilimanjaro* and *David and Bathsheba*, and yet always miss greatness.

King's forte is his astonishing perception in handling films of Americana. His best films—Will Rogers' *State Fair*, the more recent *I'd Climb the Highest Mountain* —have been sincerely and sensitively made films on various aspects of rural America. They have all been so good that one wonders why he has made so few films like that and so many big, but dull, spectacles.

Tol'able David was by far the best of King's Americana films, and quite certainly his masterpiece. It's interesting that both *Tol'able David* and *Way Down East* were re-made a little over ten years later as talkies; but already the period that they tried to evoke had begun to disappear, and the new films lacked the ring of truth of the originals.

The highest praise one can bestow on *Tol'able David* is that even had Griffith made it as he planned, it probably wouldn't have been a better picture than the one Henry King made in 1921 with Richard Barthelmess and little Gladys Hulette.

Orphans of the Storm

1921

Lillian and Dorothy Gish as Henriette and Louise, the two orphans.

When *Orphans of the Storm* had a grand-scale premiere at the Apollo Theatre in New York in January of 1922, the editor-in-chief of *Moving Picture World* went overboard with a full-page editorial rave, quite separate from the publication's equally enthusiastic review elsewhere. Headed "MR. GRIFFITH RISES TO A DIZZY HEIGHT," it read, in part . . .

"It is a triumph for D. W. Griffith to eclipse his own great productions which led the screen into new and finer realms, but with this picture he has succeeded in doing it. No more gorgeous thing has ever been offered on the screen. It has motion within motion, action upon action, and it builds up to crashing climaxes with all that superb definition which makes Mr. Griffith first and always the showman. No man of the stage or screen understands so well the art of exquisite torture for his spectators. He takes their heart-strings, one by one, then stretches them out until they are about to snap, ties little bow-knots in them, and finally seizes them by handfuls and twists them until they quiver in agony. Then he applies myrrh and aloes and sweet unguents and sends the spectators away happy in the memory of attractive sufferings that they can never forget. His detail is perfection, and its grandeur is the sum total of many perfections . . . Miss Lillian and Miss Dorothy Gish are beyond praise . . . its massed scenes surpass the greater of the European spectacles thus far on record."

I quote the above at some length because it seems such an ideal summation of Griffith's approach, and because the comments are still very valid. Although not Griffith's greatest, *Orphans of the Storm* is very fine

indeed, and, some forced comedy moments excepted, is as good today as it ever was.

The story is of course based on the old stage success, *The Two Orphans,* which has seen yeoman service on the stages and screens of the world, in endless versions with little or no variety. It is a melodramatic and weepy tale, relying to a great degree on audience acceptance of rather improbable coincidences. Griffith, realizing this, and also realizing that it was pretty trivial stuff as originally conceived, re-shaped the story considerably—to the extent of dumping it boldly into the middle of the French Revolution (which figured not at all in the original play!). Having made this decision, Griffith as usual pulled all the stops out, recreating many actual events, characters, and introducing his beloved "historical facsimiles" based on famous paintings. Carlyle's *History of the French Revolution* and Dickens' *A Tale of Two Cities* formed his "Bible" of research, and his version of the French Revolution is doubtless the most authentic and detailed ever to hit the screen, despite a certain romantic approach to Danton (played extremely well by Monte Blue). Incidentally, Griffith also shrewdly used the film to warn Americans of the Communist menace. His titles pointed out that "the tyranny of kings and nobles is hard to bear, but the tyranny of the maddened mob under blood-lusting rulers is intolerable," and that "we in the United States with a democratic government should beware lest we mistake traitors and fanatics for patriots, and replace law and order with anarchy and bolshevism."

But, of course, Griffith was more concerned with

making a good film and telling a good story than in preaching. Here the old maestro was out primarily to make a good picture that was also a good *commercial* product. Even though there are no new innovations of style or technique, all the old ones are re-employed, polished up, and developed further. The fast, rhythmic cutting in the bacchanal sequence, as the prisoners are released from the Bastille, is a tremendously exciting sequence, one of the finest ever created by D. W. And if the climatic mob scenes, the race of Danton's troops through the streets to save Lillian Gish from the guillotine seems to be a repetition of the climax of *The Birth of a Nation*, what wonderful repetition it is! Dwarfed only by *Intolerance* in size, *Orphans of the Storm* was wonderful, spectacular melodrama—rich, luxurious, and superbly played. The Gish sisters, Lillian, fiery and winsome by turn, pathetic in her pleas of innocence before the dread Tribunal, and Dorothy, as her blind sister (with an occasional scene to remind us what a pert and accomplished comedienne she was) couldn't be bettered, either visually or histrionically, as the two orphans. Joseph Schildkraut, Monte Blue, Sidney Herbert (a fine Robespierre), and Sheldon Lewis were all good too, but perhaps the best of the other performances came from Lucille La Verne, mag-

In Paris, Henriette is befriended by an aristocrat, played by Joseph Schildkraut.

One of the many fine sets; Henriette, on the balcony, hears the singing of her blind sister in the street below. But before she can reach her, she is arrested and Louise is lost again. The two orphans are parted early in the film and are reunited only in the climactic reel.

nificent as the repulsive old hag who kidnaps Dorothy and forces her to beg in the street.

Orphans of the Storm was the sort of expert combination of top-notch artistry and top-notch showmanship that seems to have vanished from the cinema today—perhaps because directors like Griffith, and stars like the Gish sisters, no longer grace the screens.

Lillian tries to choke the truth out of the old harridan who had kidnapped her sister. Lucille La Verne made a wonderful, rich characterization of this role.

Brought before the dread revolutionary tribunal, Lillian is sentenced to the guillotine by Leslie King. At right, Robespierre, played by Sidney Herbert, looks on and gloats in triumph.

Nanook himself, Eskimo hero of Flaherty's fine documentary.

Nanook of the North, 1922

Nanook of the North is often referred to as the movies' first documentary. Like so many alleged "firsts," it really wasn't. After all, all the initial movies were basically documentaries, even if they were of little more than newsreel length. But of course, *Nanook* was the first successful feature-length documentary, and indeed one of the very few documentaries that have ever enjoyed any kind of box office success. Sponsored by the Revillion Fréres, and released ultimately by United Artists, it turned out to have no commercial plugs for its sponsors at all, but instead to be a darned exciting adventure of the Far North. Its obvious authenticity gave it added novelty value in the early 20's, when location-shot films were still a comparative rarity, especially those with locations as extreme and isolated as *Nanook*'s. So deft a craftsman was writer-director-cameraman Robert J. Flaherty that he managed to resort to some decidedly non-documentary techniques to add to the excitement. Audiences didn't realize that some of his thrills were achieved through skilful editing of disconnected scenes; nor did they realize that his igloo interiors were fakes. But this is not to brand *Nanook* a dishonest film. Let us say that it achieved an honest impression of Eskimo life by imagination and ingenuity as much as by factual camera reporting!

Nanook had no stars, but its Eskimo cast, particularly wise, kindly old Nanook himself, played as though they had been before the cameras all their lives. Flaherty always had a great fondness for the "natives" who appeared in his films—although he hated that condescending word and never used it—and his love of them, and his respect for their way of life, showed through in all his films, but never more so than in *Nanook*. Because of the hardships and dangers in the Eskimo existence, the film naturally had more melodramatic and adventurous content than Flaherty's later films. It was, understandably, his most popular film. It was also, without question, his best.

Harry Lorraine rescues Lillian Hall from a Huron Indian in one of the many exciting action sequences.

The Last of the Mohicans, 1922

It is ironical that the best of the many versions of this popular American adventure tale should have been made by a French director. Perhaps it's because the Europeans often seem to have a higher regard for American history, and folklore than Americans themselves do. They look upon our themes of the West and of the American Indian much as we look upon those classics of the Greeks, the *Odyssey* and the *Iliad*. Even the Germans made a fine silent version of *The Last of the Mohicans*—with Bela Lugosi playing the Indian hero. Now almost forgotten, the 1922 American *Last of the Mohicans* is not only the best translation to the screen of that particular story, but, I venture to say, the best screen treatment of any of the James Fenimore Cooper stories.

Its director, Maurice Tourneur, although he began his career in France and went back there later, spent most of the silent period making films in America. He had a marvelous pictorial sense. Too often it overbalanced plot, acting, dramatics, and everything else, so it wasn't always a 100 percent virtue. But in *The Last of the Mohicans* it *was*. Shots of the Indian war canoes skimming along the rivers; an Indian sentinel silhouetted in a cave at dusk; the red-tinted campfires burning through the night, casting dancing shadows among the trees; the picturesque landscapes of forest and mountain; scenes like these all formed a natural background to the action and thus didn't detract one iota from the dramatics.

In its adventure material, it was first-class. The Fort William Henry massacre sequence was a real thriller—savage, ferocious, spectacularly staged. And one of the best episodes revolved around the pursuit of Cora by the villainous Indian, Magua, who wants her for his squaw. Finally, at dusk, he corners her atop a high precipice. As he approaches, she threatens to jump. Magua squats and bides his time, waiting for her to fall asleep. The night passes. In the early dawn, Cora, exhausted, falls momentarily asleep. She awakens with a start, as Magua is almost upon her, and leaps over the cliff. But the Indian is too quick for her and grabs her by the wrists. Cora struggles to free herself, so that she may complete her leap to death, and then—suddenly —she sees Uncas the Indian hero (played by Albert Roscoe) stalking stealthily up behind Magua, but still some distance away. Desperate, she now seeks to save herself, and claws at the rock. But Magua, too, has seen Uncas, and he now pries Cora's fingers loose from the rim of the rock ledge. Seconds before she can be rescued, she plunges to her death. It may not be authentic Fenimore Cooper, but it's powerful and poignant movie-making, and has remained in my memory even more clearly than the fierce and pro-longed battle between Uncas and Magua that follows —a battle that starts atop the mountain, and continues, sliding, falling and rolling, down the steep and rocky slopes, into the river below, and through turbulent rapids.

The Last of the Mohicans was wonderfully virile and exciting fare, with never a dull moment. The camera-work was flawless. The cast was headed by Albert Roscoe, Barbara Bedford and Wallace Beery (a fine villain as Magua), but the real star of the whole film was director Tourneur, who, incidentally, was ably assisted by Clarence Brown—later to specialize in far more sedate romantic and dramatic vehicles for M-G-M.

Barbara Bedford made a lovely and winsome heroine.

Albert Roscoe, at left, played the Indian hero.

Safety Last

1923

There was a wooden platform several feet below Harold—which he *might* have hit if he had fallen! Otherwise there was no faking of this scene. Note the complete lack of crowds and the disinterest of the passers-by below; human flies were no novelty in those hectic days, and that far away, the shoppers and strollers had no way of knowing that *this* one was Harold Lloyd!

Safety Last was one of Harold Lloyd's earlier comedy features, and was quite certainly his best, even though his later *The Freshman,* cashing in on the collegiate craze of the times, was commercially the most successful of all his films. But every one of the Lloyd comedies made a handsome profit and *Safety Last* certainly shows why. It is fast, clean, and optimistic; gags follow one upon the other at a breathless rate, and yet each gag is given the proper time to "build." There are no dull stretches, either in plot or in comedy, and an abundant *variety* of humor, ranging from the pathos (often over-stressed in Lloyd's films) of his attempts to impress his girl by pretending to be a high-powered executive when he is still a humble clerk, to the fast knockabout of a department store sale, the subtleties of avoiding paying the landlady her overdue rent, the speed and pep of a mad race through the streets to arrive at work on time, all climaxed by Harold's incredible building-climbing climax.

"Climax" is perhaps an understatement, since the sequence ran for over a third of the picture! These scenes, performed without a double, and without the aid of technical trickery, still thrill while they amuse, for they are so obviously real. True, cunning camera work conceals the fact that Harold is working with a net not too far below. And some of the shots were taken on a building that appeared to be much higher than it was. (Actually located on a hill, it appeared, even from one or two stories up, to be towering into the heavens, thanks to the perspective effects created by other buildings in the lower level.) But even knowing how these amazing scenes were shot doesn't make them any less impressive, especially since Lloyd had previously lost several fingers on one hand. (He uses a rubber glove on that hand, and aside from people who notice that he does most of his precarious clinging with the *other* hand, it invariably passes undetected.) There was nothing terribly subtle about Lloyd's comedies. They didn't have the pathos or invention of Chaplin, Keaton or Langdon. They were basically "formula" comedies. But what a wonderfully polished and expertly manipulated formula it was—with enough variance from picture to picture to keep audiences happily coming back for more. Mildred Davis, Lloyd's wife, made a charming and winsome heroine in *Safety Last* (as in other Lloyd pictures). Sam Taylor and Tim Whelan directed—and Lloyd probably directed *them.*

44

Lon Chaney as Quasimodo—his most unforgettable portrait.

The Hunchback of Notre Dame
1923

Of all the film spectacles built around one period or another in France's history, two stand out above all the rest: D. W. Griffith's *Orphans of the Storm* and *The Hunchback of Notre Dame*, made for Universal by director Wallace Worsley, and starring Lon Chaney. It remains the most famous of the many versions (four of them American) of the Victor Hugo tale.

Actually, Griffith would have been an *ideal* director for this film. Its whole plot, construction, and sweep cry out for his expert hand, and it contains many of his favorite ingredients. The street battles, the lost-daughter motif, the implied criticism of kingly domination, the interplay of unrelated characters and the last-minute rescue from execution are common to both *Hunchback* and *Orphans*. Griffith, however, did not make *The Hunchback of Notre Dame*, and despite its huge spectacle scenes, it emerges as a film in which the personality of the *star* rather than that of the director

creates the greater impression. This of course is no criticism of the film, merely a notation of the differing ways in which similar subject matter can be approached. Chaney's pathetic, dog-like performance as the hapless Quasimodo was a masterpiece of pantomimic tour de force, and must certainly rank among the great screen portrayals of all time. But although *The Hunchback of Notre Dame* was one of Chaney's most successful films, it was by no means one of his most typical. Generally he tried to avoid big spectacles which tended to minimize the contribution of the actor. *The Hunchback,* of course, was the film which really made him, and when it went into production he was by no means the top-ranking star that he was soon to become. Accordingly, it was not really a star vehicle and there are stretches of film in which Chaney is off the screen, and either the romantic story or the spectacle come to the forefront of attention. The elaborate

45

Patsy Ruth Miller as Esmerelda, the dancing girl.

sets, with whole Parisian streets reconstructed, are still breathtaking, and the mob scenes quite superbly handled.

With so much visual elegance and excitement to watch, it is no minor tribute to Chaney's performance that one is always anxious to get back to him. His makeup was both repulsive, and yet withal, piteous. Thanks to Chaney's marvelous acting, audiences were first frightened by his fearsome appearance, but, like the film's heroine, soon came to understand and sympathize with him. His makeup consisted of a breast-plate attached in front to shoulder-pads like those used by football players. The hump, made of rubber weighing 70 pounds, was attached to the pads in the back. A light leather harness connected breastplate and pads in such a way that Chaney could not stand erect. Over all this, he wore a skintight flesh-colored rubber suit, to which animal hair was affixed. His face was misshapen with mortician's wax, and behind fang-like teeth there was a painful device to hold his mouth open. On his head, he wore a wig of filthy-looking matted hair. All of this makeup Chaney devised, and largely applied, himself. Screen makeup, and especially Chaney's, was a much finer art in those days than it is today.

The Hunchback of Notre Dame was budgeted at a million and a half dollars—and the money really *shows* on the screen. Director Worsley, who had worked with Chaney before and was a good friend of his, used a whole battery of assistant directors for the mob scenes —one of whom was the director of the current *Ben Hur*, William Wyler. Chaney's supporting cast included lovely Patsy Ruth Miller as Esmerelda, Ernest Tor-rence as the beggar king, Norman Kerry as the hero, Raymond Hatton as the poet Gringoire (more of a comedy role in this version than in subsequent ones), Tully Marshall as King Louis XI, and saintly-looking Nigel de Brulier as the priest, Dom Claude. The villainy was in the more than capable hands of Brandon Hurst, who, it seems, was a villain with but a single thought. Only a few years after he failed to make Esmerelda his, he was at it again, on the track of Mary Philbin in another Victor Hugo epic at Universal, *The Man Who Laughs*. In the Charles Laughton re-make of *The Hunchback*, Cedric Hardwicke made the villain a good deal more dignified, but no less loathsome.

Crowned King of the Fools at festival time, Quasimodo's fearsome appearance terrifies Esmerelda.

Acting under orders from his evil mentor, Quasimodo has attempted to kidnap Esmerelda, and is now to be whipped for his crime. After his punishment, she comes to him with water—beginning the strange friendship which motivates Victor Hugo's story.

Gibson Gowland gave a magnificent performance as Mc-Teague; Zasu Pitts, whom Stroheim always considered one of the finest dramatic actresses and completely wasted in harebrained comedy roles, was almost as fine as the shrewish and frigid wife, Trina.

Greed, 1923

Greed has always been such a cause-célèbre among film esthetes as the prime example of Hollywood "butchery" of a masterpiece that its great qualities are often overlooked amid hymns of praise to its creator, Erich von Stroheim, and tirades against the studio executives who allegedly desecrated it.

It had long been Stroheim's dream to film Frank Norris' powerful novel, *McTeague*. A previous film version had been unremarkable and was soon forgotten. But in the early 20's, following a meteoric rise as a director of daring, controversial and, thus far, big box office movies, von Stroheim threw himself bodily into his version of the novel. It was a labor of love all the way. He filmed Norris' novel page by page, almost scene by scene, omitting no detail or character, and with absolute realism the keynote of the film.

It is a strange story of a dentist, his marriage to a grasping, shrewish wife whose greed for gold finally drives him to desperation—and murder—and of his ultimate enmity with a former friend. Paralleling the main story is a secondary theme of a half-wit girl who dreams of great wealth, and of her sordid romance with a grotesque junk-dealer.

Every detail of Norris' story is sketched in with loving care: the background of McTeague's father, his own early life as a miner, his introduction to dentistry, his courting of the young Trina, and picnics with her colorful German family. The theme of the film really emerges with the wedding, and Trina's chance winning of a fortune on a lottery ticket: now that she has money, she becomes obsessed by it, and lies, cheats, and scrimps to obtain more. Marcus, who had been her casual beau, now feels cheated. Had he married her, the money would have been his. And even honest, good-natured McTeague is finally driven to murder because of money. The theme of *McTeague* was that

Trina's insane passion for hoarding money finally ruins them and drives all love and kindliness from McTeague. When she refuses him money for carfare in a terrific rainstorm, he bites her fingers until she finally agrees to give him a few coins from her hoarded wealth.

greed degrades man until he is little more than an animal—and Norris' novel, and Stroheim's picturization of it, proved it powerfully and forcefully.

Stroheim's insistence on the ultimate in "realism" is of course legendary. When he wanted scenes of home life in a San Francisco apartment, he moved his cameras and crew into a San Francisco apartment. All the locations used were just those described by Norris in his book. Even the murder scene was staged in a building where a similar murder *had* taken place. And the climactic sequences in Death Valley were literally sweated out—slowly, and painfully—in Death Valley under a blazing sun, with no shade or comfort to be found on the crusty white salt flats that form the floor of the valley. Most of the crew were taken quite ill at one time or another—Jean Hersholt spent months recuperating in a hospital from a particularly unpleasant eruption of blisters that grew under the skin. Stroheim drove everybody mercilessly, and whether it was from loyalty, admiration of his unquestioned genius, or sheer hatred and a determination to show him that they couldn't be licked, he drew performances from his players and work from his cameramen that they never equalled under any other director.

And when it was all over, there was Stroheim with miles and miles of film, which he finally edited down to forty reels. If audiences couldn't be expected to sit still for eight hours, he argued, why not release the film in two parts? Not surprisingly, perhaps, the answer was no. He had started the film under Sam Goldwyn's sponsorship, but now Goldwyn had merged with Metro, and Louis B. Mayer and Irving Thalberg were in the driver's seat. Louis B. Mayer had very definite ideas about what made movies tick, and uncompromising realism wasn't one of them. Thalberg had fired Stroheim from his last Universal movie (*Merry Go Round*) and had little sympathy for or patience with him. Stroheim was in for a fight and he knew it. He finally compromised by getting his film down to twenty reels—a long film by any standards, even today's, but not an impossibly long one. However, for a film as grim and depressing as *McTeague,* its seemed to Thalberg and Mayer to be entirely too much of a good thing. They took it away from Stroheim, renamed it *Greed,* and cut it down to ten reels. Stroheim, seeing the work on which he had expended so much love, effort and —yes, genius—thus treated, withdrew with screams of "butchery" and heated curses about the mentality of

McTeague has murdered Trina, and in trying to escape is trapped in Death Valley with his bitter enemy, Marcus, played by Jean Hersholt. They fight, and McTeague kills Marcus—only to find that in their struggle, Marcus had managed to manacle their wrists together. Finally defeated, caring little now, McTeague awaits madness—and death—under the blazing sun.

the "button-hole makers" and the "money-men" who were ruining the industry by stifling creativity.

There was much to be said for both sides. *Intolerance*, at thirteen reels, with plenty of popular ingredients in the way of spectacle, melodrama and simple romance, had baffled and confused audiences. How would *Greed*, with *none* of the "accepted" popular elements, and a much grimmer mood, have fared in a version seven reels longer than *Intolerance?* Few people saw the complete *McTeague* but all who did claimed that it was one of the really gigantic works of film art. Certainly stills from deleted sections substantiate the belief that it could have been.

And yet *Greed* in its ten-reel version is such a great film that one cannot help wondering: Would its directness of theme and its hard-hitting message have been lost in a film of twice its length, with subplots and symbolic dream-sequences to divert attention from the basic theme? As cut, *Greed* represents a masterly job of editing. It looks as though it had been shot that way; there are no bad gaps in continuity, no indications of deleted episodes or characters. (The important character of the junk-dealer had vanished completely, but unless one had known that he was supposed to have been there, not one scene or reference betrayed his excision.) Reviews were mixed in the extreme; some were ecstatic, others considered it one of the vilest films ever made and termed it an "epic of the sewer." The public certainly wasn't accustomed to such strong stuff and, indeed, still isn't.

Stroheim's apparently petty insistence on actual locale and the correctness of minor details paid off. The actors played as though hypnotized into believing that they were *really* the characters they were portraying. The dentist's office, the whistle stop, the saloon, butcher-shop and kindergarten, all seemed to breathe the life of which they were in truth a part. Metro executives were not happy with the film, which didn't fit in with their policy at that time, and through the years tended to exaggerate the figures involved in its cost. It cost a fortune, they claimed—and lost a fortune. In actual fact, it cost far less than Stroheim's earlier extravaganzas at Universal—and while it certainly did not catch the public's fancy and could not be considered a popular success, at the same time it recouped its cost and made a *little* profit.

Rumors persistently float around that a *complete* print of this film—all forty reels and more, complete with all the gold tinting used in shots of money, gold teeth, and all other symbols of wealth and expense, does exist somewhere. Frankly, I think it unlikely. But if it does, I can think of no more important contribution to film history than its being made available for study and reappraisal. Even if the complete film has gone for good, however, the ten-reel *Greed*, although repudiated by Stroheim himself, remains.

Stroheim's talent was an erratic and egocentric one, and many of his films, for all their flamboyant flashes of greatness and inspiration, were often basically dull. But all the best of Stroheim was concentrated in this one film. It remains not only a movie milestone, but Stroheim's own lasting monument.

Striking exterior scenes like these—rugged, yet poetic—brought new dimensions to the western.

The Covered Wagon, 1923

Perhaps the value of *The Covered Wagon* as a film tends to be exaggerated a little today, but its importance as one of the major milestones in the history of the "western" movie can never be emphasized too much. The first real epic western, and the first American epic not directed by Griffith, it gave an enormous boost to the popularity of the western, which had begun to show signs of falling into a slump. In 1923, the

Hero and heroine: J. Warren Kerrigan and Lois Wilson.

year *The Covered Wagon* was made, only 50 westerns were produced. Yet its success was so staggering that the following year the number had risen to 125—and continued to rise during succeeding years.

Today, *The Covered Wagon*, which was directed by James Cruze, seems a trifle slow and ordinary, due no doubt to years of repetition and improvement, but in the early 20's, its effect was startling. Its deliberate pacing and almost semi-documentary style created an impression of true authenticity, even though Cruze himself knew little of the West, and the film was in fact attacked by William S. Hart as being full of boners of fact and behavior. But that didn't worry audiences or critics of the time, who were more impressed with what the film showed than with what it said. Its wondrous photography was the work of Karl Brown, a former Griffith cameraman, and later a director himself. Vast panoramas of the huge wagon train winding across the plains, the Indian attack, the prairie fire, the buffalo hunt, and the fording of the flooded river—all of these convinced audiences that the first twenty years

of westerns had merely nibbled away at the surface of the possibilities of the outdoor film, when handled with care and craftsmanship.

The Covered Wagon started out as a fairly unimportant film and grew in stature as it was made, which probably accounts for the very slight and ordinary story-line, little more than a simple triangle between hero (J. Warren Kerrigan), heroine (Lois Wilson) and villain (Alan Hale). Stealing the film quite effortlessly from these stars were those grand old character actors Ernest Torrence and Tully Marshall, cast as a couple of perennially drunken old frontier scouts.

Despite its size, *The Covered Wagon* does disappoint in terms of action. Action was just a means to end for Cruze, and he never exploited it, or built it, via careful editing the way Griffith or John Ford did. He used that old western standby, the heroine's runaway horse, only as a device to further the enmity between hero and heroine, and disposed of it in a single long shot and a matter of seconds. Even the big Indian attack, though presented on a massive canvas, was

Alan Hale made a virile and thoroughly despicable "heavy."

sharp and concise. Once Cruze had finished with a shot of a hundred charging Indians, he was through with them, and would move to something else. His attack finished at about the point where Griffith (in *America*) or Ford (in *The Iron Horse*) were just hitting their stride. However, possibly this deliberate underplaying of the sensational and the concentration on the drudgery and sheer hard work of pioneer life, was what made *The Covered Wagon* such a valuable document and such an enduring classic among western movies.

Theodore Roberts, as Moses, leads his people to freedom.

The Ten Commandments, 1923

It seems a pity that Cecil B. DeMille invaded the field of film spectacles at all. Because they made money and established him as an "epic director," he naturally stayed in that field. Yet profitable or not, most of his spectacles were basically bad pictures, redeemed in part by exciting action sequences. Critics were always harsh on DeMille, assailing him for the "vulgarity" of his spectacles and their lack of creative direction.

Yet before DeMille decided to emulate Griffith, he was a more than competent director of less ambitious subjects—scintillating comedies with Gloria Swanson, and many of the vigorous early Mary Pickford vehicles.

But, whatever DeMille's shortcomings were as a spectacle director, he did make one truly huge and impressive opus in the silent era—1923's *The Ten Commandments.* Oddly enough, however, what this film really lacked was the one quality that has always been attributed to DeMille even when his artistry was questioned, the quality of showmanship. *The Ten Commandments* was really two stories in one. The first half of the film was pure biblical spectacle, the story of Moses, with, as its highlight, the parting of the Red Sea. This was lavish-scale stuff, far bigger in scope

than his recent re-make, and also far better in its technical trickery. But, spectacle being comparatively commonplace in the 20's, DeMille thought that he needed a "gimmick" to lift his film above the general run of epics—and so he added a second story, a modern melodrama which neatly mixed sin and religion in agreeable box office proportions.

The only trouble was that this second story had no connection whatsoever with the biblical material, and being staged in smaller, non-epic proportions, also seemed a gigantic anticlimax. Just how this strange combination came about is something of a mystery. Obviously Michael Curtiz had the right idea when, just a few years later, he made a similar film in *Noah's Ark.* There, a definite parallel existed between the two stories and the same players appeared in each; more importantly, the biblical spectacle came as the climax to the picture. Somewhat lost in the shuffle of the change-over to sound, *Noah's Ark* did not duplicate the enormous success of DeMille's *The Ten Commandments.* Despite its dramatic flaws, DeMille's epic proved to be a fantastic money-maker for Paramount— very much to studio executives' surprise, for they had

Julia Faye as Pharaoh's wife, Charles de Roche as Rameses, Terrence Moore as their son, and Theodore Roberts as Moses.

felt that he had spent far too much money on the film. Indeed, DeMille had quarrelled so bitterly with Paramount executives over this film that he had left the company to set up his own independent producing outfit, and did not return to the fold until the early 30's.

The biblical half of *The Ten Commandments* was surprisingly light on star names. Theodore Roberts was Moses, Charles de Roche Rameses, Estelle Taylor was Miriam, and Julia Faye the wife of Pharaoh. Most of DeMille's big names were kept for the second half of the film: Richard Dix, Leatrice Joy, Rod la Rocque, Nita Naldi, and Agnes Ayres.

But perhaps the real star of the show was special effects wizard Roy Pomeroy, who found the secret of how to part the waters of the Red Sea while watching a child splashing a spoon into a dish of pudding!

Construction of the Union Pacific railroad was the theme of John Ford's epic.

The Iron Horse, 1924

Made in 1924 as a follow-up by Fox to Paramount's *The Covered Wagon*, *The Iron Horse* was in many ways a much more exciting and actionful epic, and remains one of the biggest and best of all the super-western films. It was directed by John Ford, who had arrived in Hollywood in 1914 and directed his first film only three years later. When he made *The Iron Horse* he was only 29, and it was his 49th movie. And 39 of those had been westerns—with Tom Mix, Buck Jones, Hoot Gibson and Harry Carey. Well-schooled in the ways of westerns, and obviously loving them, he saw in *The Iron Horse* an opportunity to make a grand-scale western rather than an epic, and that is precisely what he did. Despite its inspiring theme of national progress and its tremendous spectacle, it had a fairly

routine story-line (the search of a son for his father's murderer) and seemed like little more than a continuation on a much larger scale of his earlier routine horse operas. It was faster, bigger, more exciting than *The Covered Wagon*—yet less memorable as a film.

Shooting the film on location in the Nevada desert, Ford used but few studio sets. And what an undertaking it was! Over a hundred cooks were needed to feed the huge cast and 5000 extras. The unit built two complete towns, used a train of 56 coaches for transportation, issued a daily newspaper recording births, deaths and marriages, and altogether lived under much the same conditions as the original railroad builders—spared the dangers of Indian fighting, of course! The long cast lists a regiment of U.S. Cavalry that Ford

56

George O'Brien became a star overnight as the result of his performance in this film. Taking orders, right foreground, is J. Farrel McDonald, an old reliable at railroad building in both silent and sound movies.

managed to borrow from Salt Lake City. Also 3000 railway workmen, 1000 Chinese laborers, 800 Pawnee, Sioux and Cheyenne Indians, 2000 horses, 1300 buffalo (I rather doubt *that* figure—I can't recall more than a couple of hundred in the film!) and 10,000 Texas steers!

The Iron Horse was a long film—it ran for a full twelve reels—and occasionally a slow one, but it was never dull. When one wasn't being impressed by the size of it all, there were interesting reconstructions of historical events—and persons—to watch, and a colorful use of many authentic props, such as Wild Bill Hickok's own vest-pocket derringer.

For such an important film, its cast was surprisingly light on big names—although George O'Brien, later to become such a first-class star of westerns, couldn't have been bettered as the hero. Formerly an assistant cameraman who had worked with Tom Mix, a boxing champ, stuntman, and son of San Francisco's Chief of Police, O'Brien was new to films then. He soon became one of Ford's favorite leading men, and appeared in

no less than ten films for the ace director. Fox, giving him a big build-up as a "different" type of leading man, advertised: "HE'S NOT A SHEIK OR A CAVE MAN OR A LOUNGE LIZARD—HE'S A MAN'S MAN AND AN IDOL OF WOMEN!" Madge Bellamy made an appealing heroine, George O'Brien's brother Jack had a good role, and such Ford "reliables" as J. Farrel MacDonald and Chief Big Tree were also on hand. The villainy was in the more than able hands of Fred Kohler, and their big climactic fight was but the first of many for them. O'Brien and Kohler were still at it late in the 30's with a beefy brawl in *Lawless Valley*.

The big climax of *The Iron Horse* was an enormous Indian fight, the Indian hordes circling around the trapped locomotive, while another train, loaded with fighting workmen and troops of Cavalry scouts, dashes to the rescue. It was magnificent, pulse-quickening stuff, slammed over with tremendous vigor and showmanship—and it's still just about the best such sequence ever put on film.

Even veteran showman Cecil B. DeMille acknowledged this when he made another version of the building of the same railroad in 1939, called *Union Pacific*. Some of the most attractively-composed action shots and excitingly-designed pieces of editing were "borrowed" quite openly from John Ford's epic of fifteen years earlier.

William Fox had always wanted to make a film on Lincoln, but an independent producer beat him to the punch. Determined to let his admiration for Lincoln be known, Fox caused him to be written—quite arbitrarily—into the script of *The Iron Horse*.

Wild Bill Hickok (George Wagner) holds George O'Brien back when villain Cyril Chadwick steps out of line. Madge Bellamy is between them, and George O'Brien's brother Jack is between George and Hickok.

This film has especial nostalgia today, in that so much of its action takes place in an old, small-town movie house. You'll note that Buster didn't mind plugging his competitors (via the posters for Doug and Mary)—but he also remembered that Metro released his films, and you'll spot posters too for the Metro releases *Scaramouche* and *Mud and Sand.*

Sherlock Jr., 1924

If any one Buster Keaton feature comedy can really be said to be his best, then *Sherlock Jr.* is that one. Others were certainly more elaborate (*The Navigator, The General*) or even, on occasion, funnier (*The Cameraman* and *Our Hospitality* had some of his greatest individual sequences), but taking everything into consideration, *Sherlock Jr.* is certainly the best all-around Keaton. Significantly perhaps, it was also, at five reels, his *shortest* feature. The film zipped along at a merry pace, getting all of its characters and basic plots set up in the first reel, and leaving the last four reels for a non-stop parade of truly inventive gags, all worked out by Keaton himself (who also directed) and by his writer and co-director friend Clyde Bruckman.

Its plot was simple in the extreme, and merely served as a framework for a number of great gag sequences. Buster played a movie projectionist who fancied himself a great detective. Actually he's so dumb that he can't figure out what has happened when his rival for the girl's hand steals her father's watch, plants the pawn ticket for it in Buster's pocket and so disgraces

him. Actually, Buster never *does* solve that mystery; his girl does it for him! But it puts Buster sufficiently in the doldrums to daydream in the movie house where he is projecting film, and here is where the basic fun really gets going.

First of all, there is a marvelous sequence in which Buster (in his dream) walks right down the theatre aisle, up on to the stage, and *into* the picture. There, the editing of the film so bemuses him that he is totally lost—as he is about to dive into the sea, the scene abruptly changes before his dive is completed, and he finds himself landing on hard desert rocks! The ingenuity of this sequence is quite staggering, as is the technical wizardry that makes it all look so real. Don't let anyone tell you that the silents weren't as advanced, technically, as today's movies. This sequence is living proof that many of them were way ahead of us today!

The longest section of *Sherlock Jr.,* however is a satire of the traditional movie mystery. Daydreaming again, Buster sees himself as the great detective, his girl (Kathryn McGuire) and his rival (Ward Crane)

59

Buster dreams of being a great detective. Heroine Kathryn McGuire has a sort of dubious faith in him, but slick villain Ward Crane (at right), who wants Kathryn himself, has plans for his downfall. Second from the left is Buster's father, who frequently played small roles in his son's movies.

taking over from the characters in the movie he is showing. Since the sequence is both a spoof *and* a daydream, Buster's imagination can run riot—and it certainly does. His lampoon of the great detective (probably inspired by John Barrymore's *Sherlock Holmes* for Goldwyn a couple of years earlier) is a delightfully polished parody. One great sequence has Buster shooting pool with the villain, unaware that one of the balls has a time-bomb concealed in it. And needless to say it all winds up in a chase—one of the most hectic and insane chases ever put on film, not only a glorious satire of *serious* chases, but a darned exciting one in its own right.

Sherlock Jr. is one of those comedies that hasn't dated an iota with the passing of the years, and with a simple musical sound track could be as funny today as it was in 1924. However, since its non-stop loud laughter would certainly put most contemporary comedies to shame, it's unlikely that M-G-M will risk putting it on the market again!

Buster is the projectionist at the local movie house, and frequently daydreams himself into the films he is showing. Then the fun really starts!

Peter Pan, 1924

Betty Bronson caught the spirit of Barrie's Peter Pan admirably.

Even if there had been nothing else, the mid-20's should be remembered gratefully for the many films of gentleness and quiet charm they produced. And for the very peak of the skilled application of that charm, one need look no further than two films made by Paramount. Both were adaptations of James M. Barrie; both were directed by Herbert Brenon; and both owed a tremendous debt to the sensitivity and grace of their star—petite, winsome Betty Bronson. *Peter Pan* was the first of these two films, released in time to be the Christmas attraction of 1924; and *A Kiss for Cinderella*, discussed later, was the second.

Barrie's delicate mixture of whimsy, magic and moralizing has always been elusive screen material. Usually the beauty of his work has been mangled almost beyond recognition; even Disney couldn't pull off the trick. But Brenon managed it brilliantly, deftly catching every nuance of the tale of the little boy who refused to grow up, and lived in a fairyland of pirates, redskins, and mermaids. It's

The lesson in flying by "thinking good thoughts"; Phillipe de Lacy, Mary Brian, Betty Bronson and Jack Murphy.

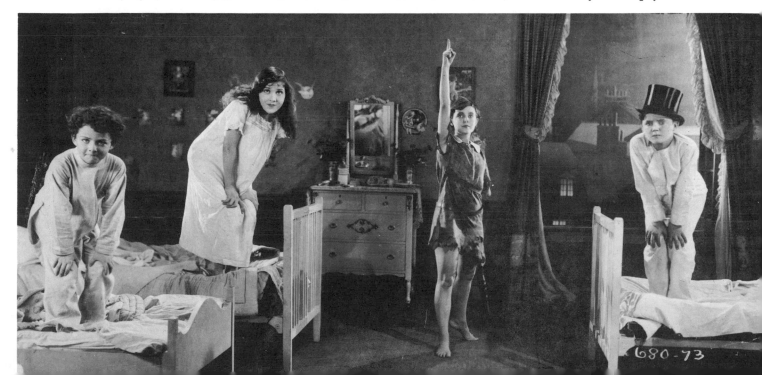

A very young Mary Brian made a most appealing Wendy.

true *Peter Pan* is open to a great deal of criticism. Perhaps because of a too reverent approach to the source material, Brenon failed to take full advantage of the added scope that the screen offered. Apart from a real ship, a real sea, and one lovely shot of the ship rising from the water and speeding through the clouds, little takes place in the film that could not also take place on a stage. The enchanted wood is deliberately a papier-mâché artificiality, and there is little camera movement as the scenes are played out in theatrical sets.

But the sheer joy of the whole production, the retention of so many of Barrie's wonderful lines as subtitles, and the admirable team work of a hand-picked cast, disarm any such criticism. At ten reels, *Peter Pan* is a long film—especially for one with such a familiar story—but it is over all too quickly. Understandably, it was a huge critical success in its day, even though it wasn't quite the box office success that Paramount hoped for. It needed the enthusiasm of childish audiences to generate warmth to the adults. And in the Christmas engagements, it got that enthusiasm. As

Peter Pan appealed to the audience to clap their hands if they believed in fairies (and thus save Tinker Bell's life) the youngsters never failed to respond gallantly. But once the holiday season was over, and the children were back at school, the film was at the mercy of the adults— those same adults that Barrie had been genially criticizing in his play. They were more interested in seeing Clara Bow in the town's other movie house!

Betty Bronson was superb and was heartily endorsed by Barrie himself, who considered her an ideal choice for Peter. (In England pantomime tradition dictates that Peter always be played by a girl.) Incredibly, her acting experience had been limited to just a few very minor roles. Her charm, her expressive face, her facile pantomime, and her ability to switch effortlessly from mischievous fun to abject pathos, won her a tremendous following overnight, and for a while it seemed that she might even surpass the popularity of Mary Pickford. And she did surpass Pickford in her appeal to younger moviegoers. For once the contribution of a star was greater than that of the director.

And what an enchanting cast of players supported

Visitors to the set included Mary Pickford, who wishes Betty Bronson well, as Herbert Brenon, immediately between them, completes the introductions.

Miss Bronson! Mary Brian made a most appealing Wendy, and lovely Esther Ralston was the essence of grace and serenity as Wendy's mother. Cyril Chadwick made an amusing Mr. Darling, and George Ali repeated his famous stage role as Nana, the dog. The Indian princess, Tiger Lily, was well-played by Anna May Wong. But despite all of these—to say nothing of a score of mermaids, and a most human crocodile, the real hit among the featured players was Ernest Torrence—a gorgeously robust Captain Hook. Nobody stood a chance against this wily old scene-stealer, and newcomer Betty Bronson was shrewd enough not to compete with him in their few scenes together. Instead she let the old scoundrel have his 'head, and his grimaces, eyeball-rollings, and other attention-getting gestures have to be seen to be believed.

As, in fact, does *all* of this enchanting film, *Peter Pan.*

The Big Parade
1924

Renee Adoree and John Gilbert in the famous "chewing-gum lesson" scene.

A giant thirteen-reel spectacle, *The Big Parade*, was much the best war film up to that time, not even excluding D. W. Griffith's mighty *Hearts of the World* of 1917. Indeed, of all films dealing with the foot soldier of World War I, it has still been surpassed only by Lewis Milestone's early talkie, *All Quiet on the Western Front*. True, *The Big Parade* seems a trifle slow today. The first half of the film is devoted largely to the bantering camaraderie between the Yank buddies, their rivalry for the pretty French girls, and so on. This was of course a deliberate build-up for the stark, horrible reality of total war when it hits the unsuspecting recruits. It paid off well in '24; if it pays off less well today, it is only because endless army and wartime comedies have made such material commonplace.

But there is nothing commonplace about the touching scenes between hero and heroine—the charming little episode in which John Gilbert teaches the French girl (Renee Adoree) how to chew gum; the bigger-scale dramatics of their parting as he leaves for the front and she hangs desperately to the truck carrying him away from her; or the tremendously moving climax of his final return to her in which he tries feverishly to run into her arms, even though he has lost a leg.

Nor was there anything commonplace about the tremendous battle scenes, which were not only brilliantly staged and directed (with a cunning assist from art-director James Basevi) but are also, according to old campaigners, some of the most accurately

The "big push": Gilbert, flanked by Karl Dane, marches off to the front, while Renee Adoree bids him a tearful farewell.

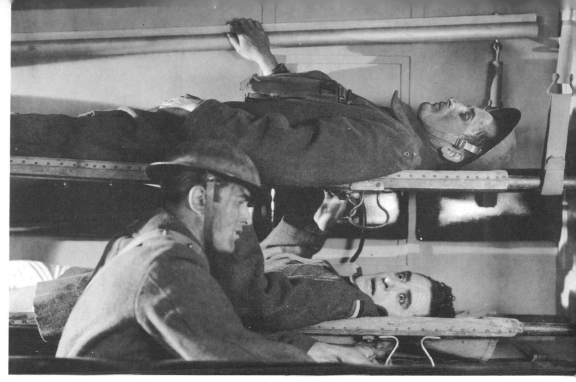

Wounded in combat, Gilbert comes to the realization that war is a murderous hell and not the glorious adventure he had expected.

reconstructed combat scenes ever put on film.

For John Gilbert, the film marked a complete about-face from his usual role as a handsome but colorless romantic idol. Minus the moustache that had become his trade mark, and in drab khaki uniform, he proved to the doubting M-G-M executives that he was a genuinely fine actor and not just a handsome profile. *The Big Parade* remains one of the very finest works of its prolific producer-director, King Vidor, and one of the artistic as well as box office landmarks of the 20's.

Director King Vidor supervises the filming of a scene with Gilbert and Adoree. Notice how the crew is down to its barest essentials—director, cameraman, and a couple of assistants. Today, union requirements alone would multiply the personnel fourfold, and there would be a small army of friends and miscellaneous assistants brought by the producer, director, and stars.

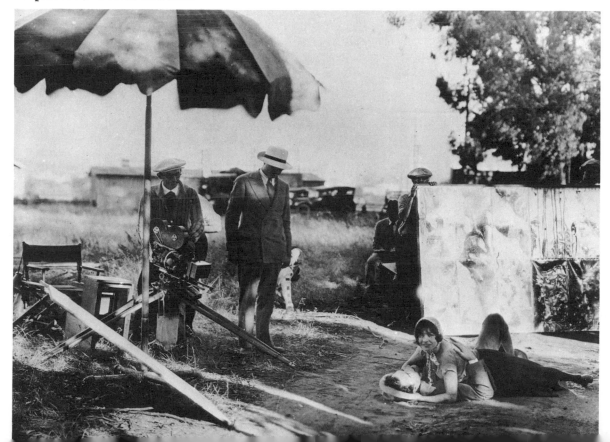

The Gold Rush
1925

When Charlie Chaplin brought out *The Gold Rush* in 1925, there was tremendous excitement. At nine reels, it was by far his longest comedy to date, and his most expensive. For that matter, it was probably the longest and costliest comedy anybody had made up to that time. The average length for the top-calibre features of Lloyd and Keaton were anywhere from five to seven reels, a length that enabled them to zip through their material without any undue padding. That *The Gold Rush* was one of the top pictures of 1925 goes without saying. But with the critics it was not the unqualified success one might have thought. Many complained of the "extreme" length (at its premiere it ran ten reels, but Chaplin edited a reel out before release) and felt that Chaplin was getting too serious, and spacing his comedy out too much. Today, ironically, and perhaps because of the dearth of good comedy on the screen, *The Gold Rush* seems to be comedy through and through, with far less plot and sentiment than usual for Chaplin. Quite certainly it is vastly superior to either *The Kid*, or *The Pilgrim*, or *Shoulder Arms* —which at the time were held up as contrasts to *The*

Throughout the film Chaplin wears his customary tramp's outfit, bowler hat and cane, making a comically incongruous figure among the fur-coated mining types.

Gold Rush to show how far, in this new film, Charlie had slipped! However, Chaplin's films, more than those of any other screen personality, have a way of emerging in a quite different light every decade or so. Today *The Kid* seems abysmally poor, and *The Great Dictator* only spasmodically good.

The Gold Rush, at any rate, despite some admittedly slow sequences, some inexcusably cheap sets (the more obvious since they are supposed to represent the "great outdoors"), and a tendency to too much repetition in gags, is quite wonderful entertainment. Some of the episodes rank among the best that Chaplin has ever created, most notably of course the famous "Dance of the Rolls" sequence. Here Charlie daydreams that the girl he loves from afar has come to his lonely cabin as his Christmas guest. Proudly he jabs forks into two bread rolls and goes into a dance. Cunningly photographed, it appears that Chaplin's huge head and the tiny roll "feet" are one body, and with a wonderful range of facial and pantomimic gestures, Charlie goes into his "dance"—an episode that has to be seen rather than described for its grace and imagination to be fully appreciated.

Scenes as spectacular as this were quite a rarity in Chaplin's always economically-made movies.

Charlie's apparently hopeless love for the saloon girl, well played by Georgia Hale along more self-reliant lines than most previous Chaplin leading ladies, produces the customary amount of expected pathos. But there's a happy ending, and comedy predominates throughout. Who can forget those classic starvation scenes, where hunger-maddened prospector Mack Swain imagines Charlie to be a chicken . . . or the meal where Charlie cooks his boots, eats the shoe laces á la spaghetti, and happily sucks the "gravy" off the nails! The big laugh of course was reserved for the climax, with Charlie and the massive Mack Swain in a cabin which has been blown to the very edge of a precipice. Unaware of their predicament, they cannot understand why it teeters alarmingly when they both stand on one side of the room. Since they are both circling the room as they go about their chores, the off-balance moments are few at first—and Charlie casually dismisses it all with an eloquent pantomime explaining it all away as stomach trouble. Ultimately of course, the cabin winds up hanging over the edge literally by a thread. Even then, despite some wild slapstick, Chaplin doesn't abandon his subtle pantomime. One of the funniest bits of all has him clinging desperately to the floor, now almost at a 90-degree angle, and trying vainly to suppress his hiccoughs—since with every one, the cabin lurches a little nearer destruction!

The Gold Rush was in production for some fourteen months, a good deal·of that time being spent on location in Nevada for the outdoor snow scenes. Chaplin

A rare production still of Chaplin directing *The Gold Rush*.

revived it in 1942, with a musical score composed by himself, and a narration which he himself spoke. It scored an instantaneous hit, and has proved to be one of the most durable of all the silent Chaplins.

One of the most poignant moments of the film: A Christmas party prepared for the girl he admires—who never comes.

The Phantom of the Opera

1925

Lon Chaney as Erik (the Phantom).

The year of *The Phantom of the Opera* was considered a bad year by the movie industry. Receipts were dropping, and radio (as later, TV) was blamed. But in retrospect 1925 can be seen as probably the greatest single year in the history of American films. What other year can claim as many successes, both artistic and box office, as this year? In addition to *The Phantom of the Opera*, the studios offered *A Kiss for Cinderella, The Gold Rush, Peter Pan, Stella Dallas, Little Annie Rooney, Tumbleweeds, The Sea Beast, The Merry Widow, Don Q, Son of Zorro, Are Parents People?, Sally of the Sawdust, East Lynne, Go West, The Tower of Lies, The Lost World, The Dark Angel, The Unholy Three, The Grand Duchess and the Waiter,* and many, many others.

The Phantom of the Opera was certainly one of the most spectacularly successful of all these films, and one of Lon Chaney's most successful vehicles. As a piece of expertly contrived hokum, the film couldn't miss. With that plot, those wonderful settings (key scenes had the added novelty of Technicolor), and the superb performance of Chaney, no director could have turned out a dull picture.

And director Rupert Julian didn't turn out a dull one. Occasionally he rose to considerable heights, in

Norman Kerry and Mary Philbin as the young lovers caught in the Phantom's insane reign of terror, brought about by his love for Mary, the Opera's brilliant young singer.

fact. The unmasking scene is a brilliant horror episode, imitated many times but equalled only once—in *Mystery of the Wax Museum* (1933). Many of the scenes in the grim caverns under the Paris Opera have very real beauty and dramatic power in their composition, evoking genuine images of terror.

Bizarre little vignettes, such as the Phantom's hand emerging from the waters to drag a victim to his doom, produce moments so good that one wishes the whole film were similarly fine. Possibly if it had been directed by Tod Browning instead of Julian it would have been a far better picture. But it probably would have been slower-paced and less commercial, for to Browning a bizarre plot and carefully-developed atmospherics were far more important than pacing and movement. Perhaps the ideal director would have been James Whale (still several years way from his first film and the subsequent *Frankenstein*), who could always be depended upon to combine artistry with commercialism and style with showmanship.

However, there can be no complaint about the excitement the film does generate, even though it is the excitement of the melodramatic serial rather than that of the subtly-contrived mystery. It is rousing melodramatic fare, reaching a lively climax with the heroes trapped in sundry torture chambers, and their fates in the hands of the heroine. If she turns a metal grasshopper, their lives will be spared; if she turns the scorpion, the entire Opera House will be blown to bits!

Unsubtle though it may be, the 1925 *Phantom of the Opera* offered—and still offers—far more excitement than the tame thrills evoked by the re-make of the early 40's, which contained far more opera than phantom.

Having kidnapped Mary, the Phantom tells her that there is no hope of rescue, and that, to quote the original titles, "You shall stay here to brighten my toad's existence with your love."

Two of the many elaborate *Phantom* sets—the underground catacombs, and the lavish Opera House interior.

The Lost World

1925

The explorers plan their trip to the mysterious plateau in the Amazon jungles—Wallace Beery as Professor Challenger, leader of the expedition, Lewis Stone, Bessie Love, and Lloyd Hughes.

Although the plot of *The Lost World* (based on a story by Sir Arthur Conan Doyle) has now been absorbed as part of the stock-in-trade of the horror film, the picture was not made, nor ever exploited, as such. When it opened at the Astor on Broadway in 1925 on a two-a-day basis, it was presented solely as a spectacular adventure story. "A Story of the Past and Not of the Hereafter" and "They sought a virgin world, untrodden by man and his passion—and even there found LOVE!"—these were two typical advertising slogans used. *The Lost World* (which had *Quo Vadis?* running as its principal competition) was one of the year's biggest stunt attractions. The reviews were all raves; nothing quite like it had ever been seen before, and in many ways it still hasn't been equalled. Even such interesting recent films as *The Seventh Voyage of Sinbad* haven't *quite* been able to duplicate the realism of the prehistoric monsters created for *The Lost World*.

Comparison with *King Kong* of the early 30's is of course inevitable. Both films used the same technical creator, the same type of monsters, and basically the same plot. Despite the fact that *King Kong* is credited to Edgar Wallce, its resemblance to the earlier film is surely more than coincidental. It utilizes the same plot construction down to the smallest detail—the slow, deliberate build-up, the journey to the sinister land where the monsters are conveniently concentrated in a small area, the sudden hysterical change of pace when the huge beasts come on the scene and create

havoc, a pace that is sustained until the capture alive of the principal monster. Then a brief lull for audiences to catch their breath, followed by even greater mayhem when the beast breaks loose in a terrified city—London in *The Lost World*, New York in *King Kong*. Even in minor incidents, *Kong* borrowed from its predecessor.

However, *The Lost World* was pleasantly off-beat and even revolutionary in its climax. The huge brontosaurus manages to outwit the stupid humans and escapes quite unharmed at the end—swimming happily up the Thames after having almost wrecked London!

Harry Hoyt, who directed *The Lost World*, was frankly a hack. Most of his films, both silent and sound, were unimportant "B" quickies. The fact that his directorial talents were negligible does not, however, affect *The Lost World*, which is essentially the work of technical wizard Willis O'Brien and that wonderful cameraman, Arthur Edeson. The story, the romance, and the dramatics matter very little, and are interesting at all only because of the pleasant and talented people involved—Lewis Stone as the English sportsman who loses Bessie Love to newspaperman Lloyd Hughes; Wallace Beery as the intrepid Professor Challenger, head of the expedition, and a heavily made-up Bull Montana as an apeman. Capturing the interest (and the footage) to a far more spectacular degree are the superbly created tricks of O'Brien—the savage fights between brontosaurus, pterdodactyl, dinasour and other monsters, all life-like in their move-

The brontosaurus that is finally captured alive and taken to London—where it escapes, of course! Scenes like this actually looked far more convincing in the film itself than on stills. Since such scenes never actually took place for a cameraman to photograph, the stills had to be faked reconstructions of scenes in the film. And technical trickery in a lab, where several negatives are matched together, can somehow never be equalled by the trickery at the disposal of the still cameraman. But take our word for it—every foot of *The Lost World* looked uncomfortably real!

ments, and given to astonishingly human eye-rollings and sneers; and, of course, the brilliantly constructed episode of the brontosaurus running amok in the streets of London. Some of the effects must have entailed a staggering amount of work, particularly a wild stampede of monsters during a (red-tinted) volcanic eruption, and a delightful shot of a playful family of some half-dozen brontosauri feeding on the carcass of another beast.

The Lost World is the grand-daddy of all the "monster" thriller—and shares with *King Kong* first place among them.

An attack by a tyrannosaurus!

The Three Faces of Betty Bronson in *A Kiss for Cinderella*: (1) As the London slavey; (2) dressed-up, storybook fashion, as Cinderella, she waits in the cold night air, near delirium, for her Fairy Godmother to arrive; and (3) as Cinderella in the dream sequence.

A Kiss for Cinderella, 1925

Even *Peter Pan* seemed almost ordinary by comparison when, the following year, director Brenon and star Bronson teamed again to make this second adaptation from Barrie. One of the loveliest and most poignant films ever screened, it was, sad to relate, a flop at the box office—putting an immediate end to further follow-ups.

This was much more penetrating Barrie fare. Although it had wonderful fairy-tale ingredients, it was too deep to be considered a real children's film. And a year after *Peter Pan*, the paying public was less interested in Barrie's philosophies than ever. Gentle charm (except in the comedies of Langdon and Chaplin) was no longer box office; even sincerely-wrought patriotism was considered quaint and old-hat. (Griffith's *America* had been box office failure.) The tempo of the times was really being stepped up; it was the jazz age, and films had to exude that same pep, if they wanted to succeed. Of course, many fine films that were not flaming-20's epics did do well, but Barrie whimsy was definitely out.

This was doubly sad because in his new film Brenon had obviously striven to rectify the mistakes of *Peter Pan*. Despite a story-line which limited itself, in stage fashion, to "acts" and to only two or three sets, this was a *film* in every sense of the word. The sets were ornate, when called for, and always solid and convincing. The photography, far more than in *Peter Pan*, captured a genuine feeling of fairy-tale magic. The trick photography—the pumpkin and mice changing into the coach and horses, to gallop proudly through the clouds to a shimmering palace—was stunning. And the elaborate dream sequence, in which the Cockney waif sees herself meeting Prince Charming at an exaggeratedly luxurious Royal Ball, staged in terms of her own Cockney imagination, was a fantastically sumptuous and magical episode.

Pictorially alone, *A Kiss for Cinderella* is a masterpiece; but by any standards—direction, adaptation, performance—it is a film of lasting greatness. Certainly it was the best film that Herbert Brenon ever directed, and it was far more of a director's film than *Peter Pan* had been. Betty Bronson had matured as an actress, and added rare poignancy to the moments of sadness. Her sprightly sense of fun was well in evidence too. In many ways, it was an even better performance than her Peter. But *A Kiss for Cinderella* was not a "vehicle" in the same way that *Peter Pan* had been, and one

Tom Moore, as a kindly London policeman, reappeared in the dream as Prince Charming.

remembers not so much the individual performance of its star as the loveliness and poetry of the entire film.

Playing with Miss Bronson this time was Tom Moore, effectively underplaying, giving a surprisingly subtle performance for a man who usually played straightforward, uncomplicated heroes. And Esther Ralston was again on hand with her beauty and charm, making the most perfect Fairy Godmother that Barrie, or anyone else, could have asked for.

A Kiss for Cinderella hasn't dated one iota; it's as moving and exhilarating now as it was over 30 years ago; what a pity that it and *Peter Pan* aren't made the perennial Christmas attraction at museums and other institutions all over the country, as they are at Rochester's Eastman House, where every year children and adults alike are delighted anew by these two wonderful movies.

Esther Ralston, as the Fairy Godmother, prepares to make all of Cinderella's dreams come true.

Son of the Sheik
1926

Valentino as Ahmed, and lovely Vilma Banky as Yasmin, the dancing girl he falls in love with.

Like Garbo, Valentino never made a really great picture. Perhaps the two most magnetic movie-names of all time, these two personalities don't have a single "classic" between them. Box-office block-busters, yes, but "art" films, no. But, apart from being grand entertainment, *Son of the Sheik* did come closest to being a masterpiece, in its own particular way.

Valentino made it in 1926, after a string of pictures that were, to his way of thinking, unsatisfactory both as pictures and as vehicles for himself. He wanted a solid hit and, away from contractual obligations, he was able to make the sort of film he wanted. And what could be safer than a follow-up to his 1921 smash-hit, *The Sheik?* It had been crudely made and was outdated even in 1921, but it established him as an idol.

Ambushed by desert brigands, led by Yasmin's renegade father, Ahmed puts up a stiff battle but is finally subdued and savagely whipped.

In his new film, he planned to correct the mistakes, and give his career a needed boost. Possibly he might have succeeded, for the film was all he hoped it would be but, alas, death struck him down before it could go into release.

Son of the Sheik has been revived constantly, both in theatres and on television, and the reasons are quite obvious. Even apart from the fact that it presents Valentino in such a colorful and famous role, the film packs in all the essential ingredients of mass popular entertainment, and they are ingredients that haven't dated to any marked degree either in their content or their presentation. It tells a full-blooded and exotic romantic story in terms that the allegedly more sophisticated contemporary cinema has "outgrown." Only veteran moviegoers from the 20's can fully realize what a loss has been sustained in favor of that "sophistication." *Son of the Sheik* is a wonderful melodrama too, replete with threatened fates-worse-than-death, desert chases, last minute rescues, stunts and furious fights. All of it is subtly tongue-in-cheek and not designed to be taken *too* seriously. (In this respect it has some of the Douglas Fairbanks flavor.) But it isn't a spoof. It invites the audience to have fun with it, but at no time does it ridicule those elements which make it so much fun. No one has ever pretended that this film was "art"—but it does represent a peak in polished hokum and showmanship backed by all the arts and techniques acquired by motion pictures in the mid-20's, when Hollywood was still a wonderland, and the movies spelled glamor. The artistic masterpieces of the period have never been surpassed, and nor have the masterpieces of "hoke" and make-believe, of which this Valentino film is a prime example. Beauty is opposed in true fairy-tale fashion by repugnant ugliness, good by unmitigated evil.

French-born director George Fitzmaurice was justly famous for his stylish adventure-romances of the period; William Cameron Menzies' sets gleam and glisten; the photography of George Barnes is rich and luxurious, utilizing the Yuma, Arizona, landscapes as well as Herbert Brenon did for *Beau Geste* the following year. Yuma was a very popular double for Arabia in the mid-20's.

Valentino's characterization is of a type that has completely disappeared from the screen today. The gentlemanly hero with dishonorable (if unrealized) intentions just doesn't stand a chance with today's production code. Thus he has been replaced by the hero whose intentions are always honorable, but who is, alas, *never* a gentleman! Valentino, Barrymore, Lewis Stone, Adolphe Menjou and Clive Brook have

In the original *The Sheik* Valentino kidnapped the English heiress played by Agnes Ayres. In the sequel they recreated their roles of the Sheik and Diana.

given over the leading ladies to the louts: the Widmarks, the Palances, the Mitchums. However, since Vilma Banky, Dolores Costello, and Norma Shearer have been replaced by Mamie Van Doren, Terry Moore, and Jayne Mansfield, perhaps matters aren't as tragic as they might be. Hero and heroine are now pretty evenly matched in aggressiveness.

Valentino played a dual role in *Son of the Sheik,* as both father (below) and son.

Mary as the tender-hearted but tough little orphan who protects the smaller fry from the evil Grimes.

Sparrows, 1926

I have selected *Sparrows* as the best of the Mary Pickford vehicles somewhat arbitrarily. They were all so good that it is almost impossible to select a "best," or

Honest sentiment, with a dash of religion here and there, was a trademark of all the Pickford vehicles.

even a "most typical." *Sparrows*, however, seems to combine best the two basic aspects of Pickford's work, aspects that were not always present in the same film —sentiment, and vigorous adventure. Mary was a boisterous little tomboy in most of her films, and she packed a good many thrills into all her pictures. *Sparrows* was certainly the most thrilling of them all. In fact, it is basically a horror story and must have caused a few healthy nightmares among youthful audiences in its day.

The story has Mary as the eldest of a group of orphans, held in bondage by a villainous farmer. He takes the kids over from the orphanage, solely for the maintenance pay that goes with them, then puts them to work night and day on his farm, and feeds them a starvation diet of potatoes—*if* they behave. And when they don't, there'd be hell to pay if it weren't for gallant little Mary and her ever-ready pitchfork. Since the villain was played by demon-faced Gustav von Seyffertitz, and since his "farm" was located in the middle of an alligator-infested and quicksand-pitted swamp, Mary had quite a problem on her hands.

The final desperate escape attempt, over sinking mud and rotting timbers that threaten to drop her and her charges to the alligators, was a real thriller! Melodramatic yes—and how!—but what superb movie-making. A few lines of synopsis can hardly hope to do justice to the film, which so expertly weaved its sentiment and thrills together under Mary's magic spell. And the superb photography and fine atmospheric sets were big plus factors, too. Western star Roy

Stewart had the official male lead, but it was actually a comparatively minor role as the father of one of the children who falls into the clutches of the villainous Farmer Grimes. And great as the magnificent skulduggery of Gustav von Seyffertitz was, it didn't stand much of a chance against the sunny smile and energetic gusto of Mary. Quite incidentally, the film provides a welcome reminder of what a really fine director William Beaudine was in the silent era, long before he became the principal director of the Bowery Boys "B" comedies.

The evil swampland farmer, Gustav von Seyffertitz, is held at bay by plucky Mary.

The escape of the orphans through the quicksands of the Florida swamp was a terrifying and exciting sequence.

If you think this scene is a thriller, you should see it in the actual film—where the rotting tree bough constantly slides and slips, threatening to tumble the youngsters to the hungry crocodiles below!

77

The Scarlet Letter

1926

Lillian Gish as Hester Prynne, one of her most memorable roles.

When Nathaniel Hawthorne wrote *The Scarlet Letter* in 1850, he doubted that it would achieve any popular success because, as he put it ". . . my writings do not appeal to the broadest class of sympathies and therefore will not obtain a wide popularity. The main narrative lacks sunshine."

It is a decidedly heavy story of a prim New England seamstress in the Puritan era, the wife of a doctor who had been called away before the marriage could be consummated, and who had since, apparently, disappeared. She falls in love with the village pastor, bears his child, and insists that he keep silent, since his spiritual leadership to the community is so important. Ultimately, the husband returns, and the pastor, tortured by his conscience, confesses his "sin" publicly, and dies in front of the congregation that has worshipped him—and scorned the seamstress and her child.

The book *was* a success, and no fewer than three movie versions were made before the Lillian Gish version for M-G-M in 1926. (There was also a talkie re-make with Colleen Moore.) Certainly Miss Gish's version was by far the best of them all, and also one of the screen's most skilful literary adaptations.

Made by the noted Swedish director Victor Seastrom, it is perhaps the most un-American film ever put out by Metro, especially during the Louis B. Mayer regime. (The phrase "un-American" is of course used in its literal, not its current political sense.) The austere theme and backgrounds, the intermingling of beauty and sensitivity with bigotry and stark tragedy, these were all elements that were second nature to the Scandinavian directors. Even the photography was affected by this Scandinavian approach. Hendrik Sartov's camerawork is magnificent throughout, but it has a cold, organized beauty, and not the lush, spontaneous beauty that Sartov had created under Griffith for Miss Gish's earlier *Way Down East*.

Notwithstanding the fine performances of Lars

The denouement: Reverend Dimmesdale (Lars Hanson) dies in the arms of Hester Prynne (Lillian Gish) after publicly admitting he is the father of her child.

Hanson as the pastor, and Henry B. Walthall as the husband, *The Scarlet Letter* has to stand on the performance of its star—and even with *Way Down East* and *La Bohème* taken into consideration, Lillian Gish's performance here is almost certainly her finest in any film.

Preparing for the long tracking shot through the woods in the early part of the film; Miss Gish at left, Hendrik Sartov behind the camera, and director Victor Seastrom at right, with hand in pocket.

79

Stella (Belle Bennett) and her husband (Ronald Colman) are interrupted by Jean Hersholt, who specialized in playing repulsive "other men" long before he became the heartwarming "Dr. Christian" of radio.

Stella Dallas, 1926

Sam Goldwyn's productions in the 20's were all real "showman's pictures"—big, glossy, laden with stars (the Ronald Colman-Vilma Banky team was a Goldwyn creation), and offering movie audiences solid entertainment. In a way, I am surprised that *Stella Dallas* is the only one of his pictures to make this top 50 listing, and I suppose one must put it down to the fact that his films were such good "all-around" vehicles that they missed the extremes of either great artistry or great box office appeal.

Stella Dallas, anyway, was one of his most successful pictures and also one of his best in a purely aesthetic sense. Its story is frankly "soap opera,"—and as such it survived for a quarter of a century on radio. It is a tale of a mother who sacrifices everything for her child through the years, the film coming to a

tear-stained climax with the mother watching her grown child's happiness through a window, being unable to identify herself without ruining that happiness, and being denied even this vicarious joy by a cop who tells her to "move along."

But Goldwyn's 1926 version was amazingly free from maudlin sentimentality. Acting and direction working together enabled it to rise above its trite content and emerge as really powerful, dramatic material. More than that, it proved to be a realistic and convincing picture of a certain strata of American life as centred around a medium-sized industrial town. Credit for this near-miracle must surely go to director Henry King, who has often shown a definite affinity with themes of Americana, ranging from *Tol'able David*, discussed elsewhere in this volume, to such talkies as *State Fair* and *I'll Climb the Highest Mountain. Stella Dallas* was helped by a fine cast, too—Belle Bennett in a most moving performance as the luckless Stella, Ronald Colman as her husband, and lovely Lois Moran as their daughter. Alice Joyce and Jean Hersholt contributed sterling performances, too, and Douglas Fairbanks, Jr., was very appealing as Lois Moran's fiancé.

Romantic stories and soap operas often succeeded so well in the 20's because they were so big, glossy and polished, in the best ladies' magazine style. *Stella Dallas* paid off in terms of conviction and sincerity rather than gloss and showmanship, and its underplayed acting and direction were extremely rare for that type of picture at that particular moment in the march of the film.

The film's climactic scene: Stella, alone and forgotten, peers through a window as her daughter (Lois Moran) is married to Douglas Fairbanks, Jr. Alice Joyce stands behind the newlyweds.

In the climactic reel, Doug—ostensibly a pirate, but actually, of course, a nobleman—finally has a showdown with the No. 1 villain, Sam de Grasse. Billie Dove (unbeknownst to Doug, she's of noble birth too—a princess in fact) waits anxiously, but confidently, for the outcome. The bearded pirate by her side (the inevitable tough old sea dog with a heart of gold) is Donald Crisp.

The Black Pirate, 1926

After four highly successful but ponderous spectacles—*The Three Musketeers, Robin Hood, The Thief of Bagdad* and *Don Q. Son of Zorro*—Douglas Fairbanks made a welcome return to at least a semblance of his former style with this 1926 swashbuckler. His previous four films had been huge, sprawling, but meticulously made films, in which Doug, obviously emulating D. W. Griffith, whose subjects warranted a more serious approach, let sheer size and story importance swamp his own brash sense of humor, and his fast-paced excitement. Even though the films had been big money-makers, Doug presumably realized that he had been slipping away from his true movie-character, and *The Black Pirate* brought him back with a vengeance. In case anybody should mistakenly take the film seriously, Doug inserted a joyful opening title about the playful habits of pirates. He made it plain that this was just to be a schoolboy romp—and it was. There was no marked increase in the comedy content, but there was much more energy to the whole thing. It was Doug's shortest film in quite a while—a mere eight reels as against the twelve reels he had become accustomed to—and there were no dull stretches. Too,

the film was superbly photographed (by Henry Sharpe) in an early two-color Technicolor, which produced extremely pleasing and restful effects, especially of green palms and golden sands.

Although Doug used a double in the famous scene in which he slides down the sail on a knife, he still had a fantastic agility and grace, and there was no doubling in the duelling scenes. One sword duel, with villain Anders Randolf, was one of the best things of its kind ever put on film. The cast was extremely accomplished, with Billie Dove—a beautiful and graceful leading lady—most appealing as the princess-in-distress, with Sam de Grasse as a fine sneering buccaneer villain, and Donald Crisp as the inevitable rough old pirate with a heart of gold. Charlie Stevens, a grandson of Indian warrior Geronimo, and a great friend of Doug's (he appeared in almost all of Fairbanks' films) was well in evidence in six or seven extra roles; no sooner was he blown up as one pirate, than he reappeared as another!

Directed by Albert Parker, *The Black Pirate* was quite one of the most exhilarating films of 1926.

Don Juan, 1926

John Barrymore seemed born to play the role of the immortal Don Juan. Errol Flynn made a commendable Don in a talkie version but there was only one Barrymore!

Don Juan was the first Warner film with a fully synchronized musical score and, backed by an interesting program of sound short subjects, was used to introduce the Vitaphone system at a great gala premiere in New York. Unfortunately, the importance of the occasion as an industry landmark has tended, through the years, to cause *Don Juan* to be overlooked as a film in its own right. A great pity this, for in its own field it was quite a wonderful film, rich, flamboyant, lush, full of pep, just the right amount of tongue-in-cheek, and with a collection of fine performances that were all larger than life, but never once approached lampoon. It was a superbly staged and directed production, one of the best of that much under-rated and now sadly forgotten director, Alan Crosland.

In contrast to some of Barrymore's earlier costume dramas, specifically the slow and dull *Beau Brummel*, *Don Juan* was full of life, from the beginning of Barrymore's appearance as his own aged father in a prologue, to the swashbuckling chase climax. A light-hearted cloak-and-dagger adventure (with the fun

John Barrymore as Don Juan with demure and charming Mary Astor, who had been his leading lady three years earlier in *Beau Brummel*.

never lessening the effect of the thrills), it was an enjoyable romp of romantic intrigue at the court of the Borgias, with John Barrymore's duel with Montague Love the highlight of the production. A classic of its kind, packing tremendous excitement, superbly photographed and edited, it remains quite unsurpassed to this day. But *Don Juan* had much more to offer as well—some delightfully boisterous orgy scenes; a wonderful episode in a torture chamber, in which Barrymore, without the aid of makeup, so contorts his features that he takes on (believably) the lineaments of his torturer (that ace villain, Gustav von Seyffertitz); an escape from a prison cell and across the turbulent Tiber; and, of course, romantic scenes done with the grace, sensitivity and passion that none but Barrymore could approach. And what a cast he had to support him: lovely Mary Astor as the lady in several kinds of distress, Warner Oland and Estelle Taylor as the Borgias, Myrna Loy, in one of her typical Oriental vamp roles, as their seductive spy, and Montague Love as the villainous Count Donati.

The film was allegedly based on the poem by Lord Byron, although scenarist Bess Meredyth seems to

83

Mary is tied to the rack in the torture chamber of the Borgias, but Don Juan soon comes to her rescue.

Below: The classic duel scene between Barrymore and Montague Love, still by far the best duel the movies have given us. Watching on the stairway, in extreme long shot, are Warner Oland, Estelle Taylor and Myrna Loy.

have used a lively imagination in adapting it. However, more than a little of it would seem to have been suggested by Barrymore himself, particularly the torture-chamber episode referred to earlier. How John loved to work bizarre little sections into his films—and how well they paid off for him!

Seventh Heaven
1927

There's no doubt that *Seventh Heaven* was the screen's most popular love story. Nobody who saw it has ever forgotten it; nobody remembers it with anything but the fondest recollections. Even younger generations who never saw it know that the title has come to represent the zenith of the filmed love story. And yet it is frankly a miracle that *Seventh Heaven* turned out so well.

Its story is maudlin, lugubrious and dishonestly sentimental. Every trick in the book is tried, re-arranged, and tried again, to squeeze the last tear out of the spectator. Even the theme music—the lovely, haunting "Diane"—is so overused that, towards the end of the film, when it is even used as a vocal* one begins to get heartily sick of it.

Why then, is *Seventh Heaven* so impressive—such a good film despite its "schmaltz"?

There are three very good reasons. Two of them are in the charming and thoroughly likeable performances of the stars, Janet Gaynor and Charles Farrell. The third, and most important reason is its director—Frank Borzage. Borzage, who started out as a villain in Bill Hart westerns, was (and still is) the screen's master of the love story. He can take the most obvious sob stuff, the most crass soap opera, and turn it into a thing of wonder and beauty. Nor is he even terribly subtle about it; sometimes he hammers away at the emotions without respite, as if to say, "This is 'schmaltz', so let's give it the full treatment!" And with Borzage it works. I don't know how or why. I only know that he can bring tears when almost any other director would bring only squirms. Take a look at his recent *China Doll* and see what I mean. It has that same old *Seventh Heaven* sentiment—"corn" if you like—but how the old maestro can shape it until it really looks like something!

Seventh Heaven is something of a rosy-hued *Broken Blossoms*—with a happy ending, of course, despite all signs to the contrary. The heroine is a street waif, consistently beaten half to death by her harridan of a guardian. After one particularly savage beating in the Paris streets, she is rescued and taken in by the itinerant Chico. At first he merely pities her, then begins to resent her as he realizes that she is falling in love with him. Finally, in spite of himself, he falls in love with her too—but before a marriage can be consummated, war is declared. And, as is the tradition in wartime

Janet Gaynor as Diane, and Charles Farrell as Chico—the immortal lovers of the screen's most popular love story. Both were subsequently teamed in other romantic stories which were very successful, but which never managed to duplicate the success of the original.

romances, within a few minutes he has been mobilized, fitted out with a uniform, and rushed to the front! Diane waits—and wonders—and works in a war factory. News comes that Chico has been killed. Despite all evidence to the contrary, Diane refuses to believe he is dead. And ultimately, as the music swells to a crescendo, he does in fact return to her.

When it was re-made as a talkie in 1937 with James Stewart and Simone Simon, all the blatant artificiality and sugar-smeared sentiment of the new version revealed the story for the sham it was. "What has happened to *Seventh Heaven*?", people wondered. "Could it really have been as good before as we thought it was?"

It was. More than three decades later—thanks to Frank Borzage—and such later films as *Camille* and *A Farewell to Arms* notwithstanding, the original *Seventh Heaven* is still the yardstick for all movie love stories.

*A silent film, *Seventh Heaven* was issued with a synchronized musical score.

The classic triangle: Lars Hanson, Greta Garbo and John Gilbert.

Flesh and the Devil, 1927

An officer in the Austrian army, John Gilbert is prepared to throw away his career for the love of socialite Garbo. But he is not prepared to throw away his honor, and it comes as something of a shock when he finds that she is actually married to an ageing nobleman, played by Marc McDermott.

Steamy love scenes like this one between Garbo and Gilbert helped make *Flesh and the Devil* a standout success, especially since it was no secret that the two stars *were* romantically inclined at the time.

Without being a great film in itself, *Flesh and the Devil*, the first of the Garbo-Gilbert romances, was quite certainly a box office milestone—and it also represents something of a high-water mark in the sheer elegance and "bigness" of movies in their most glamorous era. The sets have a solidity and glossiness which is staggering, and the technical proficiency of the trick effects—stunning matte-shots, for example, which literally make today's efforts look crude by comparison—is unsurpassed. The photography gleams and shimmers. And dramatically, the picture is big in every sense of the word. Honor, loyalty, love—strong emotions all of them, are given full expression in a story which permits no facile solutions but demands a duel, a ravaging sickness, a desperate pursuit across a frozen lake, and similar ingredients, before a happy—or at least, a satisfying—ending could be reached. And with those torrid Gilbert-Garbo love scenes to top everything off (love scenes that, Hollywood gossip had it, were very much

the real thing), this was an "audience" picture in every sense of the word.

With such polish and visual elegance, it is a pity that the film couldn't also have been a great one. It certainly had all the potentials in Hermann Sudermann's original novel, *The Undying Past*. But its basic story-line, of two Austrian army comrades whose lives are disrupted when they both fall in love with a married temptress, was so obviously an ideal subject for Garbo, that, inevitably perhaps, it was too much reshaped as a vehicle for her (even though John Gilbert got top billing) to retain much stature of it own.

But as a piece of slick, glossy romance—too stark to be called "hokum", yet still too romanticized to have much contact with a reality—it remains a thoroughly enjoyable film, possibly a trifle too slow and ponderous, but thanks to the playing of Garbo, Gilbert and the Swedish actor Lars Hanson, and the smooth direction of Clarence Brown, a consistently interesting and entertaining one.

What Price Glory?

1927

The Laurence Stallings-Maxwell Anderson play *What Price Glory?* was Fox's answer to Metro's *The Big Parade*. Critics complained that the raw, "gutsy" and bawdy humor of the play had been toned down for the movie—and perhaps it had—but Victor McLaglen and Edmund Lowe, playing the endlessly bickering (and, in years to come, endlessly imitated) Flagg and Quirt, had a field day mouthing whatever oaths they thought appropriate. And lip-readers can *still* have a field day watching curses that will probably never become commonplace on the sound screen, no matter how "adult" the cinema becomes.

Her Mexican accent unheard, Dolores Del Rio made a lovely French Charmaine.

Edmund Lowe and Victor McLaglen as Flagg and Quirt.

What Price Glory? wasn't as good a film as *The Big Parade*, but it was as big a success, and is a faster-paced, more popularly conceived affair. Its "war is hell" message came over tellingly in a few spots, but for the most part director Raoul Walsh and his crew were more concerned with putting on the biggest and most exciting war show possible. When it opened at the Roxy in New York, they were abetted in their efforts by a fantastically elaborate stage prologue. Bombs burst, scenery tumbled, red glares lit up the theatre, machine guns chattered off-stage, and just as all hell was breaking loose and patrons were thinking of heading for cover, the main titles of the film flashed on the screen!

The war scenes in *What Price Glory?* are big and spectacular, with one marvelous shot of a long trench caving in (from a bomb explosion) on the scores of soldiers huddled in it. The love scenes (particularly a torrid episode between Edmund Lowe, clad in hospital pajamas, and Dólores del Rio, a lovely Charmaine) were rough and realistic. The comedy was robust and raw. But perhaps the biggest hit of the entire show was the delightful derrière-waggling of pert Phyllis Haver, cast as "Shanghai Mabel" in the early portions of the film, set in the Far East before the outbreak of the first World War.

Marion Mack, like most of Keaton's leading ladies, was dumb and helpless. Her well-intentioned "assistance" frequently got him in more trouble than the whole opposing enemy force!

The General, 1927

Buster Keaton's *The General* is in the very odd position of being one of the classic silent comedies, while also being one of the least typical. When Keaton made it towards the end of the silent era, fast-paced panto-mimic comedy had become commonplace. Common-place, that is, to audiences of the 20's. To us, today, the best of it seems not only incredibly ingenious and funny, but also truly creative. But look at any fan magazine of the late 20's, and you will find any number of great visual comedies being passed off as "just more of the same," while pedestrian little situation comedies, relying on lengthy dialogue titles and involved plotting, were rating rave reviews for being "different" and "in-telligent." This demand for something new in comedy may have been what prompted Keaton to make *The General*. Far from being a mere answer to a public demand, it is still full of fine pantomime and visual comedy. But it is slower-paced than any other Keaton

comedy, the gags are more deliberately spaced, and there's far more substance to the story. Luckily, the story is so good on its own, and so well handled, that the reduced comedy content is amply compensated for. And we should explain that even with fewer laughs than usual, it was still funnier than any three or four of today's comedies bundled together!

The General refers not to Keaton, but to his locomo-tive, and the story is essentially a true one—the tale of the daring Civil War raid led by Captain Anderson, a Northern spy who penetrated Southern lines to steal a locomotive and wreck communications. Walt Disney told this same story—quite seriously—in his *The Great Locomotive Chase*. And yet despite its comic content, despite having hundreds of soldier extras acting like the Keystone Cops, Keaton's version was an exciting thriller too—and spun a pretty lucid account of the adventure. The climactic battle scene was staged on a

Buster's attempts to utilize a cannon almost result in his own destruction—the inevitable result of his conflict with the mechanized world. The "cannon gag" from *The General* is one of the most celebrated Keaton routines.

mammoth scale worthy of Griffith, and was exceptionally well photographed. The film ran for eight reels, and seven of those reels were devoted to a chase—first of all, Buster chasing the spies, and then the spies chasing Buster! No movie chase has ever been sustained so long, so successfully, or with such an expert intermingling of genuine thrills and hilarious comic situations.

The funniest single moment in the film must surely be the most expensive gag on record. To cut off the Northern pursuit, Buster has set fire to an enormous trestle-bridge spanning a wide river. By the time the locomotive, with its cargo of munitions and troops, arrives on the scene, the bridge is blazing merrily. The engineer hesitates, when along comes a Northern officer with a hundred or more mounted soldiers. "That

bridge isn't burned enough to stop you," he says. "You go ahead, and we'll ford the river." As the cavalry descend into the valley, the train puffs confidently forward onto the now-swaying bridge. Half way across, it gives way, and train and bridge plunge into the river in a holocaust of hissing steam, burning timbers, exploding shells, and struggling men. From this carnage, there is a quick cut to a closeup of the bewildered officer who gave the order. His expression shows quite plainly that he is not at all concerned at the havoc he has caused, but is just annoyed at having been shown to be wrong! Petulantly, he orders his men to advance. A scene that plays much better than it reads, it remains one of the screen's highpoints of purely visual comedy.

And *The General*, sadly, represents just about the

Even with the Confederate army to back him up, Buster, though determined, is none too confident. Those cannons are bound to double-cross him at any moment, he feels . . . and at least one of them does!

last really great comedy of the silent screen. It was co-directed by Keaton and his old friend Clyde Bruckman, who came to a particularly tragic end in the mid-1950's. Broke, depressed, believing himself forgotten and unwanted, he borrowed Keaton's gun and shot himself in a Hollywood restaurant. He was unaware that *The General* was still studied, and enjoyed, the world over as a masterpiece of screen comedy.

Charles "Buddy" Rogers, Clara Bow and Richard Arlen.

Wings, 1927

The Dawn Patrol and *Hell's Angels* (both early talkies) may have been *better* films than *Wings*, in a dramatic and artistic sense, but they certainly weren't any bigger! In any event, *Wings* holds the distinction of being the biggest and best air-war film of the silent screen and is one of the best war films from any period.

Forget the plot—it's the old one about two fellows in love with the same girl, and chock full of unlikely personal complications and misunderstandings. It had some touching moments, but no unexpected ones. And forget the "war-is-hell" message, which comes in occasionally. Nobody could be expected to pay too much attention to it here, and it's only there on the off-chance that somebody might be fooled into thinking this as important a film as *The Big Parade*.

You can forget—and forgive—all these things because *Wings* is such grand, slambang, adventure hokum. The World War I period is so remote now, and so outdated by contemporary politics and weapons, that films dealing with it almost come under the heading of "historical spectacle." And the heroes of the World War I air forces—the Hollywood heroes at least—were given a gallantry and chivalry so unlike the kill-or-be-killed attitude of the World War II heroes that they in themselves tend to place the adventures further back in time, almost like 1917 equivalents of the Knights of King Arthur.

Wings, at any rate, is full of rip-snorting dog-fights, huge scale bombing raids, an attack by a German giant-sized bomber, the like of which hasn't yet been seen in *any* war, brilliantly staged plane crashes, and the inevitable "big push" on land, with thousands of extras whooping it up in superlatively handled combat scenes. Paramount, with a reputation in the 20's for turning out ostensibly "big" films with a cheapness that really showed in the sparse sets and limited extras, really outdid themselves on this one. Nothing was spared to make it a big show in every way. The fantastic Paris night club set alone must have cost more than the total budget of one of their average pictures. The sheer size of the spectacle, plus the triteness of the plot, tended to make the actors seem relatively unimportant, but there were some extremely able performances. Charles "Buddy" Rogers and Richard Arlen were good as the two pals, both in love with small-town girl Clara Bow (looking extremely lovely and winsome in a much quieter role than usual). Clara spent most of the film clothed in either girl-next-door frocks, or nurse's uniform. But remembering what her fans would be expecting, writer John Monk Saunders cunningly wrote in a red-hot sequence where Clara, in order to rescue a drunken Buddy Rogers from the MP's, has to change into a daring low-cut gown and pose as a Parisian floozie! The best supporting performance came from that superb character actor, Henry B. Walthall, milking his emotional scenes (as a bereaved father) for all they were worth. There was a good performance too from a young Gary Cooper, in a telling role that lasted no more than a few minutes, but that helped to establish the rising young player as an actor as well as a husky good-looker.

William Wellman directed; he's made many war films and aerial films since—*Lafayette Esquadrille* was one of the most recent—but *Wings* is still far and away his best film along these lines.

Richard Arlen, as the tragic pal of Buddy Rogers, accidentally shot down and killed by Buddy just as he had effected an escape from the Germans and was about to land behind his own lines.

The war scenes in *Wings* were big, terrifying, and superbly staged.

The Strong Man

1927

With *Tramp Tramp Tramp* (1926) a close second (although perhaps even funnier), *The Strong Man* is the best of the Harry Langdon feature comedies—which means that it is one of the half-dozen best comedies ever made.

Harry appears in his traditional baby-faced innocent guise, this time as a Belgian soldier in World War I, carrying on a "pen pal" friendship with an American girl named Mary Brown. When Harry comes to the States after the war, he first has trouble finding Mary. When he does finally locate her in a small town, it is to find that she is blind. Those who find an affinity between certain aspects of the work of Harry Langdon

When Harry finds his sweetheart (Priscilla Bonner), he acts out his adventures for her in an eloquent pantomimic sequence.

Meek, frail little Harry is forced into posing as a muscular strong man—and somehow gets away with it!

and that of Chaplin may note the slight plot resemblance to Chaplin's later *City Lights*, but it is a purely coincidental similarity, and one that is both handled differently and solved differently. In *City Lights*, the girl regains her sight through the tramp's efforts. In *The Strong Man* she remains blind, but is happily married to the bumbling but kindly little man she has never seen.

Lest this brief synopsis give the impression that *The Strong Man* is a tragi-comedy, let me hasten to assure you otherwise. It has elements of really moving pathos—as, indeed, do most of the great comedies—but those elements are far less prominent than in Chaplin's films, and comedy, ranging from subtle pantomime to all-out slapstick, predominates from the first scene to the last. The best comedy moments are those which have little or no connection with the plot proper—such as a truly hilarious sequence in which forlorn Harry, suffering from a vicious cold, sniffs, swallows pills, sneezes, drinks medicine, and smothers his chest with a mustard plaster and lashings of vapor rub (which gets mixed up with some highly pungent cheese), all aboard a bus, to the extreme discomfort of his neighbors. There is some wonderfully funny wartime fooling at the beginning, with Harry trying vainly to hit a tin can with a machine gun, and a great bit when, for reasons far too complicated to explain here, a big city hustler (Gertrude Astor) tries to pass herself off as Mary Brown. Harry's frightened attempts to escape her seductive advances, and his bemused efforts to reconcile *this* Mary with the gentler girl he has known only by correspondence, make for a tremendously amusing sequence. When Harry finally settles down with the real Mary, there's a corrupt element that has to be run out of town, and a saloon that has to be cleaned up. All this, and more, makes for grand fun that needs to be seen rather than described.

The Strong Man is not only Harry's best picture, but also probably the best film its director (Frank Capra) ever made. He apparently remembers it well, for he repeated one of its best gags in his recent *A Hole in the Head*.

The real strong man uses Harry as a combination helper, fall guy, guinea pig and valet.

The ripsnorting climax: Harry, "bombing" the saloon with whisky bottles from his trapeze, is temporarily cornered by the town rabble. But with the aid of a cannon he soon literally cleans out the whole saloon.

95

This portrait of Jetta Goudal as she appeared in *White Gold* may be the only still from this film left. Whether it is or not, it is certainly a rarity.

White Gold, 1927

When *White Gold* was released in 1927, one trade paper summed it up thus:

"From the standpoints of production, scenario construction, directing and acting, *White Gold* compares most favorably with the best German films that have been brought to America. The production style is of the same order as *The Last Laugh.* Deeper psychology is revealed in this film than in any other ever produced in America."

Quite possibly the enthusiasm of the moment may have exaggerated its virtues a trifle. Today it is difficult to tell, for *White Gold* is one of those films of a kind that seems (in America, at least) to have disappeared completely. A few years ago there was a plan for Charles Laughton to re-make it, but it fell through because no print of the original could be found.

White Gold was set on a sheep ranch, but its strange, stylized approach to a story revolving principally around sex and jealousy deliberately suppressed the sense of fresh air and freedom its setting suggested.

It cultivated instead an oppressive, claustrophobic atmosphere, not unlike the silent Lillian Gish film *The Wind*—or the more recent *Wild Is the Wind*, with Anna Magnani. A complete box office flop, it is nevertheless regarded as one of the truly great films of the silent era, by those who remember it. George Bancroft, lovely Jetta Goudal, and Kenneth Thompson starred, and the film was produced for the Cecil B. DeMille corporation. (DeMille had left Paramount a few years earlier, and now had his own company.) Its guiding genius was William K. Howard, one of the most talented of all directors, with a superb sense of visual drama. Strangely enough, despite his great *pictorial* talent, he achieved his greatest success with a number of expert melodramas in the early talkie period, *Transatlantic* being probably the best. *White Gold* was probably Howard's only real box office flop. It was also, unquestionably, his masterpiece. When he died in February of 1954, not having made a film for eight years, he had just rewritten the script for a proposed re-make.

Realistic Highlights from "White Gold" Starring Jetta Goudal

Janet Gaynor as the wife.

George O'Brien as the husband.

Sunrise, 1927

If, heaven forbid, I had had to select the *five* great American films, instead of the 50, one of those five would most certainly have been *Sunrise*.

How can one categorize it? A love story perhaps? A drama? Melodrama? It is all of these, and so much more; it is also perhaps the only completely poetic film that Hollywood ever produced. If the term "poetic"

Visitors come to their little community for the vacations—and among the crowd is a temptress from the city.

suggests to you an arty, experimentalist, somewhat stodgy film, then my use of that phrase does the film a disservice. It is the highest form of film art; it was made with no consideration for the box office or indeed any consideration other than its creator's wish to make a beautiful and personal film. But there was nothing drily intellectual or cold about it. It was one of the warmest, loveliest, and most tender films ever made, beautifully acted, sensitively directed, and with some of the most stunningly rich photography I have ever seen.

Sunrise was a "big" picture in terms of budget. Some of the sets were fantastically spectacular—so spectacular, in fact, that they looked like the real thing (a huge carnival; a railway station; city streets; a deluxe barber-shop) and went almost unnoticed, as though the cameras had been taken on location and set up unobstrusively for the stars—and life itself—to go through their paces.

Its story is simple. A farmer, happily married, and with a child, suddenly becomes enamored of a temptress from the city. In his infatuation for her he strips his farm of its wealth, but even this is not enough. The temptress seeks to lure him to the city with her, and suggests that he murder his wife by causing her to drown. He will upset their boat—and save himself with bundles of bull-rushes that he will secrete within the boat. At first horrified by the idea, the half-bewitched husband finally agrees. Next morning, he and his wife set out across the lake. Halfway across he makes his intentions clear, but he is basically too good a man to

Infatuated with the woman from the city, the husband is unable to explain to his unsuspecting wife why he has changed so much.

At night he goes to the swamp to meet the woman. The huge swamp set, as most of the other "exterior" scenes, was created within the Fox studio.

99

Unable to carry out his plan to murder his wife, the husband tries vainly to tell her he is sorry.

have the strength for murder. His resolve weakened by his wife's pitiful pleas, he pulls at the oars desperately, rushing to the opposite side of the lake. As they land, his terrified wife flees from him, through the forest. He rushes after her, shouting his sorrow and his love. The wife reaches the point where the trolley car stops, and climbs aboard, only seconds before her husband reaches her, and swings aboard the departing car.

They ride slowly into the city—the forest slowly changing into the outskirts, suburbia changing into metropolis. All the time the husband, near tears, protests his love, assures his wife that she has nothing to fear. As they get off in the city, she gradually becomes calmer, but retains her innate fear; there is a pathetic little scene in a restaurant where the husband tries to restore her confidence by buying a plate of cakes that neither of them wants or has the appetite to eat.

Slowly, the wife's faith is restored. As they pass a church, they notice a wedding in progress, and go inside. Overcome by emotion, the husband silently, then sobbingly, re-recites the wedding vows, unseen by the young couple who are themselves reciting them to the minister. Her fear completely gone, the wife now lovingly embraces her regained husband. The middle portion of the film now becomes a very necessary lighter respite from the emotional ordeal that both the protagonists—and the audience—have been through. Desperately anxious to convince each other that everything is now all right, the couple joyously enter into a round of merriment—an elaborate meal, a visit to a photographer, a barbershop, and the carnival. Happy at the end of the day, they return home, the trolley ride and the trip across the lake that had before been so fraught with danger and doubt, now almost like a second honeymoon trip. But midway across the lake, a sudden storm arises. Within minutes their boat is in imminent danger of capsizing. Bringing out the bullrushes he had intended to use to save himself, the husband straps his wife to them and tells her to strike out for shore.

The storm subsides. The husband reaches shore safely. But there is no sign of his wife. A search finds bullrushes scattered on the now peaceful waters. Grief-stricken, near madness, the husband is led home. Thinking this to be merely part of an act, that he had in fact murdered his wife, the temptress comes to him. In a rage, he pursues her into the swamps, beating her, strangling her. . . .

Then, a cry from his mother . . . the wife has been found . . . alive! Happily, the husband rushes to her

In a restaurant in the city he tries to convince her that she no longer need fear him.

. . . and the next morning, as the sun rises, the temptress heads wearily back to the city.

I can recall no other film in which the honest emotion of love has been conveyed so beautifully, and no other film that is such a beautiful entity in itself. Even the titles, which are infrequent, have a simplicity and beauty that parallels the film itself, and often they are presented in strikingly dramatic fashion. As the temptress suggests to the husband the means by which he will drown his wife, the words themselves slide downwards on the screen, finally disappearing into the void of the black background.

Inevitably, *Sunrise* has somewhat of a European flavor. It is based on the novel *A Trip to Tilsit* by Hermann Sudermann, and while the locale in the film could be American, care is taken that it remains ambiguous. As the film's opening subtitle puts it, this is "A Song of Two Humans"—the story could be of any time, and any place. The director is the German F. W. Murnau, and it is very much to William Fox's credit that Murnau was given a completely free hand to make the film just the way it should have been made, without any interference. Murnau achieves the near-impossible: a film of tremendous style that is yet not a *stylized* film. Its beauty is not of the cold, precise, carefully pre-planned manner of his German films. Pre-planned it must have been, but what emerges is warm, natural, and spontaneous.

The credit must be equally proportioned among Murnau himself, the writer, Carl Mayer, perhaps the foremost screen poet, the cameramen, Charles Rosher and Karl Struss, and not least, the stars. George O'Brien, hitherto (and since) predominantly an action star, gives a most moving performance. His occasional tendency to overact here goes unnoticed in a role calling for overwrought emotions in the dramatic scenes, and boisterous exuberance in the light episodes. Janet Gaynor, quiet and restrained, is almost equally good, though in a less demanding role, and Margaret Livingston is fine as the seductress. Bodil Rosing and J. Farrel MacDonald are good in the only other roles of any size. Incidentally, not the least of *Sunrise's* many assets was a particularly fine musical score, which made excellent and effective use of that haunting Phil Spitalny piece, "The Enchanted Forest."

Sunrise is one of the screen's enduring classics. It can and should be seen over and over again. Each new appraisal of it brings a discovery of something new and wonderful that escaped on the previous viewing.

The aftermath of the storm: A fisherman finds the wife—kept afloat by the bullrushes.

The wife finally convinced, the couple, in mutual relief, make merry.

Ben-Hur
1927

Ramon Novarro as Ben-Hur, May McAvoy as Esther.

Ben-Hur, the biggest movie spectacle since *Intolerance* —and bigger than they'll ever make them again—was a success despite one of the most insane scripting errors of all time—that of placing the film's two biggest sequences (the sea battle and the chariot race) in the

The gigantic chariot race that was the film's highlight.

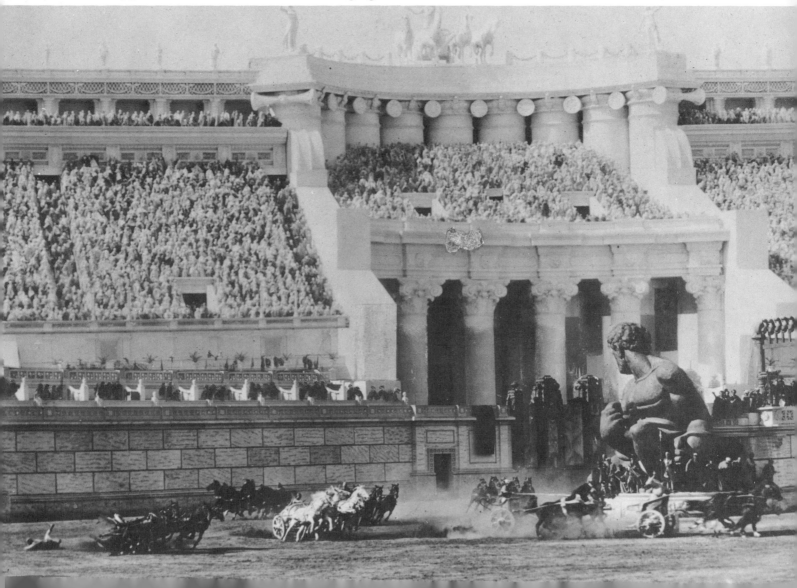

That fine old Griffith actress, Claire McDowell, played the mother of Ben-Hur.

first half of the picture! Part two not only moved slowly, but had no spectacular action highlights, and in addition spent a good deal of its footage on such decidedly unpleasant matters as the leprosy-stricken family of Ben-Hur. The stodgily presented, if sincerely motivated, religious angle slowed the picture up quite a bit too!

Truth to tell, *Ben-Hur* was a rather mismanaged picture from the start. It's a matter of Hollywood history now how reels and reels of footage, shot over a lengthy period on actual locations in Italy, were subsequently scrapped and refilmed in Hollywood. And despite its size, it was often a clumsy and pedestrian film.

Why then, is it included in our "50 Greats"? Well, for one thing its size and popularity certainly count for something. But most of all, its two really big sequences —the monumental battle at sea between the galley and the pirates and the chariot race—rate as two of the most expertly filmed action-spectacle sequences ever photographed. The chariot race, filmed on a truly colossal scale (for once that word was not misused) is tremendously exciting, magnificently organized in its tricky stunt work, brilliantly photographed by a corps of cameramen and, finally, equally brilliantly edited into a sequence that builds in tension and excitement with every foot of film. Ironically, this sequence, the

one for which the film is famous, was staged and directed not by the film's official director, Fred Niblo, but by a second unit director, Reaves Eason. (Eason's talent for handling dramatic material was weak, but he was a whiz at directing spectacular action highlights and at directing "B" westerns in which movement and fast action were the dominant elements.) Niblo was associated with some big films—films which, because of their titles, or stars, or themes, just couldn't help but be successful—but he himself was a director of workmanlike competence and no more. The real credit for *Ben-Hur's* success belongs to Mr. Eason and, of course, to its notable cast.

Ramon Novarro was a perfect choice as Ben Hur, and Francis X. Bushman made a fine opponent as Messala. The feminine side of the cast was particularly strong, too: lovely May McAvoy as the heroine, Carmel Myers as the inevitable vamp, old Griffith player Claire McDowell as Ben-Hur's mother, and, particularly effective in a brief appearance as the Madonna in the opening scenes, Betty Bronson.

Whatever its flaws, *Ben-Hur* was big film-making. This book will appear just as the new one hits the screens, but whatever its merits may be, we can be sure of one thing: With today's production costs, it just cannot duplicate the sheer magnitude of this, the original 1927 *Ben-Hur*.

The Geste family: Ralph Forbes, Alice Joyce, Ronald Colman, Neil Hamilton.

Beau Geste, 1927

P. C. Wren's famous tale of Foreign Legion adventure made such a near-perfect film of its type in 1927, under the skilled direction of Herbert Brenon, that when William Wellman re-made it as a talkie in 1939, with Gary Cooper in the role originally played by Ronald Colman, he based his new version almost scene for scene on the old.

Even during the height of an Arab attack, the villainous Sergeant Lejaune (Noah Beery Sr.) finds time to settle personal grievances with the two Englishmen (Forbes and Colman) under his command.

Wren's story was a well-knit mixture of intrigue, romance, and adventure, opening with the mysterious discovery of a desert fort manned only by dead legionnaires, and then flashing back some twenty years to the childhood of the Geste brothers. Their code of honor as children, their determination to protect their mother, and the mysterious disappearance of a fabulous jewel, all these plot threads—and others—weave neatly together until the three brothers find themselves together in the Legion, fighting not only the menace of marauding Arabs, but also the treachery of their commanding officer. It was a fine story—and Herbert Brenon, returning to movie spectacles for the first time in some years (he had been a top "spectacle" producer for years before turning to quieter stories and whimsies), made a top-notch job of it. The enormous-scale Arab attack scenes are still tremendously exciting, and the desert wastes near Yuma in Arizona made a fine substitute for Arabia.

Ronald Colman, Neil Hamilton, and Ralph Forbes made a fine trio of stalwart heroes, and Brenon and Paramount provided a great cast to support them. Noah Beery gave one of his best performances as the sadistic Commander; William Powell was excellent as a cowardly sneak thief, Alice Joyce (as the boys' aunt) and Mary Brian were in the feminine roles; reliable old character actor Norman Trevor was a Legion officer, and Victor McLaglen played a cowboy turned legionnaire. *Beau Geste* was fine, virile stuff—and it hasn't dated one whit today.

The unknown killer is one of the guests in the house, disguising himself behind a fearsome mask. He has Creighton Hale temporarily in his power.

The Cat and the Canary, 1927

The Cat and the Canary was made in a period when Carl Lacmmle was filling his studio (Universal) with imported, and predominantly German, talent. It was handed to Paul Leni to direct as his first American assignment, following years in Germany as a set designer and as a director. Universal has always been Hollywood's stronghold of horror movies, so it is no surprise that this classic chiller is so slickly done. One of what we can loosely term the "Old House" brand of thrillers, its action is restricted and its effect is dependent more upon atmosphere than sensationalism.

It was a type of horror film that was far more suited to the more methodically paced silent film than it is to the talkies. Like *The Bat* and *The Gorilla* (both also made in silent and sound versions) it was a stage derivation, and one with a marked comedy content, but it remains thrilling fare for all of that. Its plot dealt with an heiress forced to spend a night in a lonely house with a group of assorted friends and relatives, all of them highly suspicious in their behavior, and all liable to benefit from her death. One of them, needless

to say, was the hidden killer out for the loot himself. Perhaps it is also needless to say that, in established tradition, he was the most helpful of the guests, and the least suspicious in his behavior!

If the script is completely American, then the handling of it certainly shows the influence of Leni's German background. The lighting and camerawork throughout are patterned on that of *Warning Shadows* and other German films of terror and fantasy. And Lucien Littlefield's makeup as the fake doctor bears a more than coincidental resemblance to that of Werner Krauss as Doctor Caligari!

It must be admitted that the film doesn't survive the years without creaking a little, but this is not so much due to defects in the film itself as to the fact that it was really a blueprint of its own species. The format has now been repeated so many times since, the sliding panels and clutching hands degenerating through the years into such casual clichés that the original just doesn't have the same punch it had in 1927. The cards have rather been stacked against this one, but nevertheless it's still a striking and fascinating mystery

1 The opening titles of the film were most impressive; a dust and cobweb covered black slab. Hands push the cobwebs aside, revealing the titles beneath!

The Cat and the Canary abounded in fine atmospheric sets like this, along which the cameras swept almost like ghosts themselves. 4

2 The opening of the film was fine impressionistic stuff in the old German manner; a stylized, Gothic mansion, which dissolves into—

Again the suggestion of the supernatural, as wraith-like 5 **curtains** billow into a deserted corridor.

3 A shot of an invalid, surrounded by huge medicine bottles, beyond which hover evil-looking cats, suggesting the greedy relatives who are awaiting his death.

Martha Mattox is the sinister housekeeper, and Tully Marshall, the mysterious lawyer, who is murdered shortly after reading the will. 6

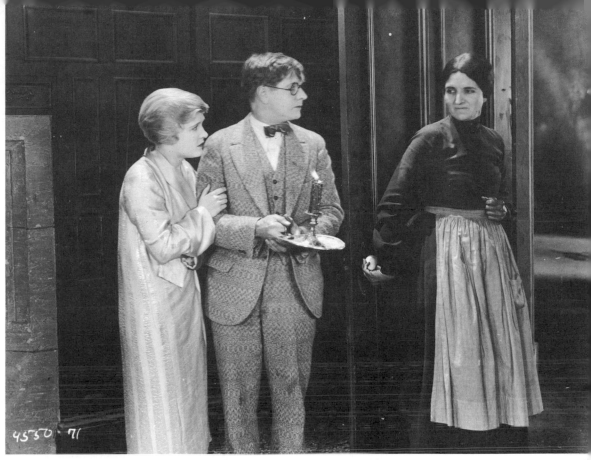

Creighton Hale appoints himself protector of heiress Laura La Plante.

thriller. Laura La Plante played the lovely heiress-in-distress, with Creighton Hale in a serio-comic role as her nervous protector. (Bob Hope played this role in the second of the remakes.) The menace, actual and implied, was in the very capable hands of George Siegmann, Tully Marshall, Forrest Stanley, Arthur Edmund Carewe and Lucien Littlefield.

The fake doctor, played by Lucien Littlefield, proceeds to terrify both Laura and (left) her friend, Gertrude Astor.

White Shadows in the South Seas

1928

This lovely film has long been something of a cause célèbre among so-called film esthetes, who complain about the "commercialism" of Hollywood being the perpetual enemy of creative artistry. Everything began late in 1927, when M-G-M production head Irving Thalberg decided to shoot a large-scale adventure film in the South Seas. He selected *White Shadows in the South Seas,* written by Frederick O'Brien, and he offered the job of directing to Robert Flaherty, the famed documentary-maker whose *Moana* had been a critical success but a box office failure for Paramount a year or two earlier. Flaherty's friends later claimed that he accepted reluctantly, only because he couldn't find work elsewhere, and because he was a friend of O'Brien. As an assistant to Flaherty, Thalberg sent

Monte Blue, as the drink-sodden doctor who becomes a force for good when he is shipwrecked among isolated islanders, and Raquel Torres as the Polynesian girl whom he ultimately marries.

along W. S. Van Dyke, an expert primarily on fast-action westerns, but a director of intelligence and integrity who had learned the business as an assistant to Griffith.

Scenes like this one give a good idea of the outstanding photographic beauty of the film.

Director W. S. Van Dyke, standing at left, prepares to direct Raquel Torres.

Flaherty however, rebelled almost as soon as work got under way on the picturesque island of Papeete. He found that he couldn't work to a studio schedule; that his co-workers were unsympathetic to the cause. In any event, he gave up on the job, and W. S. Van Dyke carried on—most efficiently.

The film that emerged may not have been quite what Flaherty envisioned, but it was, by any standards, a magnificent film. By any standards, that is, except those of the filmic pseudo-intellectuals, to whom Flaherty was a sort of God. Now I have nothing against Flaherty, and I feel that his *Nanook* is one of the greatest films of all. But I do take issue with many of his friends and supporters who promptly and triumphantly cited his withdrawal from the project as another example of the Hollywood machine triumphing over the artist. For one thing, Flaherty knew before he started that this was not to be "his" film but Metro's film, and that a certain amount of discipline would be expected from him. Secondly, it is strange that he should lose interest so quickly, for *White Shadows* was anything but a typical "Hollywood" film. It was a courageous and unusual film for *any* studio to make—and especially so for M-G-M, the most "commercial" of all the studios. And the sad despairing wails of "Oh, what a film it would have been if Flaherty had made it!" seem quite unjustified and even absurd in view of the fine film that Van Dyke turned out. It is so far superior to Flaherty's own *Moana* that it would be much more to the point to ponder how much better Flaherty's *Man of Aran* would have been if Van Dyke had directed it! Flaherty's supporters all dismiss Van Dyke scornfully because he was a slick director who made films fast and economically and without displaying any directorial temperament. This, they hinted, removed any consideration of artistry in his work. Quite to the contrary, I would have thought that those qualities were definite virtues— especially when allied to the work Van Dyke turned out with such amazing regularity. Take a look today at his *Trader Horn* and *The Thin Man* and see if you don't agree that they stand up beautifully!

Perhaps it's a little late to raise this issue. Both Flaherty and Van Dyke have passed on. The film itself is never shown outside of film societies. But with so much on the other side of the ledger, I'd like to add my two cents worth—and what better place than a book with a "Memory Lane" background?

White Shadows in the South Seas, at any rate, with its sombre story of the white man's "civilization" bringing only death and ugliness to the South Seas, and its unexpectedly tragic ending, was a tremendously moving and stirring film. A very small cast, headed by Monte Blue (possibly his best performance) and Raquel Torres played excellently, but it was the strikingly beautiful photography that was the real hit of the production; that, and the imaginative direction of Van Dyke. When it was premiered at Graumann's Chinese Theatre in Hollywood, D. W. Griffith flew in specially from New York to introduce it by saying "*White Shadows in the South Seas* is a work of art— and Woody Van Dyke is the artist who brought it into being."

109

Our Dancing Daughters

1928

Joan Crawford and John Mack Brown were co-starred; Joan as the restless, reckless flapper who finally finds happiness with quiet, dependable, patient Brown.

It's ironical that some of the best films about the 20's and the so-called "lost generation" were actually made in the 30's. Perhaps it is because we had acquired perspective by then. But if no really great films about the roaring 20's were actually made during the jazz age, at least the ones that were made then had the plus value of authenticity—the costumes, the catch-phrases, the hip-flasks, the rolled stockings—all of these were captured on film, to become a kind of documentary of the times—albeit a somewhat one-sided documentary, since those lawless times did have their credit side too!

The most famous of all the jazz-age films is perhaps Clara Bow's *It*. It also happens to be a bore which has achieved fame through the combination of star and title. Far better were such notable lesser films as *Walking Back*, which had some jim-dandy sequences in it. But I think M-G-M's *Our Dancing Daughters,* directed by Harry Beaumont in 1928, was perhaps the best of the lot. Certainly it was the lushest of the lot—and no

The film abounded in wild, w-i-l-d parties. Here, at one of them, Joan Crawford launches into a Charleston.

110

matter which of the two ways you interpret that adjective, you'll be right! It had Joan Crawford dancing the Charleston, Anita Page drinking herself to death, and ex-football star John Mack Brown as the romantic bone of contention. Nils Asther turned in a good performance, too.

Quite frankly, I can't recall too much of the plot of *Our Dancing Daughters*. I can remember Joan's Charleston—more than one, in fact—champagne glasses flowing, wild, frenzied parties in huge mansions the like of which probably never existed outside of M-G-M's stages, scores of balloons floating heavenwards, and endless short skirts swaying in fast-paced rhythm to the jazz bands.

And that, after all, is how most of us remember the 20's—or like to think we do.

Dorothy Sebastian with Nils Asther and Joan Crawford.

Another mad frolic; Joan, by the door, sits this one out, leaving the dancing to others.

Nils Asther and Dorothy Sebastian, with Anita Page. Anita's wild, drunken spree results in her death after a spectacular fall downstairs, thus paving the way for a happy ending between Brown (who had been tricked into marriage with her) and Crawford. Page's performance was quite the best in the film.

111

Husband, wife and child—reasonably happy, reasonably secure, in a small New York apartment.

The Crowd, 1928

The first real quarrel. Scenes like these were almost painfully convincing as played by James Murray and Eleanor Boardman.

The name of director King Vidor is usually associated with "big" pictures—from the silent *The Big Parade* to the talkie *Duel in the Sun*. Yet his greatest picture was not big in the accepted sense. It was an expensive picture, all right. Vidor was a precise, painstaking director, and would spare neither time nor money to get just the results he wanted. It was a *long* film—some fourteen reels. But because it dealt with "ordinary" people, and was lacking in star names, it was not regarded as a big film in the normal way.

As a rule, I don't like films about "ordinary" people doing "ordinary" things. If that sounds snobbish, I don't mean it to be. But we all see ordinary people every day of our lives. Why pay a dollar to see them on the screen when for fifteen cents or so we can see the same thing on a bus? I think that realism, for its own sake, is often very over-rated on the screen. But I have the utmost admiration for the film, or the director, who can discover and show the very real drama in ordinary people, whether they be depicted in routine, or extraordinary activities. John Ford managed it in *The Grapes of Wrath*. So did Griffith in *Isn't Life Wonderful?*. But nobody managed it better than King Vidor in *The Crowd*, one of the enduring classics of the screen. Without containing a single situation of "classic drama," it is one of the most dramatic films

The husband ponders his failure. In real life, too, actor Murray was a tragic failure.

of all time. Without a single torrid romantic exchange, it is the most poignant and moving love story I have seen.

Its plot is simply a cross-section of many human plots—the story of the meeting of two pleasant but ordinary people, their marriage, their hopes, their brief triumphs and more lasting disappointments, birth, and death. To go into more detail would be to make a great film sound trite, simply because human existence is often trite and I don't propose, even indirectly, to minimize the power and honesty of this wonderful movie.

Most of it takes place in a cheap apartment (the film created something of a stir, quite unintentionally, by being the first American film to show a certain very necessary fixture in the bathroom!) and on the streets of New York. There is a brief, ecstatic honeymoon trip to Niagara Falls—and a dreary visit to Coney Island, where only the children really enjoy themselves. There is no real climax, either happy or unhappy. Life just goes on—and we leave the hero as we find him, one of the crowd. As the "End" title flashes on, it is almost impossible to believe that fourteen reels have gone by since the M-G-M lion introduced the credits.

Photographically and directorially it is superb, but this is one case where the acting is almost of equal stature. Eleanor Boardman, as the heroine, gives a truly remarkable performance. Not a beautiful girl in the usual sense, she seems coarse and plain as we meet her in a jostling crowd, chewing a wad of gum. The initial reaction is almost one of dislike. Then, as the film progresses, we get to know and love her. Without the slightest change of makeup or clothes, she slowly seems to transform into a warm and beautiful person. The audience sees her as the hero sees her. In the latter role, James Murray is almost pitifully perfect.

Pitifully, because his real life existence later proved to be a tragically exaggerated parody of the role he here played so magnificently. A nobody when Vidor discovered him and cast him in *The Crowd*, Murray failed to exploit the wonderful chance the film had given him. He wandered aimlessly through a succession of increasingly mediocre roles, and like the hero of *The Crowd*, hit the skids. He once asked Vidor for a loan—to buy liquor—and when Vidor begged him to pull himself together and return to acting, Murray turned suddenly surly and vanished into the night. In *The Crowd*, the hero, having hit bottom at one point, is about to commit suicide and is kept from it only by his young son, playfully and impatiently tugging at his sleeve, not knowing what is in his father's mind, but urging him to move along. Murray, alas, had no one to urge him along. No one even knows whether his death was an accident or suicide. Only two or three years after he gave one of the silent screen's finest performances in *The Crowd*, his body was found floating in a river.

Charlie, temporarily employed as a street cleaner, is aghast when an elephant strolls by in a parade—and discreetly rushes his street-sweeping equipment to a different and less populated area!

City Lights, 1931

Like *Tabu*, *City Lights* was conceived, designed and made as a silent film. Also like *Tabu* it was completed after the coming of sound, but was happily released just as it was made, with no attempt to add dialogue sequences or any sound other than a simple musical score. Sound films had been a firmly entrenched fixture to the movie scene for 3 years when *City Lights* went into release early in 1931, and sound itself, while no longer a novelty, still dominated the thinking of the movie-makers. It was more important to *hear* people talking and singing, than it was to watch images *move*. Amid a welter of cynical, wisecracking dramas and tough gangster thrillers, the fragile beauty and wonderful comic pantomime of *City Lights* stood out in sharp relief. Critics and public alike took time out to consider whether sound really had added so much to the movies after all, when the best film of the year was a silent! Unfortunately, they didn't think about it too long—and *City Lights* had little influence on other film-makers, who went right on making their talkies. (In case readers feel I am prejudiced, let me say that talkies at this period did little else *but* talk.

Really outstanding movies, like *All Quiet on the Western Front* and *Hallelujah* were comparatively few and far between, and it wasn't until 1932 that the movies really began to *move* again.)

With the possible exception of *A Woman of Paris*, *City Lights* was Chaplin's most serious film to date. And Chaplin himself was in a serious frame of mind when he made it. Worried about the coming of sound, he halted production for a while to consider the advisability of continuing with the film as a silent. When that problem was settled, there were others. Leading lady Virginia Cherrill was proving difficult, and Chaplin fired her. Several other players were tried out for her role, including Georgia Hale (from *The Gold Rush*) before Chaplin relented and made his peace with Virginia again. Other players *were* replaced. And Chaplin's mother died after a long, lingering mental illness. But despite the film's rather melancholy theme, and Chaplin's own personal troubles, it had some grand comedy.

The theme of *City Lights* was the love of a tramp for a blind flower girl—and how, through his own

The tramp's buddy is an eccentric millionaire, played by Harry Myers. When drunk, Harry treats Charlie as a friend and equal, lavishing money on him, but when sober, he no longer recognizes him! Their wild evening at a night club is one of the film's many comic highlights.

sacrifices, he pays for the operation that restores her sight. One of the most poignant scenes ever achieved by Chaplin was the climactic episode, wherein the flower girl sees the tramp for the first time. Of course she does not recognize him, and is amused by his silent adoration of her. Then she feels his hand, and recognition comes. It is a beautiful scene, as delicately played by Virginia Cherrill as by Chaplin.

On the printed page, the pathos and sentiment of *City Lights* may seem old-hat and obvious. Believe me, it isn't. Nor has it dated in the slighest since 1931. When the film was reissued in 1950, more than one critic listed it as the best film of the year. Quite certainly, to my mind, it is Chaplin's masterpiece, a perfect and subtle blend of human drama, rich pathos, and often uproarious comedy.

The tramp befriends the blind flower girl, played by Virginia Cherrill. This was Charlie's favorite role—the befriender of the helpless—a role he played from such Mutual comedies as *The Immigrant* down through to *Limelight* in the 50's.

Tabu, 1931

Tabu, often referred to (quite erroneously) as the "Flaherty-Murnau" production was indeed started as a collaboration between Flaherty, the famed American documentary-maker, and Murnau, the great German master of fantasy and poetic drama. Not unnaturally, the two personalities, automatically at variance in their approach to film (one a realist, the other a romanticist), clashed. Each respected the opinion of the other and regarded him as a friend. There was no ill-will between them, but it soon became obvious to both that no good film could come from their partnership. Accordingly, Flaherty withdrew almost before the film was properly under way. The film as it emerged was wholly Murnau's, both in conception and execution, but certain film historians still knowingly falsify the facts by referring to it as a joint effort of the two film-makers, and even compound their crime by referring to Flaherty *first!*

We must consider *Tabu* an American film in that it was financed by and released by an American company, Paramount. But in that it had no stars (American or otherwise) and was the work of one man, Murnau (assisted by that fine American cameraman, Floyd Crosby), it could, with some justification, also be considered a German film. But whatever its nationality, and whatever the travails behind its making, *Tabu* was undoubtedly the greatest poetic-documentary that the American cinema ever produced, certainly a finer film even than *Nanook of the North*, which takes its place as the leader of the realist-documentary school.

Tabu, which started as a simple picturization of the life of the Polynesians, somewhat on the order of Flaherty's earlier *Moana*, was transformed into something quite different when Murnau took over the reins. There was documentary coverage of South Sea life

and customs; there were the expected vistas of palm trees and rolling surf, but these were merely the backgrounds to a story as mystical as Murnau's old German fantasies. Its story, stripped to the barest essentials, was of a girl consecrated to the gods by the islanders, and thus forbidden to love, or marry. But she *does* love—and the holy man of the islands, to prevent a consummation of that love, takes her away. Her distraught lover swims desperately after the holy man's schooner—only, eventually and inevitably, to sink beneath the waves when he is exhausted. Its story had little more substance to it than that, but Murnau imbued it all with his own particular poetry and that romantic fatalism so beloved of German directors after World War I. The figure of the holy man was really an extension of the Fate figure, that personifica-

tion of Destiny that stalked through so many German silents, and against whose will the pleas of young lovers were inevitably doomed to failure.

Although a critical success, and not exactly a box office failure, *Tabu* was obviously too off-beat to prove a resounding box office success. Too, though released with a musical score, it was, of course, a silent. When it was first shown in 1931, its breathtaking pictorial loveliness and stately visual style seemed dated and out of touch with those times, when the "movies" had become the "talkies."

Its gloomy forebodings of death and its theme of the impossibility of escape from one's fate had an ironic counterpoint in real life. Just before *Tabu* opened in 1931, F. W. Murnau was killed in an automobile accident.

Part Two
75 GREAT STARS

Broncho Billy Anderson

I wonder if G. M. Anderson really knew quite what he was starting when he established his "Broncho Billy" character back in 1908. That was five years after the man whose only connection with the West had been posing as a cowboy for a magazine cover had entered movies by working in Edison's *The Great Train Robbery* as a bit player. He got the job by claiming to be an expert horseman, but after mounting the horse from the wrong side, and later being thrown off, his deception was quite apparent and he was shifted to on-foot activity for the rest of the one-reel epic. With little to do at Edison, he moved over to Vitagraph, as a director, and a little later arranged to go to Colorado to make some westerns for Selig. They were little more than travelogues, however, and didn't "click."

Not long after that, Billy made history by forming the Essanay ("S" and "A") Company with his friend George K. Spoor. Essanay was to have a comparatively short, though interesting, life-span, with a series of Chaplin films and Anderson's own Broncho Billy westerns representing its most important product.

Anderson now sensed what was wrong with the westerns he made for Selig—they were too tame, lacking the punch of *The Great Train Robbery*. And he realized too, that if he was going to make a lot of them, he'd need a central character with whom audiences could sympathize. Billy was losing time looking around for a hero, so decided to play the lead in the first one himself. He was big and beefy, far from handsome, and he still couldn't ride. He was a long way from today's conception of the western star.

But Billy wasn't breaking precedents—he was *making* them. There were no other western stars around for comparison, so what did appearances matter? Both Billy and the film were a hit, and he decided to carry on as star *and* director, using the name he had used in that first film. (It had been taken from a Peter B. Kyne story called "Broncho Billy and the Baby".) Thus Billy became literally the first western star, paving the way for Tom Mix and Bill Hart, who were to arrive within a few years, and the scores of movie and TV western heroes who were to follow.

Anderson made literally hundreds of one- and two-reel Broncho Billy westerns. He wasn't entirely consistent: sometimes Billy was a badman reformed by love, sometimes he was strictly on the side of law and order. A couple of times he got himself killed off! But for a man who knew nothing about the West, Billy's horse operas had a surprising ring of authenticity to them. The costumes were sometimes a little strange, and the dialogue subtitles often overdone, in the manner of western pulp fiction. But the stories were strong, and the films themselves were nicely directed, photographed and edited.

They got better as they went along, and so did Billy. He never became exactly a fighting fool, but he learned to ride well enough, took an occasional leap into the saddle, and was certainly husky enough to take care of himself in a fight. For all his poundage, he was an impressive figure of a man, with sharp, steely eyes that became something of a trademark as he cowed outlaws right and left.

Marguerite Clayton was Billy's leading lady in *Shootin' Mad* and other films in the series. She was a lovely young miss, and a good actress. But apart from her, no other players of note emerged from the Broncho Billy series, although elsewhere on the Essanay lot, Gloria Swanson, Francis X. Bushman and Wallace Beery were making their first appearances on the screen.

Billy moved into feature-westerns too late, and as soon as he saw that he couldn't compete with Hart and Mix, he withdrew to concentrate on producing comedies again. He made a particularly fine series with Stan Laurel—which came to an end when Anderson, never too good a business man, found that under his releasing arrangement with Louis B. Mayer, he couldn't make enough of a profit to make all the effort worth while. So, in the very early 20's, the screen's pioneer western star retired from the industry—permanently. When he was recently asked what he had been doing during the 40 years he had been absent from the screen, his reply couldn't have been more typical. "Just driftin' along with the breeze," explained Broncho Billy.

Anderson in his familiar "Broncho Billy" get-up.

Vilma Banky

As she appeared in *The Awakening*.

Opposite Ronald Colman in *Two Lovers*.

Even if Vilma Banky hadn't been a good actress, she would be one of my foremost favorites from the silent days. She was a graceful, beautiful creature, a lady in the fullest sense of the word, with a regal bearing in every movement and gesture she made. She should never have played anything but princesses and aristocrats—and for the most part she never did. When she made her first talkie, there was almost as much excitement as when Garbo first spoke on the screen in *Anna Christie*. Vilma Banky occupied the same sort of niche that Grace Kelly did in talkies—except that Grace usually played far more down-to-earth characters. There was always something "special" and a bit unreal about Vilma. Even when she did a western, *The Winning of Barbara Worth*, she seemed to represent something far more ethereal than just the city girl beloved by both Ronald Colman and Gary Cooper.

Vilma, discovered in Budapest by Sam Goldwyn, was starred almost exclusively in lush, romantic dramas—some, like *The Dark Angel*, with some resemblance to reality; others, like *Son of the Sheik* and *Night of Love*, designed as nothing more than extravagant escapist entertainment. And how well they were designed to fulfill that aim! People who look at films like these today for the first time often dismiss them lightly as being somewhat infantile, and ask scornfully, "Who ever took them seriously?" The point is, of course, that nobody took them seriously, nor were they supposed to. They were all part of the wonderful make-believe of Hollywood's most extravagant era, when story-telling didn't always necessitate "realism" and "logic."

Vilma's career was relatively brief. In a spectacular wedding that was one of the highlights of Hollywood's social season, she married Rod la Rocque in 1927. A few years later she retired from the screen permanently, and La Rocque too began to curtail his screen appearances. Their marriage is still one of Hollywood's happiest, and wise real estate investments have brought them a handsome income. It's always pleasant to be able to put on record that two such fine people have weathered the years so happily and successfully.

And Vilma's beauty—a classic beauty that doesn't change with the passing years—is still available on celluloid to those who have never forgotten. Her two films with Rudolph Valentino, *The Eagle* and *Son of the Sheik* have been revived constantly over the past twenty years, both in movie theatres and on television.

The Dark Angel, a Sam Goldwyn production of 1925.

The Magic Flame (1927).

While Vilma was making *The Magic Flame, Rod La Rocque* was filming *The Fighting Eagle* in the same (Cecil B. DeMille) studio. The two met, fell in love, and married that same year.

vived except her classic *A Fool There Was* and a much later comedy short, *Madame Mystery,* made when she was no longer a big star and was merely kidding her former screen personality. In a way it's an especial pity that *A Fool There Was* is the only vintage Bara that remains to us. Since it is the first of the vamp films, it is fortunate that it should have survived. But as the first, it was also one of the crudest in many ways, and gives a rather inaccurate picture of the whole vampire cycle.

For that comparatively early period, it was a very good picture. Its theme was powerful and pulled no punches. It tried, courageously, to be different by showing a man's downfall at the hands of an evil woman in scenes of purely symbolic content. Scenes like this tend to seem dated today, and are likely to evoke raucous laughter from audiences that know and care nothing about the history of the silent screen. So too does some of Theda's high-powered emoting. I only wish that some of these titterers could take a look at

In *When a Woman Sins* (1918).

Theda Bara

Two exciting things happened to the movies in 1915. One was the release of *The Birth of a Nation.* The other was the triumphant rise of Theda Bara, and the coining of a new phrase in the movie vocabulary—the "vamp."

Theda Bara (the name is an anagram of "Arab Death," she being touted as being of exotic and illegitimate Egyptian parentage) was a Cincinnati girl, born Theodosia Goodman, and the film that swept her to stardom overnight was Fox's *A Fool There Was,* directed by Frank Powell. It was based on Rudyard Kipling's "The Vampire," and it was no sooner on theatre screens throughout the land than the word vampire was abbreviated to "vamp," specifying a female creature of prey.

Theda Bara films today are rarer than those of any other American star, with the possible exception of Eddie Polo. Little of Theda's appears to have sur-

certain other romantic dramas of the day, and they would realize that, for all its present-day inadequacies, it was a remarkably advanced film for those years. More than that, I wish that more of Theda Bara's other films between 1914 and 1920 were available to us today. Theda is too often classified as a vamp pure and simple (maybe *not* so pure and *not* so simple, on second thought) and she certainly did stimulate the activity of other vamp stars—Louise Glaum, Valeska Suratt, and many others. But her talents were by no means limited to femme fatale roles, and she played dramatic and romantic roles in a surprising number of non-vamp pictures. She was Esmerelda, the dancing gypsy, in *The Dancer of Paris*—an early version of *The Hunchback of Notre Dame*; she played the tragic Cigarette in *Under Two Flags* (a role Claudette Colbert essayed in the talkie version), and was Juliet to Harry Hilliard's Romeo in *Romeo and Juliet*. Just before 1920, she did a complete about-face from her usual style to play the sweet and simple heroine of *Kathleen Mavourneen*. But of course, and understandably, it is as the Great Vamp that she is remembered—in modern dramas like *Destruction*, and in stories of the great sirens of history and literature—*Cleopatra, Camille, Salome,* and *Du-Barry*

I hope that someone, someday, will do a film on the life of Theda Bara. But I hope that they do it as seriously and as well as Universal's film on Lon Chaney. To play it for laughs (like Betty Hutton's travesty on Pearl White) would do a disservice not only to the industry and the cause of film history, but to the memory of a great performer as well.

Salome (1918), likewise made for Fox. Bara was probably the biggest box office name that the studio ever had.

125

As Captain Ahab in *The Sea Beast* (1926), the first of two Barrymore versions of *Moby Dick*.

John Barrymore (in *Don Juan*, 1926).

John Barrymore

There are those who think that there was more than a touch of "ham" in John Barrymore . . . and perhaps there was. Only really great actors can get away with ham, and only really great actors can get away with not taking themselves quite seriously! On all counts, John Barrymore was one of the greatest. The pity is that that sound films arrived too late to be able to show him in the full bloom and fire of his youth. How much more wonderful his already delightful 1917 version of *Raffles* would have been had we *heard* the witticisms of the amateur cracksman, and his verbal duel of wits with his detective opponent. How much more tender and moving would his love scenes and the climactic "mad" scene have been in *Beau Brummel* (1923). Not that Barrymore needed sound; even without dialogue he was the finest actor on the silent screen.

But he was, after all, a stage player first, and that wonderful voice he deployed so well was one of his greatest assets. And when sound came in, the studios realized it. Between them, Warners', M-G-M and RKO rushed him from one film to another in the first years of talkies. He played a debonair playboy here, a sardonic attorney there; *Svengali* at Warners', *Arsene*

Lupin at M-G-M; from comedy to melodrama, pathos to whimsy; an incredible gallery of outstanding portraits in a fantastically short period.

Barrymore's initial films for Paramount, a whole series prior to 1920, had been primarily comedies. With that jaunty cock of the head, the quizzically raised eyebrow, the graceful flourish of the hand, Barrymore was a pantomimic farceur par excellence, but even in his lighter roles there was always more than a hint of the dynamic force that lay beneath the surface. One scene in *Raffles* called for John to lose his temper briefly. A mad look came into those eyes, the hand came to the forehead in that classic gesture of his, and for a few seconds we had a graphic preview of the dramatic madness that was to become so inherent a part of his later work.

For John Barrymore loved the grotesque and the bizarre. Even though exploited as a great lover, he was happiest in much stronger roles. Famed for his classic profile, he did his utmost to find parts in which his handsome features could be distorted into fearsome ugliness. Barrymore loved and respected the theatre and the acting profession far too much to take liberties with a role; but he had no grandiose ideas about

When Gregory Peck played Captain Ahab recently, the changes in him were purely psychological. Barrymore made them psychological *and* physical, as this scene from *The Sea Beast* shows; his makeup had a lot in common with his Mr. Hyde of six years earlier.

Beau Brummel: the climactic scene, as the spirit of a young Brummel rises from the corpse of the unhappy old man who has just died in the dingy French asylum.

himself, and thus had no qualms at all about playing parts that might "displease" his public, or that his advisors thought would not advance his career.

From *Dr. Jekyll and Mr. Hyde* on (and that was in 1920), he was to alternate between straight romantic dramas and swashbucklers and films that enabled him to play men with twisted minds and warped bodies. And even when there was apparently no such opportunity in a given role, Barrymore would subtly contrive a sequence in a script that would give him the chance he needed. Both *Tempest* and *When a Man Loves,* in which he played otherwise straightforward heroes, had sequences in which the hero was imprisoned and almost went mad! In *Don Juan,* to effect the rescue of Mary Astor, he had to masquerade as a fiendish torturer. And so on. In *Sherlock Holmes* he had a field day, since as the greatest detective of them all he could don some quite incredible disguises! (Interestingly enough, Barrymore was up to these same tricks much later in his career when, in the late 30's, he played in a number of Bulldog Drummond "B" movies!)

Most Barrymore movies had what we might call a "fun" sequence—an excuse for a full display of his bravura style—but when the fun was over, the serious acting remained. Barrymore's acting was of

the old, virile school—not "ham," not flamboyant theatrics, but not passive underplaying either, as is the current trend. How much he could convey with but a single gesture, or the slightest movement of the head. *Beau Brummel* (1923) was generally a weak picture, but Barrymore's performance, the only really good thing about the picture, was superb. How well Barrymore made us understand the dandy who went just a shade too far and alienated his friend the King . . . how piteously he conveyed the predicament of a man who knew that he was wrong, but who was too vain to take the few humble steps that would put matters aright, preferring instead to don a mantle of indifference, realizing that it meant a downward spiral into disgrace and poverty. In one scene, the now shabby Brummel is sitting in his attic, toasting sausages over a fire. As he eats, a morsel of food clings to his mouth. The man who was once so fastidious about dress and manners doesn't even notice it, and it finally falls from his lips, unseen—a brief little vignette, occupying but a few seconds, but conveying more eloquently than half-a-dozen fully-written scenes, well equipped with titles, the downfall of this man—and his apathy concerning it. *Beau Brummel* was full of extremely touching moments like this, one of the most moving being the brief reunion between Brummel

127

Herman Melville's *Moby Dick* had no love interest at all; needless to say, both Barrymore versions did. In the first, Dolores Costello, who became Barrymore's wife, was the heroine.

available. Because they were so deliberately "prestige" films, they gained the reputation of being on the highbrow side, which most of them actually were not. But the label stuck, and outside of the metropolitan areas, Barrymore was not a top box office name. A draw, yes—but not the spectacular draw that the greatest actor of the screen should have been.

Off-screen, Barrymore's life was often unhappy, complicated by marital misadventures, more than once involved in scandal. He was as colorfully robust off-screen as on, given to wild, reckless living. He was the possessor of a wicked wit and an uninhibited vocabulary that had to be heard to be believed. Undoubtedly, all the stories ever told about John Barrymore's off-screen antics are entirely true. Perhaps if they weren't, that troubled genius wouldn't have had the spark that *made* him John Barrymore, The Great Profile, and the finest actor of the twentieth century.

As François Villon, opposite Marceline Day in *The Beloved Rogue.*

Barrymore's last silent, opposite Camilla Horn in *Eternal Love* (1929).

and the woman he still loves. Now, after many years, she is finally free to marry him, but in his sad and poverty-stricken condition he is too proud to admit that he still loves her and sends her away. *Beau Brummel*'s climax is of course the famous asylum scene in which Brummel, now aged and insane, is visited by his faithful old butler. Believing himself back in his years of affluence, he sets about preparations for a huge feast, only to fall dead just as he has concluded a toast to his love. I have referred to *Beau Brummel* so extensively not because it is one of Barrymore's best, but for exactly the opposite reason. As a picture, it was one of his worst—and had so little of merit in it that his great performance stands out in stark relief. One can see the film solely to study Barrymore's acting, and not be concerned over having one's attention diverted by plot or subtleties of direction.

John Barrymore was Warners' big "prestige" star of the 20's. His films were long, handsomely mounted, done with the best directors and supporting casts

Richard Barthelmess

Richard Barthelmess

One of Barthelmess' rare costume roles: *The Fighting Blade* (1923).

B. Walthall, but that of Arthur Johnson. (Johnson, a fine stage player, had been with Griffith only in his Biograph days; alcoholism had brought about his death at a comparatively early age, thus cutting short what might have been one of the most distinguished screen careers of all.)

Be that as it may, Barthelmess, a top name player after only a handful of films, left Griffith in 1920 to form his own company, Inspiration, along with director Henry King, and to star in what is still considered *the* Barthelmess picture, *Tol'able David*, in which he effortlessly and convincingly played a country lad in his teens.

After such a promising beginning to his career,

Although Richard Barthelmess made his first appearance in films under the guidance of director Herbert Brenon, it was D. W. Griffith who helped form the basic Barthelmess screen-character. It was certainly Griffith who, in such films as *Scarlet Days* and the later, more important, *Broken Blossoms* and *Way Down East,* made a star of the first magnitude of Barthelmess.

In many ways, Barthelmess was the ideal Griffith hero—modest, unassuming, good-looking without being strikingly handsome, with an appearance that suggested both gentleness and a masculine strength which could be brought into play when the occasion demanded. Until Barthelmess joined the Griffith ranks, D. W.'s No. 1 leading man had been Robert Harron, a sensitive actor, but rather weak in appearance. In the right role (as in *Intolerance*) he was perfect, but he lacked the physical attributes to make him a star of box office stature.

These attributes Barthelmess possessed in full measure, and he made an appealing and virile hero in several Griffith films, including, apart from those already mentioned, two South Seas melodramas, *The Idol Dancer* and *The Love Flower*. Barthelmess was the most popular of all the Griffith heroes, but it's interesting that late in the 20's, when Griffith was asked to name the best actor he had ever directed, he gave the name not of Barthelmess nor even of Henry

In his early days under Griffith; with Dorothy Gish in *I'll Get Him Yet* (1919).

Barthelmess didn't quite carry through as expected. His standards of performance never lessened, nor did his popularity wane. Indeed, to the contrary, it grew considerably. But somehow no more pictures of the calibre of *Broken Blossoms, Way Down East* or *Tol'-able David* came his way. As a popular star with his own company, he had to be conscious of what the public·wanted, and deliver films that were as "sure-fire" as possible. The films that rolled off the Inspiration assembly-line were all slick, polished productions; in terms of entertainment value, Barthelmess never disappointed the fans.

One of his best films of the mid-20's was the fascinating *Soul Fire*, in which he played a composer. His music was symbolic of the various phases of his life—and as his concerto was performed for the first time, flashbacks told of the events which inspired the various movements, the best of them being a fine South Seas sequence with Bessie Love. Other top Barthelmess pictures of the 20's were *The Drop Kick*, a college football story, *Ransom's Folly*, an unusual story of the U. S. Cavalry (hardly a western in the accepted sense), *The Patent Leather Kid* (with some fine war scenes), and the costume dramas *The Amateur Gentleman* and *The Fighting Blade*.

In all of these, Barthelmess varied but little from the screen personality he had built up; it was only when talkies came in, and so many stars found themselves being "reshuffled," that Barthelmess began to play occasional heavies and heels, although usually ones that were repentant by the time the final reel rolled around.

Barthelmess today is a wealthy man and living in happy retirement—with no need or wish to return to the screen for an inferior role. But he has retained his good looks, his jet-black hair, and the addition of a pair of spectacles has, if anything, afforded him added distinction. Should the right role come along, Barthelmess would be an obvious asset to the screens of today.

130

Clara Bow

It's strange but true that Clara Bow, the girl who symbolized the flapper age and the roaring 20's to millions, has no one film to represent her. When one thinks of Garbo, *Flesh and the Devil* comes first to mind. With Valentino it's *The Sheik*. But with all the films she made, there just isn't a "typical" Clara Bow picture! The film she's most frequently identified with, *It,* is actually one of her quieter and least representative pictures, notable more for the pleasing performance of Gary Cooper than for any jazz-age frolics.

Clara was a long time reaching the top. She made her debut with a fine supporting performance in *Down to the Sea in Ships,* a 1923 whaling epic—one of the

As she appeared in the Eddie Cantor comedy, *Kid Boots,* in 1926.

best films of that year. As a New England miss, she looked charming in period costume, and in sequences requiring her to masquerade as a boy, revealed a fine flair for comedy. It wasn't long before she was signed by producer B. P. Schulberg to appear in a series of films for Arrow. Ostensibly starring vehicles for her, they placed her in a jazz-age environment, built her up as a flaming flapper, but never seemed quite sure how to handle her. Arrow was a small independent outfit, and the films were cheaply made. For the most part, Clara had to be the whole show, as the budget didn't run to the top names for co-starring roles. And considering how inferior some of these early films were, it's a tribute to the talent and personality of the youngster so new to acting that she was able to carry them so successfully. They were a curious group. When they had fairly strong stories, like *Capital Punishment, The Primrose Path and Free to Love,* they were singularly devoid of the jazzy elements that made Clara tick. And when they *did* have lively elements, as did *My Lady of Whims,* which poked fun at Greenwich Village bohemians, and had a couple of really wild party sequences, the stories were too dull to attract much attention. The directors were hardly out of the top drawer either. Few of Clara's Arrow pictures were notable, with perhaps the exception of *The Plastic Age,* which had an above-average script, a fine performance from Henry B. Walthall—and athletic young Clark Gable as an extra!

But when producer Schulberg moved to Paramount he took Clara with him and then her career really began to pop. Films like *It, Rough House Rosie, Dancing Mothers, Red Hair* and *The Wild Party*; popular leading men like Antonio Moreno, James Hall, Warner Baxter, and top-calibre directors like William Well-

With Lane Chandler in *Red Hair*.

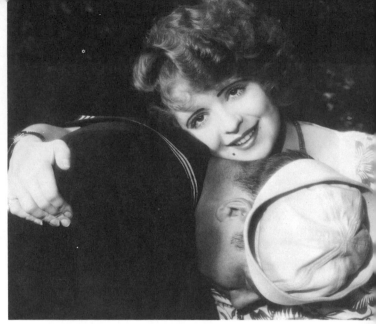

Opposite James Hall in *The Fleet's In*.

man and Herbert Brenon, all helped to make Clara the same sort of sensation in the 20's that Brigitte Bardot has become today.

Despite "naughty" titles and advertising that seemed to promise the ultimate in sex and sin, Clara's movies were basically pretty innocent. A lot was suggested, and threatened, but nothing really happened. When Clara played a "mixed-up" kid, she was less complicated about it than the youngsters in today's juvenile delinquency movies. Usually she was just raising hell because it was the era to raise hell, and to have done otherwise would have been old-fashioned. It didn't take much to straighten her out at the end of reel seven; usually all that was needed was a marriage proposal from some nice young fellow like James Hall. Basically, Clara projected a sort of flapper-age Peter Pan—a girl who'd never really grown up, didn't fully

understand the implications of the hectic life she was pursuing, and whose very naïveté and decency always seemed to extricate her from serious problems. Clara's vivacious pep, which could dissolve into tenderness so suddenly, were very much the real thing. With a far from happy home life, Clara threw herself into her movies with a tremendous enthusiasm, as though to make *them* her real life. When an era ended and the flappers were no more, Clara was momentarily at a loss. Where to put all this energy, where to direct her life from now? She made talkies—good ones—but the Clara Bow legend was over. From now on, she would be just another pretty little ingenue making pictures that any one of a dozen girls could play just as well. Wisely, she decided in favor of retirement—a happy retirement, with her new, first, and only husband, handsome cowboy star Rex Bell.

Police chief Joseph Girard hauls Clara over the coals in *Rough House Rosie*.

Because of the publicity attached to Elinor Glyn's personality theories, *It* is Clara's most famous film, but far from her best. William Austin is her escort in this scene, but Antonio Moreno, playing a yacht-owning millionaire was the man she finally won.

132

William Boyd

It's ironic that William Boyd, who achieved even greater fame in sound pictures as "Hopalong Cassidy" than he had in silents as a matinee idol, and played many a rugged hero in movies of the 20's, was one of the world's worst horsemen! When he played in a silent western (such as *The Last Frontier*) or any silent film involving riding, the script was carefully worked out so that he had a minimum of such scenes. And even those, unless the horse was practically standing still, were done by a double! When the "Hopalong Cassidy" series began, of course, Boyd really applied himself. Cliff Lyons, an expert stunt man, doubled for him in the first three or four, but by that time Boyd had had time to practice, and emerged as a really first-rate rider!

Boyd started off in extra roles, mainly in DeMille pictures, but by 1922 was beginning to get bigger and better roles. And in the late 20's he had the distinction of starring in a series of Cecil B. DeMille productions, and being loaned out to D. W. Griffith for the lead in *Ladies of the Pavement*.

An exceedingly handsome fellow, but, like George O'Brien, handsome in a rugged and breezy way, Boyd had an easy manner, a sincere smile, and a way of appealing to youngsters right away, even in fare that otherwise would be of an adult nature. Few of his films, it must be admitted, were of outstanding calibre; he was rushed from one picture to another so fast that perhaps this isn't surprising. But he himself rapidly became an important box office name, and for the most part his films—a few light comedies excepted—were rugged adventure yarns like *The Yankee Clipper* and

With Sue Carol (Mrs. Alan Ladd) in *Skyscraper*.

Griffith's *Lady of the Pavements,* with (left) Lupe Velez and (right) Jetta Goudal.

Leatherneck. Skyscraper gave him an interesting role in the William Haines manner, and afforded him the opportunity for some strong straight dramatics. And in DeMille's *The King of Kings* he made the small but important role of Simon of Cyrene into a most moving little cameo. His most celebrated film was *The Volga Boatman*—a DeMille epic of the Russian revolution—a tremendous winner in its day, but one that does not live up to its reputation when re-seen today. Another top Boyd film for DeMille was *The Road to Yesterday,* which enabled him to play a sensitive priest in the modern episodes of the film, and a swashbuckling cavalier in a second story. (A "Bridey Murphy" type of story, it traced the lives of the protagonists back to another age.) In the period story, Boyd had a particularly exciting and well-staged duel with the villain, Joseph Schildkraut—and today it is strange indeed to see our "Hoppy" wearing a long wig, period costume, and besting the enemy with a sword instead of a six-shooter!

If one Boyd silent stood out above all the others, it was Lewis Milestone's *Two Arabian Knights*, a real gem of a film, a fine mixture of melodrama and fun. But whether he was playing a doughboy (as in *Her Man O'War*), a cadet (*Dress Parade*) or a two-fisted skipper out to wrest the China tea trade away from the British (*Yankee Clipper*), Boyd was always the virile, hard-hitting, no-nonsense hero that later generations came to revere in theatres and on television as "Hopalong Cassidy."

Her most famous role—as "Peter Pan."

In the title role of *The Golden Princess*, a western despite its title.

Betty Bronson

When Betty Bronson, a New Jersey teen-ager, became a national sensation in late 1924 as *Peter Pan* in the first movie adaptation of that classic, it looked for a while as though she might usurp Mary Pickford's throne as "America's Sweetheart." Paramount head Adolph Zukor frequently referred to Betty as his "new Mary Pickford," and fan devotion throughout the country duplicated, and even surpassed, the idolatry that had greeted Mary's earlier films. After all, Mary, though still tremendously popular and still making excellent movies, *had* lost that flush of youth. Betty was the logical successor.

That she occupied Mary's throne for little more than a year was due partly to the confusion of her studio, but mainly to the changing tempo of the times. *Peter Pan* and its successor, *A Kiss for Cinderella,* had been fairy tales, whimsies—and the demand in those hard-bitten jazz-age days was for something much more substantial. Just as Griffith had been forced to abandon patriotic spectacle for more contemporary themes, so did Paramount feel that they would have to abandon the pixie-ish fare in which Bronson excelled.

But what to do with her? Their indecision wrecked the most promising star they had. They made her a flapper, and the critics were kind. "This proves that Betty can *act*", more than one of them said. Then Paramount put her into a couple of westerns, and she was less happy. Traces of her pantomimic style from *Peter Pan* and the exuberance of the flapper roles came out in her performance—and there were the first adverse, though far from damning, comments from the reviewers.

During her stay at Paramount Betty appeared in some good pictures, and was at her best in some really delightful comedies, from *Are Parents People?* to *The Cat's Pajamas.* She was popular with the exhibitors and the public. But she was no longer, because of her strangely nondescript roles, a second Pickford. If anything, she was a second Colleen Moore— and most of the studios had one of those!

It was sad that her unique talent was being wasted. When she left Paramount and went to other studios, they apparently felt the same way. There was an attempt to restore Betty to the fantasy-comedy that had been so much her forte; as for example, in the First National film, *Paradise.* But the times were still against her. The coming of sound, which brought with it a demand for a new realism, was a further nail in the

135

Betty's first film after *Peter Pan*, a delightful comedy called *Are Parents People?* Adolphe Menjou on the left, Florence Vidor on the right.

As she appeared in *Not So Long Ago*, a charming piece of nostalgia.

Between scenes of *Not So Long Ago*, Betty has fun with co-star Ricardo Cortez and (right) director Sidney Olcott.

coffin of the movie fairy tale. (There were few successful American sound fantasies, other than the films of Disney. Shirley Temple's *The Blue Bird* and Judy Garland's *The Wizard of Oz* were standouts; generally, in the talkies, fantasy, when it appeared at all, was on the much grimmer lines of *The Devil and Daniel Webster*.)

Betty appeared in a number of early talkies—among them *The Singing Fool*, with Al Jolson. Her voice was good; but somehow *any* kind of a voice would have detracted from that curious appeal of hers. As a graceful, dancing sprite she needed no words. She spoke with her lovely, expressive eyes, with a beautiful smile that started unexpectedly from a determined set of the lips, and proceeded to light up that whole radiant face. In one scene in *Are Parents People?* she "acted" only with her shoulders; her back to the camera, she had conveyed irritation, apathy and finally, fury, all by subtly different shrugs. In another scene from that film, the camera concentrated on a closeup of her ankles; without the benefit of a subtitle or a cut-back to her face, she expressed, by the differing position of those ankles, decision, doubt, delay, and finally a renewed decision. The two Barrie films especially, but also the better comedies like *Are Parents People?* were full of subtleties of pantomime such as this. And even her straight dramatic performances, notably her sensitive portrayal of the Madonna in *Ben Hur,* were the better because of her underplayed visual pantomime.

Betty Bronson made only a few talkies, but even some of those, like 1930's *The Medicine Man,* were still valiantly trying to revive the old "Cinderella" format. She retired from the screen in 1932 when she married. She made only one more film ("just for the fun of it") in 1937, when she returned to do a Gene Autry western, *The Yodellin' Kid from Pine Ridge.* Intrestingly, it was another Cinderella role!

The real tragedy of Betty Bronson's career is that she arrived on the screen just a few years too late. *Peter Pan* should have been the zenith of one phase of her career, not the beginning of it. Had she arrived on the scene just ten years earlier, in that age of innocence when honest sentiment, whimsy, fantasy, and Cinderella themes were not deemed old-fashioned and out of touch with the times, what a star she could have become! Especially as Paramount was then in the process of losing Mary Pickford, and could well have used a star with Betty Bronson's unique gift, and deployed it to advantage in such films as *The Blue Bird*. Made by Maurice Tourneur, this was a lovely and appealing fantasy as it was; but with Bronson, it could have been a masterpiece.

If I stress the "tragic" element of Bronson's career so much it is only because *A Kiss for Cinderella* and *Peter*

Pan are such lovely films, due in very large measure to her work, that one likes to think that there could have been so many others like them. But few stars are lucky enough to leave *two* such lasting testimonials to their work, so in retrospect perhaps there is more to be happy about, than sorrowful over, in the brief but joyous career of Betty Bronson.

1927, and whimsy was abandoned (at Paramount at least) in favor of slick romantic comedy. This is from *Ritzy*.

With Lane Chandler in a western, *Open Range*. Chandler and Gary Cooper were the studio's rival western stars then. Both are still active, but only Cooper made it to the big time.

Attractively gowned for a period western, *The Golden Princess.*

To Warners', and a late silent that was released with talkie sequences—in *One Stolen Night* opposite William Collier, Jr. (1929).

From one of her earlier Paramount films, *The Show-Off*. Ford Sterling and Lois Wilson were the official stars, but Louise stole the picture and the reviewers' notices.

Louise Brooks

Louise Brooks is all but forgotten in the United States, but not in Europe, where she made three of her greatest successes. Miss Brooks' films are frequently revived there by the film archives. In 1958, the huge Cinémateque film museum in France held an "Hommage á Louise" festival, honoring the star and her work.

It is strange that some stars are forgotten so quickly in this country. While at her peak, Louise enjoyed a vogue almost unequalled by any other star, and her fans were so devoted that they almost constituted a cult.

Kansas-born Louise was initially a "Ziegfeld Follies" dancer, and also appeared in "George White's Scandals." Her truly incredible beauty—"classic" seems almost too cold a term to describe it, although it certainly was that—was undoubtedly responsible for her entry into films, and at Paramount, in silent, flapper-age comedies like *The American Venus, Rolled Stockings,* and *A Social Celebrity,* everything was done to exploit her face and figure. Even her remarkable acting in William Wellman's *Beggars of Life,* a powerful drama in which Louise dressed as a boy and tramped the road with fellow hoboes Richard Arlen and Wallace Beery, didn't spur her American employers to take advantage of her dramatic talents.

But in Germany it was a different story, and G. W. Pabst tailored two grim, psychological sex stories to her abilities: *Pandora's Box* (in which, as Lulu, she came to a tragic end at the hands of Jack the Ripper)

and the much-censored and now quite notorious *Diary of a Lost Girl.* Another unusual film followed in France—*Beauty Prize*—and then she returned to the States to resume her career.

Alas, the career never did resume. Louise herself admits that she was partially to blame, feeling in an uncooperative mood at a time when producers, harassed by the change-over to sound, wanted stars who would work to orders, and not take their jobs too seriously!

One way or another, Louise Brooks' career was sabotaged, and after increasingly rare, and increasingly uninteresting roles, she left films for good. But, like Garbo, she left a legend behind. A legend of a girl with a cool Mona Lisa smile and a beauty that seemed completely unaware of itself; a legend that was strangely kept alive by, of all things, a comic strip—for the "Dixie Dugan" comic strip gave its heroine the unique Louise Brooks hair-style.

But even with only a handful of films to her credit, Louise didn't need a comic strip for that legend to live. Today, in Europe at least, the legend lives on via the films themselves, and Louise, far less of a recluse than Garbo, has recently made two trips (one to Denmark, one to France) to re-introduce her great films from the last days of the silents.

One of her finest performances was in *Beggars of Life,* an outstanding film of the late 20's. Wallace Beery, with her in this scene, and Richard Arlen were her co-stars.

John Bunny

Genial, rotund John Bunny was the movies' first comic "fat man"—precursor of a long line of successors from Mack Swain to Oliver Hardy. Indeed, he was the movies' first comedian of stature. Audiences loved him —and so did Vitagraph, his studio, who appreciated his loyalty. Like many another Vitagraph star, Bunny had come to them from the vaudeville stage. Most of the others stayed a year or so, then left for the higher pay offered by rival studios. But not John Bunny, who made all his films for Vitagraph.

Bunny was, visually especially, but also in his over-all personality, a character right out of Dickens. Indeed, he played the lead in an early version of *Pickwick Papers,* which Vitagraph filmed on location in England. And what a perfect Mr. Dick he would have made in *David Copperfield!* Bunny's talent at dialects could not, of course, be utilized by films at that time, but his other talents could, and he was a good enough actor not to rely on short comedies alone. He was quite prominently cast in Helen Gardner's *Vanity Fair,* for example, and appeared in a number of dramatic subjects at Vitagraph.

Naturally, though, it was as a comedian that he was best loved. His favorite roles were as the roaring, yet golden-hearted, sea captain—and as the lonely old bachelor, happy in the companionship of his dog. He'd give audiences a tear one moment, and a rousing laugh the next—just as Chaplin was to do several years later. His comedy was pantomimic and refined, with none of the crude slapstick that passed for comedy in so many films of that period. Some of his best were marital farces like *Polishing Up,* one of many in which he co-starred with Flora Finch. He usually played the erring husband out on the town for a little flirtation behind Flora's back. For that early period, when movies were still considered far from respectable, some of his films were decidedly on the risqué side—but they were done with such good humor and good taste, that no one was

ever offended. And after all the deceptions and near-discoveries, Flora and John would fall into each other's arms again for the fadeout, all love and forgiveness, in scenes that were often surprisingly touching for one-reel comedies.

Few stars as beloved as John Bunny ever had as short a reign. He joined Vitagraph in 1910—and died only five years later.

John Bunny: a characteristic pose from one of his best-known films, *Bachelor Buttons.*

From *Bunny Attempts Suicide.* Despite his anguished expression (and he was a good enough actor to make the straight dramatics pay off well), this little film was a comedy—and a good one.

John Bunny with his popular team-mate, Flora Finch, in 1912's *A Cure for Pokeritus,* one of the many delightful family comedies they made together.

139

With his wife, Beverly Bayne, in *Romeo and Juliet,* an early Metro film of 1915.

Francis X. Bushman

It is strange that when people today talk of Francis X. Bushman, the immediate image that comes to mind is Bushman as Messala, urging his horses onward in the chariot race scene from *Ben Hur*. Strange, because this was a villain role, while Bushman had earned his reputation as a dashing romantic hero. Yet, without doubt, Messala did give Bushman one of his finest roles—and equally without doubt, *Ben Hur* was the biggest and most successful film that he appeared in.

Bushman, like Maurice Costello, was a matinee idol of the pre-1920 audiences. Indeed, in 1914 he came out on top, beating Costello by many votes, when *The Ladies' World* invited its readers to select their favorite movie hero. Bushman at that time was a real new-comer, having only just joined the Essanay studios in Chicago. Prior to that he had been both a stage actor and a sculptor's model. Essanay undoubtedly realized

Ten years later—and still a strikingly handsome leading man; with Anna Q. Nillson in *The Thirteenth Juror*, made for Universal in 1927.

what an asset it had in his sturdy physique, and frequently cast him in Ruritanian adventures and costume melodramas requiring him to wear the most dashing and picturesque of costumes. Between these affairs, he cut a fine figure in top hat and tails, too, so he was much in demand for society dramas. His co-stars were those lovely ladies, Ruth Stonehouse and Beverly Bayne and occasionally child star Baby Parsons, better known today as Harriet Parsons, a successful movie producer. Harriet's mother—Louella—wrote some of the scenarios of the films in which her daughter and Mr. Bushman appeared.

When the new Metro company was formed in 1915, Bushman was one of the first stars put under contract, and he stayed with the company right through the 20's. One of his earliest successes was as the most muscular of all Romeos, in 1915's *Romeo and Juliet*. Juliet was Beverly Bayne, Bushman's wife off-screen, a fact very much hushed up at the time, since it was feared that a married, and thus "unattainable," hero would lose much of his romantic appeal.

Bushman had a near-classic profile, and there was more than a little of Barrymore in his acting as well. A delirium scene in a Universal film of the mid-20's, *The Marriage Clause*, is played with many of the Barrymore gestures—and their slight physical resemblance gave the scene an uncanny sense of the two personalities fused into one. But Bushman's style was one that overlapped, rather than copied, Barrymore's. He was a fine actor in his own right. And his name is still one to conjure with. Though not a wealthy man, Bushman has never sold his name for the quick dollar, never taken a bit part or played an extra—as others of his contemporaries, such as the late William Desmond, often found themselves forced to do. When Bushman accepts a role these days, small though it may be, you can be sure it's a good role, one that will get attention, and one that will not lower his standing as an actor of importance.

Chaney without makeup—a gangster role in 1928's *The Big City*.

As the vampire in *London After Midnight*.

Lon Chaney

A few years ago, in *Man of a Thousand Faces*, Universal told the story of Lon Chaney, with James Cagney playing the famous silent star. It was the best biography of a star ever filmed (I still shudder when I recall the alleged "stories" of Buster Keaton and Pearl White) and apart from some minor errors and too-sweeping generalizations, it was for the most part accurate.

Chaney was a strange man personally—moody, intensely loyal to those he loved, unforgiving to those who had wronged him, and above all, dedicated to his art. His mastery of the art of makeup has never been equalled, let alone surpassed. It was Chaney who wrote the article on makeup in the *Encyclopedia Britannica*. But Chaney's genius—and I use that much-abused word deliberately—went much further than the skilled application of makeup. He was a master pantomimist and actor, much of his sensitivity and understanding deriving from his own childhood. His parents were deaf-mutes, and in order to converse with them and cheer them up, he not only became familiar with sign language, but was also adept at creating, via pantomime, pictures of his little escapades and adventures.

Between 1913 and 1918, Chaney appeared in at least a hundred minor roles, mainly in films for Universal release. During this period he also did some directing, and even wrote scenarios. Thus when he became a top screen name, he was always more than just an actor. He was often as much of a guiding factor behind his films as were the official producer and director. It is not commonly known that many sequences in his films—such as the trial of Esmerelda in *The Hunchback of Notre Dame*—were actually directed by him.

Although in later years, he tended to specialize in the grotesque, Chaney was never just a "horror player." Behind all the makeup, there was usually a tremendous amount of pathos. Without benefit of the spoken word, he would create characters who repelled with *physical* ugliness, yet attracted by the suffering or humanity of their souls.

Chaney's truly marvellous makeups (and the duplications of them in *Man of a Thousand Faces* were but pale shadows of the originals) often involved acute pain through their prolonged distortion of muscles and limbs, yet Chaney steadfastly refused to accept easier, and less convincing, substitutes for the devices he designed. Some of his feats were almost beyond belief; one of the most astounding was in *The Penalty*, in which he played a cripple whose legs had been amputated at the knees. Chaney's legs were bound tightly behind him, giving a completely convincing picture of a man so afflicted. But not content with walking in what must have been excruciating pain, Chaney even gave himself scenes in which he *jumped* from heights and landed on his knees!

Chaney's performance as the heavy in a 1918 western, *Riddle Gawne*, was what really brought him to the attention of producers, and he remained forever grateful to director Lambert Hillyer and star William S.

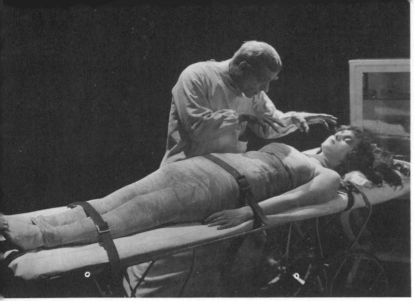

The Monster was directed by Roland West, an expert at making fine thrillers with a light touch. Chaney, as the mad doctor, played it to the hilt, but in refusing to take itself too seriously, the film confused audiences who didn't know whether they were supposed to be laughing or shuddering.

In *The Phantom of the Opera,* Chaney masked . . .

Hart for giving him that chance. *The Miracle Man* (in which Chaney played a cripple) followed, and made a star not only of him but also of Thomas Meighan and Betty Compson. *Treasure Island, The Penalty, Oliver Twist* (Chaney's performance as Fagin drew the praise of the critics) and *Victory* were other notable pictures before *The Hunchback of Notre Dame* (discussed at length elsewhere in this book) arrived in 1923 to establish Chaney as one of the half-dozen greats of the silent screen. His performance in that film is still intensely moving and poignant.

Thereafter, with the exception of *The Next Corner* for Paramount, and *The Phantom of the Opera* back at

Universal, Chaney made all of his films for Metro. They were all strong, "gutsy" films, but not all were melodramas or thrillers. Films like *The Tower of Lies,* made by the Swedish director Victor Seastrom, and also featuring Norma Shearer, gave him a chance to show what a really fine straight actor he was. For seven of his M-G-M films, Chaney teamed with an old friend who had directed him earlier, Tod Browning. Browning was a master of atmospheric chillers that aimed at far more than the superficial goose-pimple, and he and Chaney made an unbeatable combination for such films as *The Blackbird, The Road to Mandalay, The Unknown, London After Midnight* and *The Unholy Three.* Despite his success in off-beat and somewhat gruesome roles, it was in a straight adventure film, minus any kind of makeup, that Chaney scored one of his biggest

. . . and unmasked.

One of his most taxing portrayals, the memorable *The Penalty* (1920).

In *Where East is East.*

hits. This was as the tough sergeant in *Tell It to the Marines*—still one of the most subtle portrayals of its kind, with far more depth than the average current "tough-soldier-with-a-heart-of-gold" performance.

Chaney was dismayed when sound came in. He had a good voice, but he was afraid (and events have proved him right) that talkies would do away with the visual art of pantomime. However, he was persuaded to re-make, in sound, his great silent success *The Unholy Three,* which concerns a trio of weirdly assorted criminals, one of whom (Chaney) is a ventriloquist who masquerades as an old lady. Despite the modifying of some of the stronger elements of the original, and the introduction of added scenes to pacify the now more militant censors, the new *The Unholy Three* was a better film than the old. And it proved to Chaney that, in his case at least, pantomime need not necessarily be killed by the talkie. Audiences were fascinated by his great portrayal, in which he utilized four different voices. Sound, it seemed, would make Chaney a greater star than ever!

All sorts of vehicles were planned for him, including *Dracula,* which, of course, was ultimately done by Bela Lugosi. But a growth in his throat had begun to give him increasing trouble. As usual, he had not spared himself during the shooting of *The Unholy Three,* and undoubtedly the unusual strain on his vocal chords had only aggravated the condition. He entered a Los Angeles hospital, and cancer was diagnosed. He died on August 26, 1930—in silence. Towards the end, he had been completely unable to speak, and had been forced to return to the sign language and pantomime of his youth.

With Herbert Brenon, who directed him in *Laugh Clown Laugh.*

In *Laugh Clown Laugh.*

Masquerading as the old lady in *The Unholy Three.*

The clown in his familiar costume.

Charles Chaplin

With at least a dozen complete books written on Chaplin's career and films, what can one say about him that hasn't already become a platitude through years of repetition? There are those who feel that Chaplin is a god, at least cinematically, and can do no wrong.

I am not one of them. I have a tremendous amount of respect for his work, and consider him one of the foremost craftsmen of the screen. But to me Buster Keaton was a far superior comedy creator. Keaton stopped at comedy, however, whereas Chaplin's work often went far deeper. Conversely, there are those who despise *all* of Chaplin's work because of his political beliefs, alleged or actual, and who find in his films tendencies to inject scenes or thoughts to support those beliefs. (Even though if the exact same film had been made by someone else, no one would dream of interpreting them in that way!) This, of course, is quite unfair, and all that matters is what shows up on the screen. If Chaplin made bad films, they deserve to be criticized; if they were good, no other considerations matter.

The thing that impresses me most about Chaplin is what remarkable strides he made in his early years. The initial Keystones, made under Mack Sennett, were often unutterably crude and vulgar. The humor consisted of everyone running around at top speed, falling down on the slightest provocation, and delivering as many kicks to the posterior as the footage would allow. I am forever baffled by those historians who find a "grace" and "poetry" in the early Sennetts. They provided valuable training ground for a number of top comics, both players and directors, in their formulative years, and are not to be despised. They played a valuable role, and some were even very good. But the great Sennetts—and the great Chaplins—all came later. However, it is apparent that as Chaplin took over direction of his own Keystones, they began to show definite signs of improvement. Amid all the hectic buffoonery, there were often great little vignettes of subtle pantomime and genuine comic invention. Films like *His Trysting Place*, in which Charlie had Mabel Normand and Mack Swain working with him, were quite superior to the

From 1916's *Easy Street*, one of Chaplin's funniest two-reelers.

Chaplin's grace is quite apparent in this still from *The Rink*.

general run of Sennetts. Chaplin's Sennett period, beginning and ending in 1914, produced some 35 films, mainly one- and two-reelers, including also the feature, *Tillie's Punctured Romance,* with Marie Dressler, and Mabel Normand—a weak film, but important as the first feature-length comedy. In 1915, Chaplin moved to Essanay in Chicago, where he wrote, directed, and starred in sixteen one- and two-reelers, and also the now famous *Burlesque on Carmen,* which, in one brief scene, contained his first really serious acting on the screen. The Essanays stressed slapstick as had the Keystones, but they had better stories, and elements of pathos began to creep in now— in films like *The Tramp.* The Essanays were not by any means great comedies— but they were infinitely better than the Keystones—and they seemed to improve as they went along. Best of the batch was *A Night at the Show,* a really polished comedy with some very funny and well-developed comic routines.

From Essanay Chaplin went to Mutual where, in 1916-1917, he made the twelve two-reelers that, in my opinion, represent his greatest period. Films like *The Cure, Easy Street, The Pawnshop* and *The Immigrant* represent a flawless welding of brilliant comedy and really moving pathos. Edna Purviance, as Chaplin's perennial leading lady, lent her beauty and effective underplaying to all of these films, inevitably cast as either the poor, downtrodden girl who is rescued by Charlie or the well-to-do girl who seems out of his reach. Charlie's move to First National in 1918 seemed another big step up. The first film he made there, *A Dog's Life,* was considered by many to be his masterpiece up to that time. It's still one of his best.

Then came *Shoulder Arms,* a wonderful spoof of World War I heroics which somehow still managed to convey the tragedy of war without holding up any of the fun. *Shoulder Arms* doesn't have quite the same impact today, since so many of its ideas and routines have been copied endlessly through both the silent and sound periods. But its best sequences—Charlie's pantomime as he duels with an unseen sniper, his adventures in a flooded dugout, his masquerade as a tree in order to pentrate the enemy lines—are still hilariously funny.

But after *Shoulder Arms,* something happened. The critics had been noting, and praising, the deeper meaning in some of Charlie's films, and in their enthusiasm for subtleties and symbolism they went overboard, often reading into the film philosophic content that Chaplin had hardly intended. But Chaplin was impressed, and changed the format of his films. They

Chaplin in one of his rare sophisticated roles—with Edna Purviance in 1921's *The Idle Class.* But Charlie had a dual role, played his usual tramp character as well.

With Edna Purviance (who worked only for Chaplin) in his famous World War I comedy, *Shoulder Arms.*

A typical moment of slapstick from *Shoulder Arms.*

Chaplin, as director, explaining to his cameramen a scene that he is about to do in *The Circus*—his last comedy of the 20's.

were still comedies, but the pace slowed, the laughs were fewer and more obvious, and the pathos and drama were stepped up. The remainder of his films for First National—*The Pilgrim, The Kid, The Idle Class, Sunnyside,* and others, all with glorious moments, were, as a whole, a distinct retrogression from the great Mutuals and the first two at First National. They did nothing to lessen Chaplin's enormous popularity, however, and with the release of *The Gold Rush* through United Artists it was apparent that the Little Tramp was back in form again. The "serious" material remained—and indeed was to increase in subsequent Chaplin films—but the great comedy scenes were back.

Along with Griffith, Stroheim, Keaton and Fairbanks, Chaplin remains one of the half-dozen immortals of the American screen.

One of the funniest moments in *The Circus*—Chaplin, substituting for the tight-rope walker, believes he is supported by a wire. No sooner does he discover that it has fallen off than he is suddenly "attacked" by monkeys, one of whom insists on putting its tail into Charlie's mouth.

A rare still—Chaplin as Napoleon in a serious film that never materialized. A few stills showing costume and make-up are all that emerged from this fascinating idea.

Chaplin remained loyal to the concepts of the silent film longer than any one else. His last silent film—and one of his very best—was *Modern Times* (1936).

Marguerite Clark

With Eugene O'Brien in *Come Out of the Kitchen.*

With Harrison Ford in *Girls.*

Marguerite Clark

One of the great frustrations of those of us who love the silents is the lack of opportunity to evaluate the work of many of the stars who enjoyed a tremendous popularity when the movies were young, but whose careers were literally at twilight with the arrival of the 20's. The films themselves have not survived in many cases, and since comparatively little serious film criticism was being written in those days, one cannot even find contemporary opinions of real value. Marguerite Clark is a case in point. Brought to the screen from the stage by Famous Players in 1914, she was, only a year later, one of the most popular players on the screen, ranking with Chaplin and Mary Pickford in terms of audience approval. Yet today she is forgotten; and in books such as the recent *The Movies* one finds not a single mention of her!

I think it's interesting that in 1916, a leading fan magazine, *Motion Picture Magazine* (and fan magazines had far more substance and influence in those days than they have today) polled its readers to determine their opinions on the greatest screen performances to date. Performances that are *still* considered great were appropriately appreciated. Walthall's in *The Birth of a Nation* was in third place, those of Mae Marsh and Lillian Gish in the same film were farther down the list. Notable performances by Mary Pickford, Norma Talmadge, William Farnum, and others were duly recorded. Yet Marguerite Clark's performance in

Wildflower—her *first* picture—was voted into second place. Since she was beaten only by Earle Williams (for *The Christian*), the indications are that the public at large considered her the screen's finest actress. And at least *six* other Marguerite Clark performances placed prominently in the voting!

I must admit to never having seen a *complete* Marguerite Clark film—but from the snippets that I have seen, it is quite apparent that she was not just "a second-string Mary Pickford" as she is so often called. She was a sensitive and captivating little actress—and I have a sneaking suspicion that Mabel Taliaferro, Charlotte Burton, Ruth Blair and others of that 1914-1920 period must have been just as talented and charming.

We are making important rediscoveries in the realm of old films all the time. But the old nitrate stock is decaying fast; many prints and negatives have gone beyond recall; much more is decomposing even as I write. There is a desperate race against time to salvage (at great cost) as much of this material as possible before it has gone forever. To those of you who may be keeping old prints in your attics or basement, unseen for years, probably forgotten until now, I would say that while their monetary value might be slight, their cultural value (whether the film be good or bad) might be inestimable. *Please* see that such film is examined and preserved. If you don't know how to go about it, get in touch with me.

Who knows, maybe one of my readers has in his possession a print of *Wildflower*—the film that in 1916 was considered to have the finest performance by any screen actress to date.

Opposite Vilma Banky in *Two Lovers*.

Ronald Colman

Colman's polished performance was one of the greatest assets of Lubitsch's version of Oscar Wilde's *Lady Windermere's Fan*. With him here are Bert Lytell and May McAvoy.

Even though it is for talkies such as *Lost Horizon* and *The Prisoner of Zenda* that Ronald Colman is best remembered, and even though the silent screen could not exploit one of his greatest assets, his beautifully modulated and cultured voice, Ronald Colman was an enormously popular leading man in the 20's. He was without question the leader of the small but select band of "gentleman" heroes. Even when he was playing a gypsy outlaw or a fiery lover, he always somehow contrived to remain suave, debonair—and above all, polite and well-mannered. And if this sometimes lessened the conviction of the performance he was giving . . . well, that was amply compensated for by the charm and grace he exuded.

Born in England in 1891, Colman came of parents with no great wealth but a considerable "cultural" background. He was raised a gentleman, and so he remained, on screen and off, until his death in 1958. Today, unfortunately, the word "gentleman" is often used with a sneer, as though it were now quite out of date. Let me hasten to add that that is *not* my interpretation. Everybody who knew or worked with Colman loved and respected him. In the movie business, you can usually find somebody who is out to malign a prominent personality, no matter who he is. I've yet to come across anyone who feels so inclined towards Ronald Colman. He conducted his personal life via a code of honor and chivalry that seems to have forestalled the making of any enemies.

After notable service with Kitchener's forces in World War I, Colman turned seriously to the acting that had interested him casually, prior to the war. After some years on the British stage, and in some minor English films, Colman came to America. Some good reviews on the New York stage produced only disappointing film offers—at first. Colman bided his time in a couple of good programmers for Selznick (one of which starred George Arliss). Then the big break came. Impressed by his work in a New York play with Ruth Chatterton, director Henry King and star Lillian Gish offered him the male lead in *The White Sister*. As the tragic soldier hero, Colman was fine, and when the film was released in early 1924, he found himself an immediate star. It was natural that King and Miss Gish should use him again for their (and his) next picture, *Romola*. Like *The White Sister*, this was an elaborate film made in Italy. This time, unfortunately, Colman was sadly wasted. Though nominally the hero, he had literally nothing to do, and was quite overshadowed by the work of the Gish Sisters and William Powell as the villain.

But Colman was too good an actor—and too fascinating a star—to be downed by one bad role. Interesting films, light dramatics with Blanche Sweet, polished comedy with Constance Talmadge, followed fairly quickly, but it wasn't until 1925 that he really hit his stride again, making his first of many films for Sam Goldwyn, and the first of a long series of co-starring romantic adventures with Vilma Banky. The film that did it was *The Dark Angel*. A succession of hits followed for the now permanently established star—*Stella Dallas*, Lubitsch's *Lady Windermere's Fan, Kiki, The Winning of Barbara Worth*, the particularly fine *Beau Geste* (Colman's best performance to date), *The Night of Love*, and several others.

With talkies just ahead, Ronald Colman was on the threshold of a long and brilliant career. Now that he's gone, and his old films are reappearing on television, it's suddenly apparent how vital a part of the movie scene were his courtly manners and graceful good humor—and how very much he'll be missed.

Colman's last silent film: With Lili Damita in *The Rescue* (1929), a Joseph Conrad tale directed by Herbert Brenon.

Jackie as he is best remembered.

A star in his first film. With Chaplin in *The Kid* (1921).

Young Jackie was frequently cast in roles in which he brought joy into the lives of lonely old men, like Cesare Gravina in *Daddy*. But not all of the old men were as sympathetic as Gravina. Russell Simpson, seen above in a typical Coogan scene, certainly wasn't.

Jackie Coogan

Jackie Coogan has been coming back into the limelight again of late, with guest appearances on several TV shows, and dramatic roles in a number of movies. And nothing could be further from the Jackie Coogan of old than the Jackie we saw recently in *High School Confidential,* as the slimy head of a dope-peddling ring! Roles like that one are happily soon forgotten, but I don't think anyone who ever saw him as a child player can ever forget his performances in *The Kid, Oliver Twist,* and a dozen other movies of the 20's, made for First National and, later, M-G-M—where Joan Crawford was one of his first leading ladies!

Next to Shirley Temple, Jackie was about the most phenomenal child star Hollywood ever saw. No one could resist that round little face, those wide eyes which tried so often and so valiantly to hold back the tears, and that ragamuffin outfit of his that soon became his trade-mark—the cap turned around backwards, the oversized trousers, and the well-worn sweater. But quite apart from the pathetic and lovable figure he presented, Jackie was a good little actor too. He was fine in *The Kid,* his first film, but there were those who doubted that he had real talent. It was all Chaplin, they said. Jackie was merely a puppet on the master's strings, and on his own, he'd be helpless. They were

wrong. In his subsequent films, Jackie showed not only that he had a great natural gift for acting, but also that he was a very shrewd observer. Although only four and a half when he made *The Kid,* he had been sufficiently aware of what was going on to study Chaplin's pantomime—and to use it to his own ends in such subsequent films as *My Boy.*

The Kid and *Oliver Twist* apart, Coogan made no really *important* films. Important, that is, in an aesthetic sense. They were most decidedly important to the exhibitor, who found Jackie a little goldmine whether he was playing a mischievous little brat in *Peck's Bad Boy,* or a pathetic orphaned waif who befriends an old sea-dog in *My Boy.* Jackie's films were unashamedly sentimental. They played mercilessly on the heartstrings of the audience—and they succeeded with a vengeance. They were made for very little, and grossed a small fortune. While movie audiences of today have (to their loss, I feel) outgrown the honest sentimentality of the 20's to such an extent that Coogan's type of film will never be made again, his films still hold up surprisingly well. Their charm is still remarkably preserved, and little Jackie's performances are as moving and effective now as they were well over thirty years ago.

With John Barrymore in *The Sea Beast* (1926).

Dolores Costello

Along with her sister Helene, Dolores Costello made her bow in films in the distinguished company of her father, Maurice Costello. Both sisters were merely children then, and had little to do but add their juvenile good spirits and curly-haired prettiness to papa's one-reel dramas for Vitagraph. Dolores left the screen thereafter for a considerable period, to follow a career in the theatre and as a model, not returning to the screen full-time until the early 20's.

Dolores Costello was one of the loveliest leading ladies ever to grace the screen. She had poise, dignity, and a patrician beauty. That, in itself, would almost be enough, but she was also an extremely able actress. Few of her roles, however, made any very great demands on her acting ability. With her regal features and slim figure, she was usually cast as the aristocratic lady tamed by love—or as the pure and virtuous heroine threatened by sundry fates worse than death—with the oldest and most reliable of those fates usually well to the forefront, whether it be in a modern melodrama like *Old San Francisco* (in which only the 1906 earthquake saves Dolores from being sold into Oriental white slavery by Warner Oland) or a biblical spectacle such as *Noah's Ark*, wherein the Deluge itself, plus George O'Brien, saves her from the evil designs of Noah Beery.

However, once in a while a role came along that required beauty *and* brains, and then Dolores Costello was able to prove that she wasn't just a beautiful decoration. One such film was *When a Man Loves*, a stylish version of *Manon Lescaut*. Another was *The Divine Lady*, in which Miss Costello, beautifully photographed by John Seitz, played Lady Hamilton.

Best remembered, perhaps, of all the Dolores Costello films is *The Sea Beast*, the first screen version of *Moby Dick*. There was, of course, no heroine in Melville's novel—but for a John Barrymore special, there had to be one! The beautifully done love scenes between Dolores and John Barrymore more than compensated for a rather artificial-looking whale. (Barrymore's second version of the story, this time a talkie, had a much better whale—but less satisfying love scenes.) One of the reasons for the power and conviction of the Barrymore-Costello romantic sequences may have been their very real off-screen love for each other. Miss Costello became Mrs. Barrymore in 1928.

A 1923 portrait. No longer a leading man, Costello applied his virile good looks to mature character roles.

A vacation shot of Costello with his wife and daughter Dolores.

Maurice Costello

Like so many of the early stars, Maurice Costello came to the movies from the stage, where he had been a top performer for nearly twenty years. He became one of the movies' first matinee idols—but because he was already mature, his tenure of the top rung of the ladder of stardom was brief. In 1921 we find him playing an ordinary villain role in Selznick's *Conceit*, the trade papers of the period noting that "old-timer Maurice Costello has a small part."

Costello had joined Vitagraph in 1909, after a couple of years with Edison. His biggest hit for Vitagraph had been as Sydney Carton in *A Tale of Two Cities*, with Norma Talmadge. That was in 1911. And less than ten years later one of the biggest stars of them all was being referred to casually as "an old-timer." But of course, the movies were developing so fast in those days that anyone associated with the movies' early days was automatically regarded as a veteran.

Maurice was not exactly handsome, but he was good-looking and attractive, with a kindly face and greying hair that added to his mature appeal. Like Henry B. Walthall, he had a happy knack of underplaying a scene, and of giving convincing sincerity even to the most commonplace of roles. In his skilled hands, even little one-reelers like *What a Change of Clothes Did*, a most unlikely melodrama in which he appeared with Clara Kimball Young, seemed important.

He tackled everything from serial hero to romantic lover with the apparent conviction that it was the performance, not the role, that mattered. And even when his short-lived reign as a star was over, he stuck to that same principle—through the late 20's and on into early sound films—sad perhaps that movies had arrived a little too late for him to stay on top a little longer, but always giving of his best. And despite the several later, more elaborate, versions of *A Tale of Two Cities*, I still think that his Sydney Carton was the most moving of them all.

westerns. But Miss Crawford took all this in her stride. Just how well her patience paid off, when she became the queen of high-grade soap operas in the 30's and 40's, is now a matter of record.

But actually she made some of her best films in her earliest years in the business. *Tramp Tramp Tramp* with Harry Langdon was one of the finest of all silent comedies and Joan made a most appealing heroine as

As the Charleston and Black Bottom flapper in *Our Dancing Daughters* (1928).

Joan Crawford

Joan Crawford may not have been one of the biggest stars of the silents in terms of drawing power (her peak box office period was in the 30's), but for a newcomer she got to the top in an awful hurry—and appeared in as many hits as most of the more firmly established stars. A former dancer, Miss Crawford hit Hollywood when the Charleston rage was at its height, and it's not surprising that in films like *Our Dancing Daughters* Metro exploited her as their own, slightly more serious, Clara Bow.

Clara went wild in her movies, because it was the jazz age and it was the only way to have fun; Joan was usually motivated by other factors in her films. The end result was pretty much the same, although since Joan varied her flapper roles with more serious ones and more than a few nonedescript heroine supports to (then) bigger stars like Harry Langdon and Jackie Coogan, she was never typed as a "jazz baby."

Good films, a much-publicized marriage (to Douglas Fairbanks, Jr.) and frequent tiltings with the reigning queen of Metro, Norma Shearer, kept Joan's name before the public at all times. Few stars before or since ever worked so hard, on screen and off, at being a star, and no star earned her status more than Miss Crawford did. At times, back in the 20's, M-G-M thought she was trying a little *too* hard, and "disciplined" her by putting her into a couple of inexpensive Tim McCoy

With Harry Langdon in *Tramp Tramp Tramp* (1926).

the object of the little clown's attention. *Sally, Irene and Mary* was another particularly good one, and she had a strong role in *The Unknown*, one of the meatiest of all the thrillers Lon Chaney made for director Tod Browning. Chaney played an armless wonder who threw knives with his toes; Joan was the girl he loved; while *she* was in love with Norman Kerry. It was grim but powerful stuff.

Despite her Academy Award in later years, I'm sure that Miss Crawford would be the first to agree that she has never been among the great actresses of the screen. But sometimes it means as much to be a *personality* as an actress. Often it's considerably more difficult. Always a good actress, always steadily improving, Joan has been star and personality material from the very first, and today, whether she be on the sound stages or making a personal appearance—or simply walking into a hotel lobby—Joan Crawford remains one of the few active reminders of the glamor that made Hollywood great.

In *The Taxi Dancer* (1927).

Marion Davies

I've always felt that Marion Davies has been unfairly overlooked by writers on the film and unjustly maligned by those who point only to her sponsorship by William Randolph Hearst. It's true, of course, that Hearst did force Metro into starring her in expensive pictures at a time when her name was not "box office." But, after all, many a studio has followed this path with contract stars, and it seems unreasonable that just because the mechanics were a little different in this case, it should be singled out for condemnation. All the fuss over the ultra-determined push to establish Marion Davies as a top-rank star has quite obscured the fact that she had what it takes to achieve star status on her own and, indeed, would probably have emerged as a much bigger star had she been able to chart her own course and achieve the top more slowly, with exhibitor support rather than antagonism. Miss Davies herself has always been discreetly silent on this point, and charitably passive to those who have attacked her. Now wealthy, happily married and a successful business-woman, I hope she occasionally looks at her early talkies on television, and becomes aware of the pep and charm she put into films like *Peg o' My Heart*.

Marion may not have been one of the top box office stars of the 20's, but in retrospect one can see that she appeared in some mighty good pictures—from spectacular period pieces like *When Knighthood Was in Flower* and *Little Old New York* to modern, zippy comedies of the calibre of *The Fair Co-Ed, The Patsy*, and *Show People*. King Vidor, who directed her in the latter, obviously has a high regard for her abilities as a comedienne, and praises her work at length in his autobiography, *A Tree Is a Tree*. Marion is much more a veteran of the silent screen than most people realize. She entered show business in a typically decisive fashion, leaving a convent to becoming a dancing girl with a *Chu Chin Chow* troupe. She was in films by 1918, with Pathé's *Runaway Romany*, and followed that with one or two films for Paramount (*Restless Sex, April Folly*) before signing with Metro.

Marion would be the last to regard herself as a great dramatic actress, though she was at least a good one. But her greatest gifts lay outside the fields of realistic drama; she could ring a tear effortlessly in a piece of schmaltzy sentiment, and she could stop the show with her pantomime and wicked mimicry (she and Jimmy Durante kidded Garbo and Barrymore in *Blondie of the Follies*).

Marion Davies in 1928.

Marion Davies was a gifted comedienne and a gallant trouper, and she well deserves her place in this book as one of the greats of the silent screen.

Satirizing a movie queen in one of the best of her silent comedies, King Vidor's *Show People*.

Carol Dempster

The name of Carol Dempster, a Griffith heroine who started as an extra in the 1916 *Intolerance*, hasn't survived the years as well as those of the Gish Sisters, Mae Marsh, and other "Griffith girls." While she was never a top box office name, she enjoyed the unswervingly loyal devotion of her fans. And they have remained loyal throughout all the years. Nine out of ten silent filmgoers may have forgotten Carol by now; but if the tenth was a Dempster devotee, his eyes will light up as her name is mentioned, and every detail of her performances will be recalled with glowing admiration.

Miss Dempster was a curious actress, and a very promising one. Reputedly, D. W. Griffith was very much in love with her and asked her to marry him. Miss Dempster declined. Ultimately they came to the parting of the ways (in the mid-1920's) and Carol's star waned. Apparently she relied too much on Griffith's guidance to be completely successful without him. Indeed, sometimes in Griffith's own films, her reliance on him was a little too evident. All through *America*, for example, one has the distinct impresion of Griffith telling her: "Now play this scene like Mae Marsh in the homecoming sequence from *The Birth of a Nation*;" or "Do this scene the way Lillian Gish would." The utilization of different acting techniques for different scenes proved most disconcerting. The fault, of course, was as much Griffith's as hers.

But at her best, Carol could be, and was, superb. Films like *Scarlet Days, Dream Street* and *Sherlock Holmes* (a nondescript role in a film where *everybody* was overshadowed by Barrymore) didn't give her too much of an opportunity. But she was most touching in *The White Rose*, another Griffith film, even though her romance with Neil Hamilton tended to be given secondary treatment in favor of the Mae Marsh-Ivor Novello story. In *The Love Flower* (opposite Dick Barthelmess, for Griffith), a melodramatic South Sea romance, she was flawlessly photographed and looked stunningly beautiful throughout. She came to life for perhaps the first time, with real vitality and blooming womanhood shining through her rather wan and fragile appearance. That physical appearance stood her in good stead, however, in *Isn't Life Wonderful?*, Griffith's several-years-ahead-of-its-time study of inflation and poverty in post-war Europe. Again opposite Neil Hamilton, Carol played a young, homeless girl in those chaotic years, lining up day after day for food to feed her aged father, striving desperately to restore hope to her disillusioned fiance, weak and ill from a wartime gassing. Even Garbo's performance in a similar role in *The Joyless Street* (which followed, and largely copied, Griffith's film) was no match for Carol's sensitive, intensely moving, and completely convincing performance, in this film. If she had made no other films, that performance alone would justify Carol's inclusion among the "greats" of the silent screen.

From a bit role in *Way Down East* to the heroine in *Sally of the Sawdust* (which starred W. C. Fields), Carol appeared in Griffith's films over his peak years. Her work, though erratic, certainly warrants a great deal more recognition than it has received in recent years.

Carol Dempster with Ralph Graves in *Dream Street* (1921).

In Griffith's great epic of the Revolutionary war, *America* (1924), Lionel Barrymore played the notorious Captain Walter Butler; Carol was a (fictional) Southern belle who became embroiled in his plans for conquest.

Reginald Denny

Denny as he appeared in the popular Leather Pushers films, a series of two-reelers made for Universal in the early 20's.

Reginald Denny

As we go to press with this volume, Reginald Denny has just ended a lengthy run on the New York stage in the fabulous *My Fair Lady*. Denny has become best

With Laura La Plante in the best of his silents for Universal—*Skinner's Dress Suit*.

known as the amiable and slightly foolish Englishman in a score of comedies, or as the reliable and honorable "other man" who really should get the girl but stands nobly aside at the end. But in silents, he projected quite a different type—at first the virile man of action (he starred in Universal's fine "The Leatherpushers" series in the early 20's) and later the adventurer-comedian in something of the Doug Fairbanks manner. Denny's films for Universal—be they comedies of manners, or comedies of action—were enormously popular in the 20's. Exhibitors and public alike looked forward to them as much as they did to the new Bob Hope film in the 40's. No mere programmers, they were expensively mounted pictures with top directors and fine production values. They zipped along at a fast pace, all dominated by the ebullient and breezy personality of Denny. His films were often very similar to Fairbanks' in overall *idea*, but very much more down to earth. Doug was always so full of self-confidence that he never had to prove himself to anyone—least of all himself. Denny often did. And whatever Doug's problems, they were never ordinary ones. But Denny had to cope with such things as paying the rent, keeping up the installments on the furniture, and finding a way to break the news to his wife that he had been fired. But, withal, there was a definite affinity between the comedies of Doug and Reg—without there being any attempt to *pattern* the Denny films on Fairbanks'.

Reginald made so many fine comedies for Universal that it's difficult to remember them all. And I use the term "comedies" only loosely to generalize the whole series. Many of them packed in some pretty exciting action too. *Skinner's Dress Suit*, with Laura La Plante—and a lively Charleston sequence—is my personal favorite; a thoroughly refreshing comedy of manners directed by that maestro of filmic froth, William Seiter. Another fine one was *Oh Doctor*—with lovely Mary Astor just on the threshold of big things. Then there were *On Your Toes*, and the wacky, zany *California Straight Ahead*—with a cross-country motor trip, a horde of animals escaping from a circus to plague the tourists, and a whale of a motor-race finish. Denny never put a foot in the wrong place in those expert films of the 20's—and might have continued indefinitely in that vein if it hadn't been for the coming of sound. There was nothing *wrong* with Denny's voice. It was a fine speaking voice—and he knew how to use it. But, like Doug, he had been playing brisk young Americans. And his voice was very plainly and unmistakably that of a brisk young *Englishman!*

Denny's career didn't falter. But he did more than his share towards having sound scripts doctored so that a key role could be identified as an Englishman—or at least a Canadian.

A typical Dix situation—In *Icebound* (1924), directed by William de Mille.

In *A Man Must Live.*

Richard Dix

The phrase "strong, silent he-man" has become something of a cliché used in describing leading men of the silent screen. It was an apt phrase, even if over-usage has made it seem a trifle corny today, but actually there were relatively few stars to whom it really applied. William S. Hart was certainly one of them. So was Jack Holt. But most of all, perhaps, it applied to Richard Dix, who made fewer westerns than either Hart or Holt, but who carried those "strong, silent" western characteristics into all his roles. He was the quiet, reliable, often noble type, ever ready to stand aside and sacrifice his own happiness, willing to shoulder the blame for misdeeds that were not his in order to protect the weak, but he was also a man of two-fisted courage when the time finally came to swing into action.

Dix's was an idealized hero, the kind born of fiction rather than real life, and as such enjoyed a big vogue in the 20's when the predominant mood was for entertainment and escapism first. Dix's strong, rugged features, determined yet kindly, also made him an ideal "pioneer" type—whether he was carving an empire from the old West, or "creating" in contemporary surroundings. (He was frequently cast as a construction engineer, tackling anything from huge buildings to an underwater tunnel from England to America.)

One of his biggest silent hits was for Sam Goldwyn in *The Christian*. But most of his work was done for Paramount—in a variety of roles ranging from the hero in the modern section of DeMille's *The Ten Commandments* to *Nothing But the Truth* (a comedy). In *Lucky Devil* he was an ace racing driver, opposite Esther Ralston; in Zane Grey's *The Vanishing American* he was an Indian hero of World War I who comes back to the West to find his people being persecuted by white politicians and business grafters.

With Bebe Daniels in *Sinners in Heaven.*

Douglas Fairbanks

A racial stereotype like this would hardly get by today. But Doug poked fun at everyone—and everything—so genially that no one took offense. This scene is from *The Nut*.

To most moviegoers today, the name Douglas Fairbanks conjures up only one image: a swashbuckling cavalier hero—D'Artagnan, or the Black Pirate—a cloak cast over his shoulder, a sword in his hand, and a gleaming smile beneath a neat moustache. Actually, this was the *later* Fairbanks—the real Doug was the fascinating character that emerged in his movies between 1916 and 1920. These were films that abounded in action and dizzy stunts, but which were essentially comedies rather than melodramas or adventures.

In these films Doug created a unique screen character: the super-all-American boy—more resourceful and athletic than Charles Ray, less inept and dependent upon luck than Harold Lloyd. (Both of these made the all-American boy their special forte, too.) Doug was the super-athlete and super-optimist. He won through in the end because he was on the side of right, and because his philosophy was a cheerful, ebullient, optimistic one. That, he implied, was all that was necessary to defeat any kind of enemy, whether it be a human one, or such intangibles as gloom or monetary worries. To a nation depressed by World War I, he became a shining beacon of hope. Because he invariably played the good-natured American kid, he could be identified with by every man and boy in the audience.

That audience didn't realize two things, however. Doug's victories were usually brought about by physical prowess and agility, and while he made it all look deceptively easy, he was something of a superman in the gymnastic field. Secondly, his screen characters were invariably wealthy. Problems of making a success in business before he could marry never arose; backed

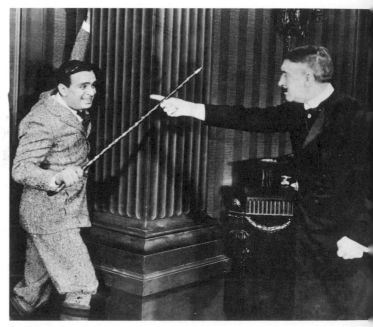

His Majesty the American (1919) was Doug's first for the newly-formed United Artists. A wonderful spoof on *Prisoner of Zenda*-type adventures, it was packed with action, excitement, and comedy.

As Zorro, he protects Marguerite de la Motte from the villainous attentions of Robert McKim. *The Mark of Zorro* paved the way for a new career in costume swashbucklers for Doug. (1920.)

160

With his old pal Charlie Stevens in *Robin Hood*—one of Doug's biggest, though not necessarily best, films.

With Lupe Velez in one of his best, though more serious, films; *The Gaucho* (1927).

As *The Thief of Bagdad*.

by unstressed but ever-present wealth, he was free to play the gallant perpetually and to indulge his every whim for twentieth-century chivalry. Perhaps that was one of the secrets of his success—his films were frankly escapist, yet didn't appear to be. They told every man in the audience that *he* could be this successful if he'd just stop worrying and tackle life with a smile. Nobody seemed to worry that it was never explained just how to go about this. After all, what did it matter? It was a healthy and constructive philosophy, and it was no wonder that Doug was everybody's idol.

Films like *Wild and Woolly, His Picture in the Papers, American Aristocracy, The Nut, Man From Painted Post, Knickerbocker Buckaroo* and *Manhattan Madness* were all breezy stories of contemporary life. Some lampooned current sabotage and other war scares. Others kidded the American craze for publicity. None took themselves seriously. And Doug, skipping around, never still for a minute, rarely with that infectious grin very far from his lips, took himself less seriously than anyone. If he had one favorite role, it was that of the repressed city dweller who longs for the life of a cowboy—and ultimately goes out West and proves himself a tougher customer than the real westerners! At the same time, William S. Hart was displaying a fondness for stories about the westerner who comes East and proves more than a match for shrewd city tricksters. Doug and Bill worked for the same companies—first Triangle, then Paramount.

Doug had so little interest in stepping out of his established character that he once incorporated into one of his films, *A Modern Musketeer*, a hilarious and action-packed sequence lampooning all the swashbuckling tricks that he was later to take so seriously. As D'Artagnan in a daydream sequence he pulls out all the stops, and packs more fun—and daredevil stunting—into a mere five minutes than he managed to get into all eleven reels of the later *The Three Musketeers*, in which he again played D'Artagnan!

With Mary Astor in *Don Q, Son of Zorro*.

161

William Farnum

Dustin Farnum

William & Dustin Farnum

The name "Farnum" on a theatre marquee in the early days of the movies always meant a top picture and top business. Even before Doug Fairbanks and Bill Hart had established themselves, the Farnum brothers, William, via *The Spoilers*, and Dustin in *The Squaw Man*, both in 1914, found themselves in the front rank of the then newly-emerging star system. Both had had extensive stage experience, and both came to the top in rugged western characterizations. And although both, not unnaturally, continued to specialize in action roles, they didn't by any means limit themselves to such fare. Straight dramatic and romantic roles were given their fair share of attention too, and the appeal of the Farnums ranged from adventure-loving youngsters to romantically-minded spinsters!

Dustin faded from the screen relatively quickly, but as his star was waning in 1919, William was at his peak as a star for Fox. Early in the 20's however, Bill had a serious accident on a Paramount movie, and was off the screen, except for minor parts, until the end of the silent era. Then, like Henry B. Walthall, his stage experience and his rich voice made him a natural for talkies, and he remained active in films

right up until his death in the early 1950's. Quite often he found himself cast in supporting roles in re-makes of films which had starred either him (as, for instance, Fox's *Last of the Duanes*) or brother Dustin (*The Corsican Brothers*).

Bill was probably the better screen actor of the two, and could tackle anything from Zane Grey to Dickens. One of his biggest hits was in an early Fox version of *A Tale of Two Cities*. But his big, almost beefy, build, made him seem more at home outdoors than in, so it's not surprising that so many of his early films were westerns. Dustin didn't adapt so easily to films as did Bill, and remained essentially a stage actor in a rather unfamiliar medium. But except for that occasional colorful flamboyance, a fire sadly missing from the screen (and stage) today, Bill showed few traces of stage technique in his screen portrayals. He had a wonderful face, strong and determined, yet genial and kindly, with a big smile, and eyes that crinkled into a sort of smile. (It was doubtless this facial quality of strength and gentleness that resulted in Bill being given so many "padre" roles in the 30's and 40's.) Accordingly, Bill's directors usually exploited this face by giving him rather more closeups than

Bill in a typical scene, from Fox's *Drag Harlan*.

usual—another step away from stage technique.

It's unfortunate that so few of the important early Farnum films have survived the years. When I played Dustin's *The Corsican Brothers* on my program recently, the response proved quite definitely that the Farnum name is still an honored, well-loved, and well-remembered one.

Dustin as the great English actor David Garrick in the 1916 film of that name.

GRETA GARBO Metro-Goldwyn-Mayer

Greta Garbo

It has often been said of Greta Garbo that she never made a great picture. I wouldn't go that far—but it *is* true that for such a fine actress, she made surprisingly few important pictures. Certainly one cannot associate with Garbo's name a gallery of outstanding films such as one can with the names of Barrymore or Gish.

It is very much of a tribute to her that she made sense of some of the idiotic roles she was given to do in the silent period—high-grade soap operas, improbable melodramas—none of them selected, it would seem, with any view to being a showcase for one of the great dramatic talents of the time. Possibly M-G-M felt that the mere name of Garbo was enough. Her name would sell the film to the big European market, where she had started, in Swedish and German movies; her name would sell the film to the intellectual audience in this country. The implication, then, is that the story-content was aimed at the "popular" audiences, who might be unimpressed by the Garbo name, but who would be drawn into the theatre by torrid love scenes, by a femme-fatale theme, or by the thrill of a bursting dam! When sound came in, Garbo began to get roles more worthy of her mettle——presumably because the sort of fare she had been making suddenly

became (in the minds of the movie-men at least) antiquated and corny.

But whatever their deficiencies in terms of plot material, Garbo's silents for M-G-M were handsome productions, with all the polish that M-G-M films were justly famous for. And in a grand, overblown way, they were good movie-making too. Her first American film was *The Torrent* (1926), a surprisingly short adaptation of an Ibáñez novel, with Ricardo Cortez starred. It had a wild finish—Ricardo in a small rowboat, paddling through a man-sized flood, pleading with a stonily disinterested Greta to marry him—which even the off-beat, unhappy ending couldn't quite overcome!

Greta was a femme fatale again in *The Temptress*, playing the role so well that even the melodramatics of a bloody whip-duel and a bursting dam seemed logical! The plot zipped from Europe to South America and back again, and when the much re-filmed final version finally reached completion, the critics were most enthusiastic. The film had had its troubles—players had been substituted along the way and Swedish director Mauritz Stiller had started the film, then been replaced by Fred Niblo. (Where one left off and the other began was painfully apparent by a complete change not only of style and pacing, but also of such other things as costuming, hairstyles, and so on!) But apparently the effort was worth while—the critics loved it, especially the dramatic ending, in which Greta, having wrecked the life's work of Antonio Moreno and indirectly caused his great dam to be destroyed, returns to Paris, becomes a streetwalker, and dies in poverty! But M-G-M apparently felt this ending a little raw for American tastes and eliminated

Garbo arriving in America in July, 1925, accompanied by the fine Swedish director Mauritz Stiller—who hoped to be allowed to guide her American career but who, alas, never had that chance.

With Antonio Moreno in *The Temptress*.

A rare scene from *Love*—rare because M-G-M, a studio with such a penchant for "fussing" with films that it was known in the trade as "Re-take Valley", completely eliminated Lionel Barrymore from the version finally released.

Garbo's death completely. Instead, the title "Five Years Later" was inserted—and at the re-opening of the repaired dam, Antonio Moreno introduces the woman to whom he owes all his success, who is now free to live happily with him—one of the most abrupt changes of character in movie history!

The reliable old "Five Years Later" title was useful too in *Love*, the first of Garbo's two versions of *Anna Karenina*. Europeans were privileged to see Tolstoy's original, tragic, ending; over here, after the convenient five-year period, Anna and Count Vronsky

Typical of the strange publicity shots released to promote the furtherance of the "Woman of Mystery" tag for Garbo.

(John Gilbert) married and settled down happily!

Of course, not all of Garbo's silents should be dismissed so casually or so flippantly. Even basically bad films like *The Temptress* had a lot of good things in them. And the good Garbo films were often *very* good. *Flesh and the Devil*, best of the Garbo-Gilbert films, was a beautifully done romantic tragedy. And perhaps best of all was Garbo's last silent, *The Kiss,* made in 1929, when most of her contemporaries had already either made the adjustment to talkies or had shown that they never would. As if in defiance of the current demand for talk and more talk, it took a basically talkie story—and told it supremely well in the language of the silent cinema.

The following year, when Garbo made *Anna Christie*, the whole selling campaign was built around the simple slogan, "GARBO TALKS!"

She talked so successfully, her deep, heavily accented voice so perfectly matching the aura of feminine mystery that her slim body and beautiful face projected, that she went on to far greater heights in sound films than she had ever attained in silents.

Garbo fans shudder when they recall how close Garbo came to being out of the movies almost as soon as she was in them. Initially, Garbo was not happy at M-G-M at all. She had few friends in this country, didn't even speak the language well. She thought she was wasting her time posing for silly publicity pictures and doing films with idiotic story-lines. But she knew how much her pictures were making at the box office, and even though not a businesswoman, she recognized that that seemed to be sufficient justification for their being made. But she was being paid only $16,000 a

With Conrad Nagel in *The Kiss* (1929).

year as opposed to the $400,000 that Lillian Gish was getting, and finally in 1927 she went on strike. If she couldn't have good pictures, at least she'd have the satisfaction of being paid what she knew she was worth. The old M-G-M regime was a ruthless one, and it fought back hard. The publicity department released stories to the denigration of Miss Garbo. She was even told that unless she behaved, she could be—and would be—deported. But Miss Garbo held firm, and M-G-M knowing what a goldmine she was, finally gave in to her demands. It was an unprecedented victory, for one woman alone, a foreigner, and not versed in the ways of Hollywood business, to defeat a huge Hollywood corporation. It earned Miss Garbo added respect from exhibitors, who were also having their troubles with M-G-M in those days.

Garbo has been off the screen for a long time now —wisely, I think. I hope she never returns. In her time, she was a living legend, a cinema goddess. If she came back, it could only be as an actress—a fine, sensitive actress, but, withal, a human being. We have too few living legends, almost no goddesses. Those that we have, we should keep intact.

Garbo comes between friend (Lew Ayres, in his first major role) and husband (Anders Randolf) in one of the dramatic highspots of *The Kiss*.

Adrian outdid himself in creating a stark, "martyred"-look costume for Garbo to wear in the climactic murder trial sequence.

John Gilbert

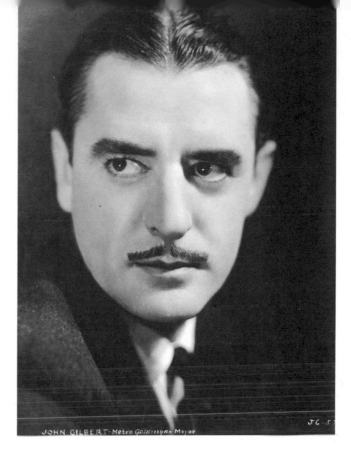

JOHN GILBERT - Metro Goldwyn-Mayer

I am so weary of hearing the fiction repeated over and over again that John Gilbert was ruined when the microphone revealed his voice to be high-pitched and tinny, that if this book accomplishes nothing else but putting a stop to that hoary old legend, I shall be well satisfied.

The impression is that Gilbert made but one or two talkies, and literally crawled away, ashamed and crushed, to die of a broken heart. Actually Gilbert made a great many sound films over a period of several years. At the beginning, his voice was not particularly good—but it was no worse than those of a dozen other stars I could name. And it improved. Gilbert worked hard with voice tutors, and in a very short time his voice was, if not the voice of a Colman, quite satisfactory.

The real cause of Gilbert's decline lies elsewhere: The sound cinema had killed the type of extravagant romantic fare in which he excelled. Garbo continued in love stories of course, but in a far less exuberant vein. There is a world of difference between her *Camille* and the silent *Flesh and the Devil*. Gilbert had also made swashbucklers—*Bardelys the Magnificent* was one—but that cycle was dead, too, at least until the mid-30's. Even Fairbanks resumed modern roles. John Barrymore had to exchange the colorful costume dramas of the *Beau Brummel* and *Don Juan* variety for a far different, and more modern, type of characterization.

Gilbert was a good actor—a very good actor, in fact —but he wasn't a *great* actor, as was Barrymore. He couldn't as Barrymore did, merely shrug off one style and step into another. He tried hard, and he gave good performances. But the roles that came along, many of them gangster and "tough guy" roles, just didn't give him any kind of opportunity or incentive. His era had gone with silent drama—as had Clara Bow's, and Harry Langdon's, and Mary Pickford's— and Rudolph Valentino's, had he lived. His voice had little or nothing to do with it.

Gilbert had started out inauspiciously enough, as an extra in Bill Hart's *Hell's Hinges*. (Another extra in that very fine western was Jean Hersholt.) In that

In *The Love Gambler*, a 1922 Fox production.

As M-G-M's premier romantic star, Gilbert restored his moustache. He shaved it off only once, as the doughboy hero of *The Big Parade*.

With Mae Murray in *The Merry Widow.*

King Vidor (with glasses) directs Gilbert in *Bardelys the Magnificent.*

first film, Gilbert, easily recognizable in crowd scenes, was a good-looking fellow with a moustache. But apparently he didn't like the moustache, for in the bulk of his subsequent pictures for Triangle he appeared clean-shaven.

Gilbert's features were attractive, but irregular; he hadn't known it, but the moustache had helped a great deal. Without it, he looked definitely less handsome. Triangle saw in him a good, but slightly weak-looking, fellow, and cast him accordingly. When he had a sympathetic role, as in another western, *Golden Rule Kate,* it was usually a subsidiary one. In that film he played an outlaw who reforms, but Louise Glaum was starred and got most of the limelight. In other films he was the unpleasant "other man" who *didn't* get the girl—an obnoxious rich youth who loses out to the pleasant poor boy in *Happiness,* the smalltown bigwig who loses Colleen Moore to Charlie Ray in *The Busher.*

However, once he left Triangle, his luck seemed to change. He played opposite Mary Pickford in one of her better films, *Heart of the Hills.* With a moustache, and still calling himself Jack Gilbert, he rapidly gained popularity at Fox. He had the title roles in *The Count of Monte Cristo* and that famous old riverboat melodrama, *Cameo Kirby,* directed by John Ford. He joined M-G-M in the mid-20's, by that time sufficiently popular to justify their launching him as their own, and somewhat more sophisticated Valentino.

What happened is a matter of Hollywood history. Gilbert scored in hit after hit: *He Who Gets Slapped, The Merry Widow, La Bohème, The Big Parade* (a film that showed he could really *act* as well as do convincing love scenes), *The Cossacks, Man, Woman and Sin* (a fine film with Jeanne Eagles), *Bardelys the Magnificent,* and of course, most successful of all, his high-powered love stories with Garbo—*Flesh and the Devil, Love* and *A Woman of Affairs,* in all of which he rated billing over Garbo. (Their one talkie together, *Queen Christina* [1933], for which Garbo had insisted on Gilbert as her leading man, showed quite clearly how star values change in only a few years. Now she was starred, and he given mere featured billing.)

Gilbert never became quite the legend that Valentino was, and his period of peak stardom lasted a mere four years, but in those four years he was, next to Valentino, the most idolized romantic star the screen ever knew. His love scenes still ignite the screen when *Flesh and the Devil* is shown today. In talkies, not even Gable and Colman, to take two extremes, ever quite re-kindled those sparks.

The classic triangle from *Flesh and the Devil:* Gilbert, Garbo, and Lars Hanson.

Dorothy Gish

Dorothy Gish in her earlier days.

Later: a more sophisticated Dorothy.

Dorothy Gish, who made her film debut with sister Lillian in a Biograph one-reeler, *The Unseen Enemy*, in 1912, is rather unjustly neglected by film historians today. They give her a nod in passing, and then turn to the more famous Lillian. To a large degree, this is because so few representative Dorothy Gish films have survived the years. I know of no prints, for example, of *Remodelling Her Husband* (in which Dorothy was directed by Lillian) or such early delights as *Nugget Nell*. Yet Dorothy made many more films than Lillian and in their films together usually stole the show. This, I hasten to add, was not because she was a better

actress than Lillian (*was* there a better actress than Lillian?), but rather because of the conception of their roles when they played together.

Lillian was always the ethereal, somehow unreal, heroine, to whom went all the heavy dramatics. Dorothy was inevitably presented in a lighter vein, or given a role with more meat. In *Hearts of the World*, for example, Dorothy played "The Little Disturber," a young French girl of slightly dubious morals, but full of warmth and a spirit of fun. In *Romola*, while Lillian played the aristocratic heroine, having literally nothing to do but look exquisitely

A rollicking western role in *Nugget Nell*.

With Kate Bruce—perennial mother in the early Griffith films—in *Betty of Greystone*.

Two scenes from *Orphans of the Storm*. As the blind Louise (left) she is taken to Paris, and is there kidnapped by a family of beggars, dressed in rags, and forced to sing on the streets (right).

beautiful in Italian Renaissance costumes, Dorothy was given the far more colorful role of the girl betrayed by scoundrel William Powell. With an illegitimate baby, and a tragic death scene as she drowns in a canal, she couldn't help but engender far more audience sympathy than Lillian. However, both Gishes were pretty evenly matched in *Orphans of the Storm*.

Lillian, of course, was essentially a dramatic actress of the first order. Dorothy was a fine actress too (as she has proved on the stage many times), but her true forte was light comedy. She had a bubbling sense of fun and a magnificent talent for mime and mimicry that made her, to my mind, the finest comedienne on the silent screen, bar none. She threw herself into everything with such gusto, improvising little bits of pantomimic business as she went along, obviously enjoying herself to the hilt—and communicating that

enjoyment to the audience. And I'm not forgetting her sterling dramatic work in films like *Fury* and *The Bright Shawl* when I say that she was really at her unbeatable best in such enjoyable frolics as *Clothes Make the Pirate* and the western spoof, *Nugget Nell*, and in a whole parade of sparkling comedies for Paramount in the pre-1920 period.

In the late 20's, she made a group of films for England's Herbert Wilcox—among them *Nell Gwynn*, in which her performance is still a remarkable and subtle blending of pathos and high-spirited fun. The career of the boisterous Nell, actress-mistress of King Charles II, was obviously made to measure for Dorothy, and she played it to the hilt.

Dorothy, still a very lovely and chaming person, has been making occasional stage appearances in recent years—but a return to the screen is long overdue.

1916: In a Griffith production, Dorothy is directed by Elmer Clifton, who also started as an actor under Griffith. The cameraman is Karl Brown, who later photographed *The Covered Wagon* and then became a director himself.

Lillian Gish

Lillian Gish today, still beautiful and fragile.

Lillian Gish

To me, Lillian Gish, more than any other star, has always symbolized the silent screen heroine. Of course, she was more than just a "heroine" and all that that hackneyed word implies. An actress of fragile beauty and astonishing sensitivity, she was not only the first lady of the screen, but one of the great actresses of all time. John Barrymore, excited over her work in *Way Down East,* wrote to her that she had even surpassed the work of Duse. And Griffith (several years after Miss Gish had made her last film for him), when asked if he *really* thought that she was the screen's foremost actress, shrugged his shoulders and replied: "Who is greater?"

Initially it seemed that Lillian Gish was more valuable to Griffith for her looks than for her acting ability. She had (and in fact still has) that ethereal, not-of-this-world look, a birdlike fragility from which emerges sudden, unexpected strength. She was the epitome of what Griffith wanted in a heroine visually. But, in the early Biograph days at least, and through the Triangle period (until 1917) it was Mae Marsh who was the better actress. Or at least, it was Mae who was given the roles that demanded acting ability rather than a beautifully wistful and expressive face. In early one-reelers like *The Musketeers of Pig Alley* (1912), and *The Mothering Heart,* Lillian was exceptionally fine, but she really began to mature as an actress after 1917, in films like *Hearts of the World* (the scene in which she wanders through a war-torn battlefield, clutching her bridal veil, searching for the body of the boy who was to have been her husband, was heart-rending), and the lovely little rural romance *True Heart Susie,* one of the unsung classics of the American screen. Then came *Broken Blossoms* and *Way Down East,* which, by 1920, quite firmly established her as the screen's foremost actress. Strangely enough however, although she had learned so much from Griffith, and was so devoted to him, some of her best work came after she left him. To Griffith, the story was the thing—and for him, it was the right way to work. His pictures justified his methods. And those methods did not include "showcases" for virtuoso performances, although *Way Down East,* with a simpler story-line than usual, and more stress on the one character of Anna Moore (played by Miss Gish) came closest to being a star vehicle. Lillian's scenes with her dead baby are still among the most poignant moments to be found anywhere on the screen.

Miss Gish of course had no complaints against Griffith's methods, and went on to make *Orphans of the Storm* for him. But it was obvious that as an actress she could develop no further in Griffith's films, and so the two, quite amicably, came to a parting of the ways. Miss Gish's films thereafter were more infrequent, and more carefully selected. Not all were

With sister Dorothy in *Orphans of the Storm* (1922).

Griffith's *The Romance of Happy Valley* (1918), one of several charming romances the great director-star team made in this period.

In *The Wind* (1928).

wisely selected, and *Romola,* despite a huge budget and lengthy location work in Italy, was a cold and stodgy film, lovely to look at, but little else. Miss Gish's role gave her little to do but look exquisitely lovely in Renaissance costumes. The earlier *The White Sister* had been an enormous popular success, of course. Moving to M-G-M, Miss Gish was more than just the highest-priced feminine star on the lot. She had very definite ideas about the art of the film, and managed to imprint these ideas quite positively into her films. King Vidor and others who directed her were impressed. Even when they sometimes disagreed, they respected her integrity and creativity. Most of all, they respected her devotion to the art of acting, and her endurance of hardship and discomfort in the interests of a finer performance. In his autobiography,

A Tree Is a Tree, King Vidor describes at great length the rather appalling ordeal Miss Gish subjected herself to in order to simulate death so convincingly in *La Bohème.*

Miss Gish's best M-G-M films, *La Bohème, The Scarlet Letter,* and *The Wind* presented her with strikingly mature roles, in contrast to the innocent and girlish roles which had fallen to her under Griffith. And yet, of course, so much of that innocent charm remained. Who could resist Lillian sitting placidly and uncomplainingly in the stocks (in *The Scarlet Letter*), forcing a smile while her wide eyes were filling with tears, or entreating a pawnbroker (in *La Bohème*) to pay just a little more for her mittens, so that she can pay her rent? (Of course, how anybody could refuse an unspoken plea from Lillian's eyes, let

In Triangle's *Sold for Marriage* (1916) with Walter Long.

Opposite John Gilbert in *La Bohème* (1926).

On the frozen Connecticut river for the climactic scenes of *Way Down East* (1920).

alone be inhuman enough to be mean to her, is a point that often bothered me as I watched her suffering so beautifuly in so many silents!)

Miss Gish was devoted to the silent screen, and felt that it had just about perfected a universal language of the arts when sound came along to destroy it. She has made many talkies and has always been superb. But now that the silent screen has gone, her main love is the theatre—and what a rare privilege it is to watch such an outstanding artist at work today! Styles and standards have changed, "The Method" and other modernizations have come and will probably go. Amid all the mumbling that passes for acting today, Lillian Gish's power and sensitivity and force remains a vibrant and living link with an acting school that has never been surpassed—the school of silent cinema.

A charming pose from *Orphans of the Storm*.

Corinne Griffith

Billed and publicized as "The Orchid Lady" of the silent screen, Corinne Griffith had a spectacular beauty that tended to eclipse her other talents. People wanted to look at her rather than study her acting, and as a result she never really got roles which showed whether she *could* be a notable actress or not. When talkies came in, Corinne, mindful of her existing "movie queen" status, was reluctant to change it. "Why should I go on until I am playing mother roles?" she asked—and promptly retired. One or two later films confirmed the wisdom of her first decision; her voice was not good, and a return to star status eluded her.

But Corinne had made money when she was on top, and didn't need the movies to support her. Instead she turned to big business, politics, and the writing of books—and recently, to the financing of a movie.

In the fourteen years that she was on top, she enjoyed the sort of popularity accorded Hedy Lamarr in the 40's. Audiences just went to *look;* critics, often unfairly, dismissed her good performances because of the general unimportance of her elegant but superficial movies. But for all the slightness of films like *Syncopating Sue* and *Mademoiselle Modiste,* Corinne was one of First National's biggest feminine stars, both in heavy dramas like *Black Oxen* and in trifles like *The Lady in Ermine.*

Perhaps she was seen at her very best in an enjoyable imitation—Lubitsch film of the late 20's, *The Garden of Eden.* Directed by Lewis Milestone, it was a sophisticated sex comedy, stunningly photographed, handomely designed by William Cameron Menzies, and displaying Miss Griffith's beauty and her neat sense of fun to their very best advantages. *The Garden of Eden* is one of a group of silents that you'll be seeing on television quite shortly, giving you an opportunity to make—or renew—acquaintance with "The Orchid Lady."

Corinne Griffith in a typical pseudo-DeMille farce of the early 20's—*It Isn't Being Done This Season.*

A lovely portrait of Corinne Griffith as she appeared in *The Divine Lady.*

William Haines

Bill Haines, now a highly successful interior decorator, hasn't made a film since the early 30's. One hardly hears his name mentioned when talk turns to the silent screen—and yet in the 20's he was one of the hottest male properties under contract to M-G-M. Good-looking, breezy, optimistic, he was in some respects a development of the Harold Lloyd character, but minus slapstick, of course. Haines' speciality was the self-confident kid out to make good, but, unlike Lloyd, he was usually a wisecracking know-it-all, who had to eat humble pie somewhere along the line before finally succeeding. Haines was a unique type of hero in the 20's, which is doubtless why he stood out; when sound came in, giving new scope to the flip comment and the fast wisecrack, his type became standard—with variations ranging from Pat O'Brien and Lee Tracy to James Cagney and Ben Lyon. He was ahead of the parade by several years, and his performances are still among the most likeable of his particular school.

Haines was spotted in New York by a Goldwyn talent scout, and entered in a "new faces" contest. He and Eleanor Boardman won and promptly were sent out to Hollywood—both to more than fulfill the expectations of the contest organizers. His first film was *Three Wise Fools* in 1923, and other notable films like *The Tower of Lies* (with Lon Chaney and Norma Shearer) followed. But his snappy personality soon asserted itself, and it wasn't long before he was being placed in roles specifically tailored to it. With fellow contest-winner Eleanor Boardman he played in *Tell it to the Marines*, as the rebellious recruit who learns (the hard way) to love the service and all it stands for. Lon Chaney was the marine sergeant who showed him how! *Tell it to the Marines* had a plot that has since been imitated and reshaped endlessly, but in its day it was a whale of a picture. Basically it still is, but, like Haines himself, it has suffered through the familiarity bred by the years of similar movies. *Brown of Harvard, Alias Jimmy Valentine, I'll Tell the World, Slide, Kelly, Slide* and *West Point*—all of these are titles that should be dear to the hearts of those to whom Bill Haines was everything that a movie idol should be.

Haines (in *A Man's Man*).

Haines' extrovert manner was an excellent match for Mary Pickford's equally rambunctious cavortings in that excellent mixture of pathos and comedy, *Little Annie Rooney,* made in 1925.

One of Haines' best roles, as the raw recruit in *Tell It to the Marines.* Dallying with this island maiden provokes a fierce brawl with the natives—from which Chaney has to rescue him.

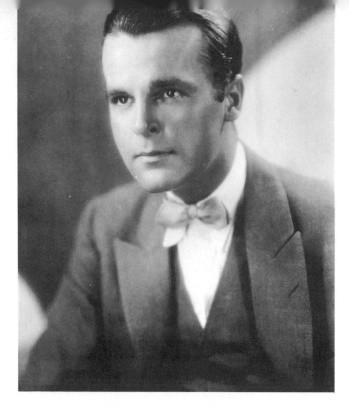

Neil Hamilton

After a long stage career and a couple of false starts in films, Neil Hamilton finally achieved film stardom when, in 1923, D. W. Griffith cast him as one of the two male leads (Ivor Novello had the other) in *The White Rose*, a charming and tender romantic story filmed in the bayous of Florida. Hamilton's quiet manner, good looks and pleasant personality made him an instant success. Critics were quick to acclaim him a new Richard Barthelmess and to point out that,

since he was huskier and more rugged looking than Barthelmess, he obviously had quite a career ahead of him. And of course he did. He made three more pictures with Griffith, proving quite definitely that he had solid dramatic ability plus athletic know-how. In *America*, for instance, he had a lot of hard-riding sequences, and as he led the troops to the rescue for the spectacular climax, he sat his saddle like the most accomplished western star.

After he left Griffith, Hamilton signed with Paramount. He never did become quite as big a star as Barthelmess, but he was one of Paramount's most popular leading men. And since economy-conscious Paramount kept all their players working as much as possible, Neil appeared in picture after picture during the last half of the 20's. Although he played an occasional heavy in the sound period, Hamilton was strictly hero-material for silent-day audiences. His heroics however were not of the spectacular variety, and generally his roles were patterned very much after the Barthelmess model—a quiet, unassuming, but dependable fellow. (As it happens, that is just what Neil Hamilton is off-screen, too.) One of his most notable silent successes was as the third Geste brother (the others were Ronald Colman and Ralph Forbes) in *Beau Geste*; and then there were such films as *The Little French Girl*, the Zane Grey western *Desert Gold*, Scott Fitzgerald's *The Great Gatsby*, *Street of Forgotten Men*, *The Patriot* and Elinor Glyn's *Three Weeks*.

Hamilton's resolute good looks are still with him, but his acting these days is limited to the stage. In these days of mumbling types, I for one would welcome his soft, pleasant, clear diction back to the screen again.

The Golden Princess was an interesting and off-beat western, co-starring Betty Bronson. Clarence Badger (in white cap) directed.

Griffith made a popular team of Neil Hamilton and Carol Dempster in a trio of top pictures, one of which was *America*.

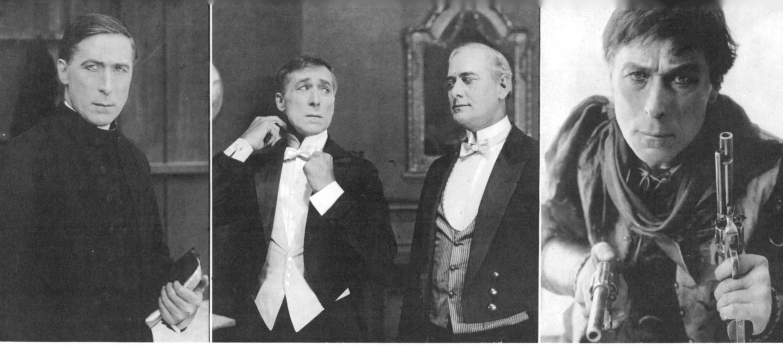

Hart often played an evangel-ical type of westerner—some-times even a priest, as in *The Apostle of Vengeance* (1916).

Hart got a lot of fun out of the situation of the cow-boy going East. This scene is from *Branding Broad-way* (1919). Like most of Bill's best pictures, it was directed by Lambert Hillyer.

One of the best, and most typical, poses of the two-gun westerner.

William S. Hart

Of all the western stars who have ever galloped over the California landscape, the first three undoubtedly remain the most important—and the most beloved. Broncho Billy Anderson literally created the western star; from him all else sprang. Tom Mix gave the western showmanship, color and excitement. No one else has ever quite equalled him. And the greatest of them all, William S. Hart, brought realism and a rug-ged poetry to the "horse opera." Indeed, he may well have rescued the western from an untimely end, for the species seemed to be dying, mired in a rut of clichés, when Hart arrived on the scene in 1914 as an actor, and later as a director, to breathe new and vigorous life into what were literally the first "adult" westerns. And even today, they remain the *best* adult westerns!

Hart, born on December 6, 1870, in Newburgh, New York, travelled the West as a youngster. (His father was a wandering miller.) He grew up with Indians and trail herders, and acquired a deep love of the West which was to remain with him all his life. But stardom in westerns came comparatively late; he spent twenty years first on the Broadway stage as a Shakes-pearean actor. It was from this period that the erroneous supposition grew that the "S" in his name stood for Shakespeare; actually his middle name was Surrey. Even in his Shakespearean period however, Hart went in for a number of rugged roles, ranging from Messala in *Ben Hur* to *The Squaw Man* and *The Virginian*. Drifting into westerns for his friend Tom Ince in 1914, he initially played a heavy, but was soon starring in his own pictures, with a fondness for "good badman" roles. Hart was a tremendously sentimental man, and also a man so devoted to the lore of the West that nothing but the real thing would do for him. His rugged early adventures had an almost documentary-like realism to them. There was nothing glamorous about Hart's West, with its shabby wooden-shack towns, dusty exteriors, and practical rather than colorful costumes. And what rugged titles his pictures had: *Hell's Hinges; The Return of Draw Egan; The Aryan; The Cradle of Courage; The Testing Block*. Despite his sentimental streak, Hart was a big, rugged fellow, too, and took his chances in the fight and rid-ing scenes along with his loyal crew, and his beloved little pinto pony, Fritz.

But times change. With the coming of Ken May-nard, Hoot Gibson, and the new streamlined cowboys of the 20's, Hart's vogue waned. He was an older man now too. He was told to change his pictures and their "out-dated" style; to forget realism, and give his audiences showmanship. Hart refused, and lost his Paramount contract. Valiantly, he started up on his own again—with the memorable *Tumbleweeds* in 1926. It was a fine film, climaxed by a spectacular recon-struction of the Cherokee Strip land-rush. It vindicated Hart in many eyes, proved that his theories still worked, but it wasn't the success he hoped. Tired—

With western writer Buck Connors, center, and Thomas H. Ince. Ince is often erroneously credited with being the director of Hart's films. Actually, he never directed a foot of them, but he does deserve credit for recognizing Hart's talent and giving him a free hand to make his westerns as he felt they should be made.

too tired to have to fight to produce his pictures—he retired to his ranch in Newhall, to write his memoirs and books of western stories.

His last screen appearance was in 1939, when he appeared in a prologue to a reissue of *Tumbleweeds*. His fine old voice, with the range and emotion that comes only from years of stage work, boomed out as he told of the early days of the West, of his love of the West, and of his love of motion pictures. It was probably the most moving eight minutes ever put on film; literally a man delivering his own epitaph. It is a pity that an actor as fine as Hart never had a chance to star in talkies. Had he been a little younger, he might well have occupied the position that Gary Cooper soon assumed in the mid-30's. He died in a Los Angeles hospital on June 23, 1946.

Hart and his beloved little pinto, Fritz, in *Pinto Ben* (1915). The film, which he directed himself, was based on a poem he wrote, dedicated to Fritz.

An off-beat role for Hart; as the Aztec chief in *The Captive God*. With him in this scene are Robert McKim and Enid Markey.

Hart was a sentimental man, and it showed in his films. *The Testing Block* with Eva Novak is a good example.

Opposite Fannie Ward in 1915's *The Cheat.*

Sessue Hayakawa

Sessue Hayakawa, who made recent screen "comebacks" in *The Bridge on the River Kwai* and *Green Mansions,* has never really been away from the screen. But at frequent intervals through the years, when he'd make a picture after a sojourn in his native Japan, or a return to the theatre there, critics (and publicity men!) would jump on the current film as representing the "triumphant return of a silent screen idol"! This is something Sessue himself has never quite understood.

Sessue, who is married to lovely Japanese star Tsuri Aoki (likewise a veteran of the silent screen), chose to be a Shakespearean actor after being educated for a Naval career, but made his greatest screen successes in roles anything but Shakespearean. His first American films were made for Thomas H. Ince, and in those early years, starting in 1914, he varied Oriental roles with some decidedly American ones. In *Last of the Line,* for example, he played an American Indian—although Ince, possibly unsure of audience acceptance of a famous Japanese player as an Indian, made certain that there were no closeups of Sessue in all of the film's two reels. But in long and medium shots he made a convincing Indian warrior.

Sessue played villains too, of course, but his kindly face and nature did a lot towards dispelling the traditional conception of the Oriental as a sinister man of mystery. One of his biggest hits while with Ince was *The Typhoon,* in which his wife also appeared. The title was a symbolical one only. The film was not a sea spectacle; quite the opposite, it was a strong political melodrama of a man who deliberately sacrifices his life, confessing to a murder that was actually committed by a diplomat. The murder was a crime of passion, and it is deemed more important that the diplomat complete his mission than that he pay for his crime with his life. Hence, the false con-

fession by a patriot willing to sacrifice life, and more important, honor, for the sake of his country. In a strong role like this Hayakawa was exceptionally fine, and brought a distinctly "different" type of hero to American screens.

Hayakawa moved from Ince to Famous Players and there, in such films as *The Bottle Imp* and *Forbidden Paths,* he continued to be a top name in consistently off-beat films that ranged from fantasy to romantic tragedies built around racial problems. His first really "sock" hit under Lasky was in the illustrious *The Cheat,* produced by Cecil B. DeMille. Fannie Ward was Sessue's co-star in this hackneyed but powerful old barnstormer. It's interesting that Sessue re-played his same role (a villainous one) in a French talkie remake over twenty years later!

Unfortunately, it hasn't yet been possible to pry any of Sessue Hayakawa's early films loose from the Paramount vaults. But at least there is a measure of compensation in that he is *still* appearing in films, consistently delivering performances that can make most of the newer stars look to their laurels.

1924: *The Danger Line.*

Jannings in 1928.

Jannings—whether he was playing Henry VIII or Othello or a jealous suburban husband. It was obvious that he enjoyed himself hugely in every role—but it was definitely not "ham." It was acting in the grand manner perhaps, with more than a trace of the stage, but when done by a master like Jannings (or Laughton) it was a tremendously effective bravura style. And when Jannings underplayed he could be, and frequently was, extremely moving.

His main fortes were great historical figures—and films of strong melodramatic content with a good deal of "soap opera" to them. His American *Street of Sin* and *Way of All Flesh* were typical examples of this category.

But undoubtedly his best American film was Josef von Sterberg's supremely stylish and multi-camera-angled *The Last Command* of 1927, in which Jannings played an ousted Russian officer, a refugee from the Revolution, who in later years turns up as a Hollywood extra—to find that his director is the same former espionage agent (well played by William Powell) who brought about his downfall. A fine movie—and a fine performance.

Emil Jannings

Although we are concerned solely with the American silent screen in this book, and Emil Jannings was of the German cinema (its leading actor in fact), he was so fine in a number of American films that he made for Paramount in the late 20's that it would be unfair not to include him. Especially since it was his association with director Josef von Sternberg in *The Last Command* that led to the two of them making that great early German talkie *The Blue Angel* together—and starting the slightly waning Jannings off on a whole new career! And, too, via Emil Jannings, we can pay tribute to all the other fine German players who came to work in Hollywood at that time—Lil Dagover, Lya de Putti and Conrad Veidt among them

Jannings was an actor of the old school—a school to which George Arliss also belonged—in which the character to be played was somehow always subordinated to the player. In other words, Jannings was always

In *Street of Sin*, a heavy melodrama directed by Mauritz Stiller for Paramount in the late 20's.

With Evelyn Brent in *The Last Command*, as the ruthless yet innately decent Russian officer.

In *The Last Command* again—the officer reduced to being a mere Hollywood extra.

Jannings in *Sins of the Fathers* (1928). The scene, incidentally, was borrowed from Jannings' great German triumph of a few years earlier, *Variety*.

Leatrice Joy

Leatrice Joy, DeMille's No. 1 star in the late 20's—and No. 1 showcase for Adrian's gowns!

At a time (the mid-20's) when femininity was very much the thing on the screen—whether sweet and simple, Norma Shearer style, or wild and sexy á la Clara Bow—Leatrice Joy created a unique type of screen heroine in the mannish, sophisticated, ultra-efficient society girl. It was the forerunner of the type essayed by Rosalind Russell in so many talkies. Leatrice would play the business-woman with no time for love (as in *Clinging Vines*) or the bored, spoiled society girl who is humanized only when she comes into unpleasant contact with stark reality. *Vanity*, a really rugged melodrama, was easily the best in that category.

She cut a most imposing figure in tailored men's suits, and her boyish bob started a whole new hairdo fad. Leatrice is remembered best for these roles because they were unique in their time, but actually they represented but a small part of her large and impressive list of film credits. And, exquisitely gowned by Adrian, she could be, and usually was, one of the most elegant of all screen heroines. She was Cecil B. DeMille's favorite leading lady, and starred for him not only in the first *The Ten Commandments* and in *Manslaughter*, but in a whole series of films made for his own production

In *You Can't Fool Your Wife*.

company in the late 20's after he had left Paramount.

Leatrice's screen career dates back to the year 1915, when she played an extra in a Mary Pickford film. She was also Billy West's leading lady in some very funny slapstick comedies; West of course was the outstanding Chaplin imitator, and his take-off on Chaplin was staggeringly good. Leatrice entered into these slapstick frolics energetically and genially, usually as the romantic bone of contention between hero Billy West and comic villain Oliver Hardy. But it was in the 20's that Leatrice's star was highest in the heavens; it was then that she married John Gilbert; and it was then that she was most in demand for loan to other producers, such as Sam Goldwyn. *Java Head, A Tale of Two Worlds, Eve's Leaves,* and *The Blue Danube* will be familiar titles to many of you.

Leatrice still makes an occasional movie—just for the fun of it—but there haven't been more than a handful over the past twenty-five years. The last was one of Marilyn Monroe's early Twentieth Century-Fox comedies, *Love Nest.* Miss Joy still respects and loves the silent cinema too much to want to become a very active part of talkies—and is quite content in Connecticut, as one of Greenwich's glamorous grandmothers.

Leatrice contributed a good deal to the popularity of the boyish bob in the 20's. Sporting a bob here for Clive Brook in *For Alimony Only,* she is cast as a super-efficient business woman.

1924's *The Marriage Cheat,* made for Thomas Ince, with Percy Marmont playing opposite Leatrice Joy.

Alice Joyce

Alice Joyce was in the photoplay from its earliest days, when she was a popular player with Kalem and Vitagraph. Because her unusual face—attractive, intelligent-looking, not really beautiful, but with character and sensitivity—was familiar to moviegoers from the beginning, she acquired a "veteran" status while still younger than many of the newcomers! When she was at her most popular (in the 20's), most of her roles were the "mature" ones of wives and mothers—she was young enough to be chased by the villain, or involved in romantic intrigue, but too old, at least in the minds of the casting directors, to play flapper types. But in any event, Alice Joyce was always much too serene and gentle ever to make a convincing flapper!

One of her best performances was in Paramount's *Dancing Mothers,* as the wife of a philandering business-playboy (Austin Trevor) and mother of flapper Clara Bow. Tired of the senseless, butterfly existence they lead, she rebels and goes "on the town" herself, only to find herself romantically involved with Conway Tearle. In a genuinely surprising and off-beat ending, she is almost reconciled with husband and daughter, but finds that their apparent concern for her was actually only selfishness. Whereupon, she leaves them both, determined to find a new life for herself free of their influence. Clara was a vivacious youngster then, but even her never-ending pep and vitality couldn't take the film away from Miss Joyce, whose quiet and authoritative performance was the best thing in that curious and interesting film.

Possibly you may also remember her fine performances in *Sorrell and Son, Stella Dallas,* as the mother in *Beau Geste* and in both versions of *The Green Goddess.* She appeared with George Arliss in the silent and the sound versions, the first in 1923, the second six years later. Miss Joyce did make talkies successfully, but soon decided to retire and concentrate on her family. With her death in 1958, Hollywood lost a gracious and charming lady.

Herbert Brenon, under whom she gave such fine performances in *Beau Geste, Dancing Mothers,* and *Sorrell and Son,* also directed her in *The Little French Girl* (1925). The young lady is Mary Brian.

1923: with George Arliss in *The Green Goddess.* This version was made for Sam Goldwyn; in 1929 the same two stars made a second, talking, version for Warners'.

Buster Keaton

I think it's a measure of Buster Keaton's greatness and unique comedy talents that no other comedians ever tried to imitate him. They would "borrow" his gags perhaps, but no attempt was made to copy his style and personality. Keaton was unique among screen comics in that he never relied on pathos and never even tried for audience sympathy. He was the eternal pessimist who didn't expect people to feel sorry for him, and in fact didn't even feel sorry for himself. He *knew* things would go wrong no matter how hard he tried, and somewhere along the line he'd just give up trying. Then, somehow, something would work out to his advantage. But even this elicited no response from Buster. Once in a while, the law of averages demanded a lucky break, but he knew there'd be more trouble ahead.

Buster's gaunt, unemotional, never-smiling face was the perfect facade for the defeatist character he projected. He was the exact opposite of the bubblingly optimistic Harold Lloyd, not only in personality, but also in the way he confronted life. Lloyd's girl friends for example, were usually adoring creatures who knew that ultimately he would make good, and always gave him credit for far more ability than he had. Buster's leading ladies, however, usually cared little whether he lived or died. They would misunderstand his motives, turn down his proposals of marriage, and think the very worst of him. In addition, they were *stupid;* when Buster finally did get things organized properly, along they would come with some scatter-brained idea or action which would undo all he had so carefully done, plunging him into chaos again.

Most important, Buster's troubles were never of his own making. Harold Lloyd frequently landed in hot water by the misfiring of his own zeal, but Buster, never! He was cautious and correct, and did everything by the rules. But the complexities of modern life, especially the mechanical things (anything from an ocean liner to a movie camera or an ordinary deckchair), would always defeat him. Buster never understood, but he never complained either. Like a man from Mars suddenly dumped in the middle of Times Square, he stumbles blindly along, accepting the fact that he can never figure out what's what, and content to be out of step with everyone and everything, as long as nobody bothers him too much.

Buster Keaton in a typical pose (one that he repeated often), scanning the horizon (and his own future) with the detached air of a casual traveller, secretly convinced that whatever is waiting for him is hardly worth the effort of going to meet it! This particular scene is from *Our Hospitality*.

It was an intriguing and unusual character for a screen comic to adopt, but a tremendously effective one. I've used a great many words describing Buster's

One of Buster's earliest comedies, the two-reel *His Wedding Night*. Buster is between Fatty Arbuckle and Al St. John (1917).

Marion Mack carried on the tradition of dumbell heroines in *The General* (1927). Here she refuses to believe Buster's story that he was first in the line to enlist but was turned down.

Kathryn McGuire was one of the dumbest of all of Buster's screen heroines. In *The Navigator* (1924) she and Buster are stranded aboard a "runaway" ocean liner. The principal comedy derives from their problems in performing operations actually designed to be done on an assembly line basis—such as, here, feeding the furnaces, or attempting to boil two eggs in a huge vat designed to cook hundreds!

modus operandi; he could do it on the screen in a matter of seconds, with a single gag and some eloquent pantomime. Audiences understood Buster right away—sometimes more so than the critics, who were so anxious to attach sociological meaning to Buster's films that they often missed half the fun. And what fun they were! From his earlier two-reelers to his later features, I don't think Buster ever made a bad comedy. His pacing was upset by the use of sound, and his talkies weren't a tenth as good as his silents, but they still contained some very funny moments.

Silent screen comedy should be seen rather than described, and I don't intend to dwell too much on the gags themselves, except to say that they were brilliantly imaginative and magnificently executed. Keaton's acrobatic training (he had had a long career in vaudeville) was not only an asset to the fast slapstick (Buster rarely used a double), but perhaps more importantly in-

stilled in him a perfect sense of timing, so that each gag built marvelously and paid off at just the right moment for the maximum laugh reaction. I don't think there was a funnier man on the screen than Buster Keaton—and that includes Lloyd and Chaplin.

Luckily, a good deal of Keaton's material has remained intact, and can still be seen today. At least three of his great two-reelers are still around: *The Haunted House, Balloonatics* and, best of all, *Cops.* A good number of his features can still be seen, too. *Sherlock Jr.* and *The General* are discussed elsewhere in this book. Almost as good—and perhaps I should drop the "almost"—are *Steamboat Bill Jr., The Navigator, The Cameraman* and *Our Hospitality*—all of them full of the most wonderful visual humor.

Keaton's humor was so far ahead of its day in the 20's that it's not surprising that he was not quite the box office draw that Chaplin and Lloyd were. Those who really appreciated his work were unstinting in their praise; but there was a subtlety and methodical pacing to his films that made Harold Lloyd's faster and more obviously slapstick of more immediate appeal to the average audience. Keaton was big, make no mistake about it, but in terms of box office returns, he ranked third to Charlie and Harold. However, his work has endured better. There are Chaplin and Lloyd films that seem dated, or forced today, but Keaton's comedies are less affected by time. Advanced in their day, they are *still* sufficiently revolutionary and ahead of the times to be fresh and boldly imaginative today.

Go West (1925) was one of the weaker Keatons, perhaps because it veered towards straight slapstick so much. But it had fine moments—and Kathleen Myers was an appropriately useless heroine.

In 1922, with Claire Windsor in the Goldwyn production, *Brothers Under the Skin*.

Norman Kerry

Rochester-born Norman Kerry might well be described as a silent-era Errol Flynn. Handsome, dashing, he even looked a little like Flynn, and while he cut a neat figure in a tuxedo, he was seen to his best advantage in the costumes and uniforms of swashbucklers. However, he was not as athletic as Flynn, and his roles in costume films were usually far less demanding physically. Critics gave him the same sort of brushoff that they gave Flynn, regarding him as an amiable enough player, and good-looking enough to please the ladies, but no actor. Flynn of course, in later years, proved that he was an actor. Kerry never did—nor did it worry him. He knew he was no great dramatic performer, and had no illusions about his talent. But he was a competent actor, and always did his best. Free of temperament, ever ready to take advice and direction, he was extremely popular with his crews and co-stars. Valentino was a particularly good friend of his and, in fact, Kerry—who made a success of acting in films a little before Rudy did—was instrumental in getting Valentino minor roles in those early, pre-*Sheik* days.

Kerry's first film appearance was in a minor supporting role to Douglas Fairbanks in *Manhattan Madness*. Playing thereafter with Mary Pickford, Constance Talmadge and Alice Brady, he managed to get himself reasonably well established as an actor, before leaving for service in the Army during World War I. Some of his better-known pictures in the 20's, when he was at his peak (principally as a leading man for Universal) were in the Lon Chaney films, *The Hunchback of Notre Dame* and *The Phantom of the Opera*, in *Merry Go Round*, and with Lillian Gish in *Annie Laurie*. He made only a few talkies. Comfortably off, he died at the age of 60 in Paris in the mid-1950's.

A year later, with Patsy Ruth Miller in *The Hunchback of Notre Dame*.

In *The Phantom of the Opera*, Norman was never very effectual in saving lovely Mary Philbin from the clutches of Lon Chaney. The script had him faint away at the moment he was needed most! But he was handsome and dashing in the love scenes.

A typical pose of the baby-faced clown.

Harry Langdon

It's sometimes difficult to realize that Harry Langdon was once considered a serious threat to Charlie Chaplin as the screen's leading comedian. Occasionally on "Memory Lane," when I've shown one of Langdon's old Sennett comedies, I've remarked on his greatness, and viewers have written in to ask why. They've enjoyed him—but haven't found any sign of true genius.

But, believe me, Langdon was one of the greatest. Unfortunately, his genius was of a very specialized kind. It needed careful, delicate handling. Almost as soon as it reached full fruition on the screen, Harry decided he could handle his own comic career. After all, he had created his screen character—why shouldn't he produce, and direct, and write as well? This, alas, was his undoing. Directors like Harry Edwards and Frank Capra knew what he was trying to do, perhaps better than he did—and they knew how to handle him, how to express it best. When Langdon took over, he

became bogged down in his character for its own sake. Plot and comic invention were shunted aside; misfire pantomime and large doses of pathos took over. The tragedy is that Harry himself never knew what was wrong and went on trying, each picture being less successful than the one before it. When he died in the mid-40's from a stroke, he was still in harness—playing in "B" pictures, planning and dreaming of a comeback, still trying to figure out what had happened to him.

But before the decline started, he left us two of the greatest feature comedies ever made—*Tramp Tramp Tramp* (with Joan Crawford) and *The Strong Man*, discussed elsewhere in this book. Less funny, but with some marvelous sequences, was *Long Pants*. And he left dozens of Mack Sennett two-reelers—many of which are an uneasy mixture of Sennett slapstick and Langdon pantomime, but some of which (*There He Goes* is a good example) were among the best silent comedy shorts ever turned out.

Sennett once described Langdon as a "lovable, confused little man." This describes both his on-and off-screen personality. His chief comic characteristic was the projection of complete, babyish innocence—he was so trusting and stupid that he didn't realize when harm had been done to him, and thus his complete blind faith in everyone and everything helped him win through in the end. He'd blink those big eyes with happiness and humility—wave his hand in that odd hesitant gesture of his—anxious to be friendly, but afraid of being thought "not good enough"—and achieve more pathos in a few feet of film than many stars can attain in a whole reel. His films weren't all quiet charm either—they had some roaring slapstick sequences too, like the devastating cyclone episode in *Tramp Tramp Tramp*.

The tragedy is not so much that Langdon is forgotten, but that while he was on top, he was too impatient to start on his own ideas to let the wisdom and experience of others guide him for just a little longer.

Harry's best picture—the First National feature, *Tramp Tramp Tramp*, with Joan Crawford as the leading lady.

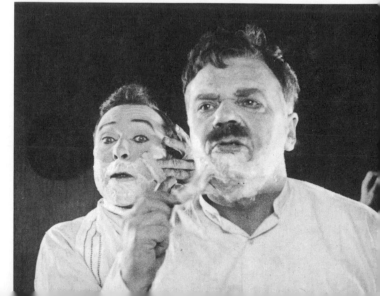

A fine comedy moment from Mack Sennett's *Luck of the Foolish:* Harry trying to shave in a swaying train, to the consternation of the other passenger using the same mirror.

Laura La Plante

I saw most of Laura La Plante's movies well into the sound era—at least ten years after all of them were made—and was always bowled over, not only by her loveliness, but by her charm and sense of fun. And it was a double pleasure when, a couple of years ago, I finally caught up with one of her very first talkies, and found that her voice had exactly those same qualities, and was in fact the sort of voice I had imagined while watching her silents!

For years Laura was Universal's No. 1 feminine star, and meant as much to them in the 20's as Bette Davis did to Warners', or Greer Garson to M-G-M, in later years. She had started off, frankly determined to be a movie star, as an extra (and a very lovely one) in Christie comedies at the age of fifteen. Charles Ray's *The Old Swimmin' Hole* (1921) gave her her first real break, and a contract with Universal followed not long after.

She was a strikingly beautiful girl, yet there was nothing exotic or extraordinary about her beauty. It was the kind of beauty that the publicity agents are always telling us is the "typical American girl" type, or the "girl-next-door" type. This may be true, although it seems to me that the "girl next door" is always next door to somebody else! Anyway, with her handsome features and lovely honey-blonde hair, Laura was an asset to dozens of Universal features. Her good humor and neat timing made her especially at home in come-dies like *Skinner's Dress Suit*, with Reginald Denny, and *The Teaser*. But she made a most fetching damsel-in-distress in *The Last Warning* and *The Cat and the Canary*, as well as adding distinction to such Universal deluxe specials as *The King of Jazz, Captain of the Guard,* and *The Midnight Sun*.

Laura made a surprise return to the screen a few years ago—playing Betty Hutton's mother in *Spring Reunion*. She still looked so young and lovely that she was almost unconvincing in the role!

One of Laura's best performances was in *Smoldering Fires,* an excellently-done "soap opera" (directed by Clarence Brown) with Laura as the girl who inadvertently falls in love with the man (Malcolm MacGregor) her older sister (Pauline Frederick) had planned to marry.

Laura became a brunette temporarily for her role in *Show Boat* (1929), which was released in both silent and part-talkie versions.

Oliver Hardy (left) and Stan Laurel.

A scene from *You're Darn Tootin'* that sums up much of Laurel and Hardy's basic formula: society, outraged, points an accusing finger at the boys, who express bland innocence despite being so obviously responsible for all the chaos!

Laurel & Hardy

Laurel and Hardy made so many films, features as well as two-reel comedies, that for years they were taken for granted. Everybody loved their films, but few people took the pair seriously as truly creative comedy craftsmen. Fewer still regarded them as comedians entitled to rank with the greatest of their profession. Only now is coming the belated recognition that their contribution to screen comedy is as important and unique as that of Buster Keaton. The pity is that so much of this recognition and latter-day enthusiasm has come after Oliver Hardy's death.

Individually, Laurel and Hardy had been in movies for years before they finally got together, both starting out around 1917. Laurel had starred in a particularly good series in the early 20's for Broncho Billy Anderson, who had by then reverted to plain G. M. Anderson, producer. One of that series was the famous and hilarious *Mud and Sand*, a delightful spoof on the Valentino *Blood and Sand.* Later he was a solo comedy star, and a director, for Hal Roach. Hardy had started out with Sennett, and through the years had specialized in playing comedy heavies—most notably in a good series of two-reelers with Larry Semon. Once in a while, Hardy's grandiose gestures and jolly face would betray the fact that he knew he was just an actor playing a villain, and the wonder is that his obvious comic potentialities weren't spotted much earlier.

The boys didn't get together until 1927 when they began appearing together in Hal Roach comedies, such as *Slipping Wives*. They were merely supporting comedians, and didn't operate as a team. Their screen characters varied from picture to picture. Then, almost by accident, they were cast as a team in *With Love and Hisses*, a good army comedy. The short was a tremendous hit with the public, and a team they remained—although it was to be several pictures before they really established their basic screen characters, and longer still—not, in fact, until after Hal Roach's move to M-G-M—that they were granted recognition of their worth by being accorded star billing.

A lot of interesting people worked with Laurel and Hardy in the early days—people who soon graduated from two-reelers (to the two-reelers' loss, unfortunately). Their No. 1 cameraman was George Stevens, now producer-director of such films as *The Diary of Anne Frank.* Leo McCarey wrote and directed many of their best ones; he too became a top-flight producer-director. Many other first-rate directors learned the ropes on Laurel and Hardy comedies. And they built up a wonderful "stock company" of comedy performers

—scrawny James Finlayson, with his walrus moustache, plump Billy Gilbert, eternally frustrated Edgar Kennedy (who proved to be a fine director on a couple of their silents), Mae Busch, Charlie Hall, and so many others.

But of course the basic contribution was that of Laurel and Hardy themselves, for they devised most of their own material and, in a sense, directed themselves besides. As a team they complemented each other perfectly, not only physically, but also in terms of personality. Laurel was the eternal innocent—trusting, babyish, so stupid that when a good idea comes to him it is gone before he can grasp it and make use of it, and with a streak of childish maliciousness in him which comes to the surface when pressed a little too far. Hardy on the other hand, was completely adult—the bon vivant and gallant of the old school, with flowery gestures and eloquent speech, pompous and opinionated, and only temporarily deflated when his ego is punctured—as it always was, without fail!

Their comedy was primarily of the violent slapstick variety, although they did make films which were basically situation comedies, in which slapstick was purely incidental. The dominating aspect of their work was precision; they built their comedies methodically, almost like children playing with a set of toy bricks. Sometimes they were a little too methodical, and their deliberate pacing confused many. But when their style paid off—and it usually did—some gems of comedy resulted. One of their trademarks was the incredible savagery of their encounters with rivals; yet it was a sportsmanlike savagery, and despite the most fiendish indignities, nobody was ever really hurt. Faced with an enemy, Laurel and Hardy would start off casually by snipping his tie. He would retaliate in kind by ripping the crown from Hardy's hat. Then—*kerplunk!*—an enormous armful of mud would be dumped on the offender. And so it would go—the victim accepting his fate passively, making no attempt to avoid it, even waiting with curiosity to see what indignity would be inflicted next. Then it would be *his* turn, and Laurel and Hardy would display the same sportsmanship in taking their medicine. Sometimes a whole film (like *Big Business* or *Two Tars*) would be constructed around such an idea, building finally to a mad orgy of destruction in which houses, cars, everything in sight, would be totally destroyed. Then, sheepishly embarrassed that their anger had taken them so far, yet at the same time grinning boyishly at the fun they'd had, Laurel and Hardy would make it up with their opponent and take themselves off with a courtly bow.

One of their last silents was 1929's *Double Whoopee*. It was also one of the *first* films of blonde bombshell Jean Harlow.

As convicts in *The Second Hundred Years*, they jail-break their way right into the warden's office!

Again from *The Second Hundred Years*: they escape from prison by posing as painters, and to make their deception convincing, proceed to paint everything in sight!

Two Tars started out like so many Laurel and Hardy comedies, with the boys, at peace with the world, full of good will towards all, starting out to enjoy a day's drive in the country—

Also like so many Laurel & Hardy comedies, *Two Tars* wound up in an orgy of frenzied destruction, all arising, of course, out of the simplest misunderstanding!

Laurel, it seems, was the one who did most of the work behind the cameras, while Hardy was the one who was most creative in front of the cameras. Quite apart from his wonderful comic pantomime, he was also an extremely winning personality, and a good straight actor, as his few non-comedy performances proved. But it's difficult, and pointless, to separate the contributions of the two. Individually, both were fine; togther, they were great. The best of their silent comedies—*Battle of the Century, You're Darn Tootin', Big Business* and *Two Tars*—rank with the best silent comedies ever made. And few players made the switch to sound with such facility as did Laurel and Hardy. Their voices matched their figures and personalities perfectly; after a few hesitant pictures, in which they rather uncertainly tried to adapt their mathematically precise silent style to the new medium, they hit the right formula and were off again to even greater public acclaim. But while most of their sound comedies were fine, the bulk of them were actually re-workings in one way or another of their silents. Almost all of their sound films, including the 1938 feature *Blockheads*, had gags or situations lifted from their films of 1927-1929, the "Golden Age" of Laurel and Hardy.

Lincoln's one and only great role—as "Tarzan of the Apes." This scene is from the first of all the Tarzan thrillers, made in 1918.

Elmo Lincoln

If ever there was a one-character star, it was good old Elmo Lincoln! The screen's first Tarzan was on the screen since *The Birth of a Nation*, in which he played several roles, including White Arm Joe, proprietor of the dingy gin mill broken up by Wallace Reid. Next, in *Intolerance*, he had a field-day as Belshazzar's "Mighty Man of Valor"—a huge, muscular warrior, fighting off the hordes of Cyrus the Persian. Then, in 1918, he was cast as the lead in the first movie adaptation of the popular Edgar Rice Burroughs novel, *Tarzan of the Apes*. Although some of the apes and lions were palpably phoney, it was a good adventure film, and made a fortune. Because of his gigantic frame, Elmo's tree-swinging was kept to a minimum, although for such an enormous man he was surprisingly agile. He had a whale of a fight scene with a lecherous native who tried to carry off the heroine, Enid Markey. The fact that Lincoln was not a polished actor mattered not at all, of course, for the Tarzan role; indeed, Lincoln's occasional awkwardness, particularly in the romantic scenes, was happily and surprisingly apt. He was certainly a fine figure of a man, clad in a leopard skin which covered most of his chest as well as his loins (censorship at the time, surprisingly unrestrictive where feminine nudity was concerned, found the bare male torso objectionable apparently!), and he made a most convincing Jungle King, even though a less nimble one than some of his Olympic successors.

Lincoln later made *The Return of Tarzan*, a serial full of good jungle action, and such other serials as *Elmo the Mighty*. Unfortunately, his physique prevented his ever becoming a really top star. In a later period, he might have become a tough character performer, as did Nat Pendleton and William Bendix, but such a type did not exist on the screen in Lincoln's time, at least not on the star level. Even a fine actor like Louis Wolheim found the going decidedly rough. So Elmo, who seemed on the threshold of stardom in 1918, never quite made it. But he didn't give up in despair either. He loved movies, and was determined to keep making them—even if star status was to elude him. He was still doing the work he loved as a small part player in Charles Starrett westerns at Columbia when he died in the early 1950's.

193

Harold in his most familiar and characteristic pose; a scene from 1921's *Never Weaken*. It's difficult to realize that Lloyd did scenes like this missing most of the fingers on one hand!

Harold Lloyd

If you've never sat in a crowded theatre and rocked with laughter at Harold Lloyd's hilarious and thrilling antics (and if you're under 35, the chances are that you haven't), then you've really missed out on one of the best treats the movies ever offered. The sharing of continued and hearty laughter in a theatre was one of the silent era's happiest contributions to the welfare of mankind, and Lloyd was one of the principal benfactors.

Lloyd was by far the most talented of all the comedians who weren't really funny in themselves. Keaton, Chaplin and Langdon were unique personalities. Even if their material had been inferior, their pantomime would have put them over. But Lloyd was different—like the later sound comedians, he relied almost exclusively on his material, and it was material that could have been as effective in the hands of another comic.

This is no disparagement of Lloyd. Far from it. His

Bumping into Broadway winds up with a mad melee in a gambling house, with seemingly every cop on Broadway after Harold personally.

great talent lay not so much in being a comedy performer as in being a comedy creator. Because he dreamed up so much of his own material, he was naturally the best practitioner of his own form of humor, which his breezy personality socked over to its best advantage.

Lloyd started as "Lonesome Luke," a hayseed character with more than a few of Chaplin's tramp traits. Although in later years Lloyd dismissed these early comedies as unimportant, they were actually of a very high standard. They seldom rose above straightforward slapstick, but it was slapstick of the first calibre. Around 1918, however, Lloyd graduated into his more familiar character—the breezy young go-getter with the

With Bebe Daniels in *Bumping into Broadway*, his first two-reeler. It was made for Hal Roach in 1919. The gallant Harold, as a struggling artist, comes to the rescue of Bebe, who is about to be evicted for not paying her rent.

horn-rimmed glasses. Whether by accident or design, this Lloyd emerged as something of a composite of Charlie Ray (the small-town boy) and Doug Fairbanks (the All-American boy). His principal asset as he set out to conquer the world (he usually started in a hick town, and made his way to the big city right away) was a tremendous zeal, backed by unflagging optimism and self-confidence, and a firm belief in the Horatio Alger (and Cinderella) stories. His ideas for "getting ahead" were often good, but they always assumed the 100% full cooperation of everyone with whom he came in contact. Inevitably, Harold's little world would slowly fall apart when he came up against the complications of big business, the city, and rivals who didn't see the need to play fair. Ultimately, his basic honesty and perseverance won the day for him—but not before he'd been made to take himself down a peg or two, and substitute common sense for daydreams.

Lloyd's open, trusting and perpetually cheerful face made him a natural for this sort of role and he played it to perfection. (Incidentally, he is very much the same type of person off-screen, too.) Quite apart from the likeability of his screen-character, he scored on the breathless pace of his gags, and the variety of gags within a single picture. Everything was planned almost mathematically, but it plays as effortlessly on the screen as though it was all taking place off-the-cuff. Slapstick predominated, of course—the wild, chillingly convincing, and always hilarious scamperings over skyscrapers (as in *High and Dizzy*, *Never Weaken*, *Safety Last* and others) or the zany, high-speed car chases in which Harold eluded the cops by the most fantastic stratagems. *Girl Shy* was the funniest of these, perhaps. But there was grand comedy material of a quieter nature too—the department store sequences in *Safety Last*, eluding the landlady by hanging himself up in a clothes closet (a gag he repeated several times), the wonderful episode in *The Freshman*, in which the suit he had collected from the tailor in too much of a hurry begins to fall apart on the dance floor, *just* as he is trying to impress his girl. There was pathos in the Lloyd comedies, but never too much. Eternally optimistic Harold never let set-backs deter him for long.

Harold Lloyd comedies need an audience. They need the chain-reaction of audience laughter far more than do the quieter films of the other great silent comedians. They were paced and designed so that one laugh led into a bigger laugh to be topped by another, fol-

One of Harold's biggest feature successes, *Grandma's Boy*, in which a country youth gains courage and manhood by being told the story of his ancestor's heroic exploits in the Civil War. Harold, of course, played both the modern lad and the Confederate hero.

Captain Kidd's Kids was the last of his films opposite Bebe Daniels—

—thereafter his leading lady (on screen as well as off) was Mildred Davis.

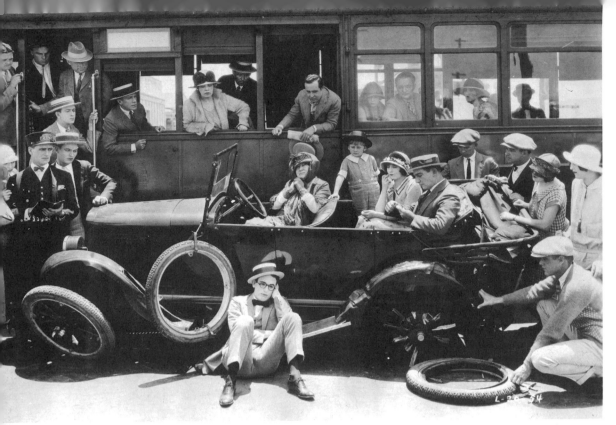

Old cars—and the systematic wrecking of them—fascinated all silent screen comics. This scene is from *Hot Water*.

lowed by a moment of repose for the audience to get its breath back before the next onslaught. Thus if Lloyd ever releases his old classics to television, you won't by any means be seeing them to their best advantage, or in the proper environment.

One of Lloyd's more off-beat features was *Dr. Jack*—which wound up with Harold and a mad killer chasing each other around a crumbling old mansion.

It seems likely that before any TV sale, Lloyd will try some theatrical reissues—and if he does, those of you who have never seen Lloyd, or his charming dimpled wife, Mildred Davis, who appears in most of his films with him, have a real treat in store!

Another automobile adventure, *Get Out and Get Under*. Juvenile comic Sunshine Sammy offers some of his usual unwanted assistance. When Sammy wasn't making life difficult for Lloyd, he was getting in the way of Snub Pollard or "Our Gang," elsewhere on the Roach lot.

196

Typical poses of Bessie in her early Triangle days.

Bessie Love (1917)

Bessie Love

Bessie Love, who is still a very beautiful woman and remains active in movies in England and Europe, used to be referred to as Hollywood's "Peter Pan." (In fact, she was tested for that role in the Paramount film version, and was the leading contender until Betty Bronson came along.) She never seemed to "grow up" as far as films were concerned. Always looking about sixteen, she seemed to be forever on the threshold of top stardom, but never quite made it. Every few years there would be an exceptionally good role, and the critics would hail her "comeback." And then she'd be overlooked again for a few more years. Her biggest comeback of all came with the introduction of sound, when her dancing and singing talent made her much in demand for *The Broadway Melody* and other "monster" musicals of the period.

Perhaps Bessie's main problem was that she was too much of a mixture of other stars. She had the ethereal innocence of Lillian Gish; the gamin tomboyishness of Mary Pickford; the child-wife naïveté of Mae Marsh. Too many of her roles were ones that would have been better suited to one of those stars, stars who, being tied up by other contracts, just weren't available. But when Bessie had a role tailored specifically to her talents, she

really made good! Griffith recommended that Bill Hart use her in *The Aryan*—and as the girl who softens the bitter old Westerner she was superb. That one role did much to boost her then-young career, and she was perhaps the most eminently satisfactory heroine that sentimental old Bill ever had. She was exactly what he wanted in a western heroine.

In the 20's, she had another fine opportunity in *The King of Main Street*, a charming and touching little film (made by that unjustly forgotten director, Monta Bell) about a European king who falls in love on a state visit to New York—but has to give it up for an unhappy marriage that will benefit his country. Bessie was excellent as the American girl who returns his love but has to settle for a conventional, loveless marriage with the boy next door. The film also gave Bessie a chance to introduce the Charleston to the screen.

Another exceptionally fine role was as the island girl in Richard Barthelmess' *Soul Fire*. She never looked lovelier, nor danced more enchantingly. But roles like these were disappointingly infrequent for Bessie. When she landed in a big smash-hit like *The Lost World*, her role was too conventional to attract much attention—especially with a herd of dinasours for competition!

In the 20's, Bessie switched to heavier dramatics, as in *Sundown* for First National (1921).

And starring roles in pleasant programmers like *Young April, Dress Parade,* and *Rubber Tires*—enjoyable though those films were—did little more than keep her name before the public, and prompt critics to remark periodically that her talent was being sadly wasted.

Bessie Love's career was sadly mishandled from the beginning, and the dramatic potential displayed in *The Aryan* was never fully realized. But if nothing else (of course, there *were* good films and fine performances), she brought a perpetual youth, beauty and grace to all of her many films, and the silent screen was very much enriched for her being a part of it.

Mae Marsh

If I were ever asked to name the three finest actresses of the screen, and if I ever had the temerity to attempt it, there are only two that I would include without any hesitation at all. One would be Lillian Gish, and the other Mae Marsh. (Discretion, as well as indecision, dictates the leaving of the third name open!)

Mae, like Lillian, started out with Griffith at the old Biograph company. She was by far the finest actress he had working for him, and the most suitable for his purposes. She had that frail, wispy look that he liked in his heroines, yet there was maturity and strength, too. She could play an older woman with far more conviction than could Mary Pickford, for example. Mae's real specialty was playing the girlish heroine suddenly confronted with adult reality. In a moment, the childish hand-clappings and jigs of joy would disappear, to be replaced by anxiety and despair. Mae had a beautifully expressive face which mirrored these emotions perfectly, and fine as most of Griffith's Biographs were, she was usually one step ahead. The Griffith Biographs were notable mainly for their outstanding artistic, directorial and photographic innovations; with rare exceptions, emotional depth was not one of their strong points. Mae played in a great variety of roles at Biograph, big and small. In *The Lesser Evil* and *The New York Hat* she was merely an extra. In *Lena and the Geese*, a charming fairy tale of old Holland, she co-starred with Mary Pickford. *Man's Genesis* and *Brute Force*, Griffith's films on the history of man, saw her as Lilywhite, a Stone Age maiden. And in *The Telephone Girl and the Lady*, a really exciting melodrama, she was the wide-awake telephone operator who saves society matron Claire McDowell from bandit Harry Carey.

Mae idolized Griffith, and stayed with him when he moved to the coast. She was in *The Battle of Elderbush Gulch*, one of the last (and best) of the Biographs. *Home Sweet Home* and *The Avenging Conscience* followed, and then, as Griffith was ready to leave two-reelers and program-features behind him, *The Birth of a Nation.*

Her role in this great film was an enlargement of what had come to be her most familiar one—the girl growing to young womanhood, suddenly brought face to face with tragedy. Mae's reactions to a guerilla raid, her excitement at receiving a letter from her big brother, away at the wars, the pathetic tenderness with which she greets him when he returns home, all of these were memorable highspots from a performance climaxed by a most moving death scene.

Mae had advanced even further as an actress when,

Mae Marsh

With Henry B. Walthall in *The Birth of a Nation.*

In Griffith's *Man's Genesis* (1912).

199

Two scenes with Bobby Harron from *The Wharf Rat;* Mae as a playful youngster, unable to believe in the young hero's romantic interest; and as the suddenly matured young woman.

the following year, she was seen in *Intolerance.* I have discussed Mae's great performance in this film in the section devoted to it, so I won't cover the same ground again, except to reiterate that at this time Mae was quite certainly the finest dramatic actress on the screen.

As well as playing in the big "spectaculars" like *The Birth of a Nation* and *Intolerance,* Mae was also appearing in a number of Griffith-supervised productions which gave her Mary Pickford-type roles. There were rousing melodramas like *The Wild Girl of the Sierras* and *A Child of the Paris Streets,* and Cinderella romances, of which *The Wharf Rat* and *Hoodoo Ann* were typical. Expertly made "little" pictures, they proved tremendously successful, and did much to boost Mae's popularity. In many of them she was co-starred with Bobby Harron, who had been appearing with her since the old Biograph days.

In time, however, Mae left Griffith, and found, as had Henry B. Walthall, that her career came to somewhat of a standstill. She remained a top name in terms of box office, but nobody, not even Sam Goldwyn, for whom

One of her most enjoyable lesser films, *Hoodoo Ann* (1916).

she made many films, seemed to know quite what roles were right for her, or how to direct her to her best advantage. Roles that under Griffith would have been charming now seemed maudlin and cloying. She was always better than her material, never given a role that she could really get her teeth into.

This disturbed Mae—but not too much. She was now happily married, and being a wife and mother mattered to her far more than being a movie star. But there was one more great role ahead for her—back with Griffith in *The White Rose* (1923). It was a strong emotional part again; she played an inexperienced youngster who is attracted to Ivor Novello. There is a mutual seduction and he disappears, contrite and ashamed—for he is a minister. Mae's child is born, and because she is unmarried, she is fired from her job and evicted from her lodgings. In her performance in this scene, Mae even surpasses the acting of Lillian Gish in an identical sequence in *Way Down East.* No matter how desperate her plight, Miss Gish always somehow suggested an inner strength which audiences knew would see her through somehow. But in *The White Rose,* Mae's abject helplessness and bewilderment, and her defiant refusal to name the father of her child, for she still loves him deeply, is even more moving. In other hands, *The White Rose* (which piled complication upon complication until a final happy ending was reached) would have been unendurably sentimental. But with Griffith directing, and with Mae in the lead (Neil Hamilton and Carol Dempster carried a subsidiary love story), *The White Rose* was a tender and touching love story, beautifully photographed on location in the bayou country. It represented Mae's last really great performance on the silent screen; or perhaps I should amend that to say that it was her last really good role.

Mae retired from the screen in the late 20's, but re-

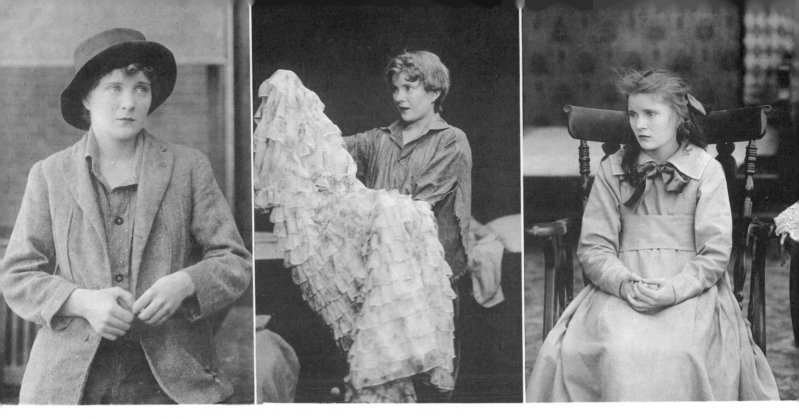

Three shots of Mae's haunting, expressive face.

turned in the early 30's to star in Fox's re-make of that fine old Mary Carr tear-jerker, *Over the Hill*. Mae had a good voice, and with her always mature face, which now, as in 1912, made her look older than she was, she was a "natural" for strong character roles. She has been at it ever since, contributing outstanding cameos to a number of movies—including a good proportion of John Ford's films. And you may remember her superb little cameo as the hysterical plane passenger in *Julie*, a Doris Day film of a few years back.

Like most of the Griffith group, Mae Marsh remains a staunch supporter of "The Master," ever ready to launch into a lengthy testimonial to his work. Only recently, discussing the collaboration between Griffith and his ace cameraman, Billy Bitzer, Miss Marsh said in that small, yet firm and determined voice of hers, "Billy Bitzer always did what Griffith told him because, of course, Mr. Griffith was always right!"

What a pity that Mae didn't work more with "D. W." after 1917. When Lillian Gish struck out on her own, she had the strength to make the gamble pay off. When Mae tried, it didn't work so well. It is sad to look at her magnificent portrayal in *Intolerance* and to realize how little her great talent was really utilized thereafter. But Mae never complained, and had a happy home life to compensate for a career that never developed as it might. And we still have Mae at the peak of her artistry in *The Birth of a Nation*, *Intolerance* and *The White Rose*—performances that, if anything, seem to improve with the passing of the years.

1922, and *Till We Meet Again*, a comparatively minor independent film. One year later she was back on top again with *The White Rose*.

With Billie Burke in *The Mysterious Miss Terry* (1917).

Thomas Meighan

It is difficult to tell just what makes a star. Personality and good looks aren't always the answer, and Thomas Meighan is a case in point. His work today seems to lack the youthful vigor of a Wallace Reid, or the mature polish of a Lewis Stone. In both looks and performance he seems to be almost a composite of Milton Sills and Richard Barthelmess. And yet the record is there—

The Miracle Man (1919) with Lon Chaney—the film that really established Chaney and gave Meighan a further big boost.

Meighan was a top star from 1919, when he made his first big hit in Lon Chaney's *The Miracle Man,* right through the 20's. That his appeal hasn't stood the test of time as well as John Gilbert's or Valentino's is no fault of his own; rather it is a reflection on the changing tastes (and age-groups) of movie audiences.

In the 20's, movie audiences were dominated by adults, with teen-agers occupying a less prominent position than they do today. And so naturally there was less stress on the young, dashing hero as a box office necessity. Adults liked mature leading men too—the thoughtful, dependable type, neatly dressed, physically able to raise a fist in the heroine's defense if need be, but smart enough to find some other way out of the difficulty. Conway Tearle, Henry B. Walthall, Ralph Forbes and Lewis Stone fell into this category; and so, certainly, did Meighan. Indeed, he was the biggest star name of this category. He played in everything from melodrama to romance, satire to whimsy—but his basic screen character, like George Arliss's, rarely changed. You may remember him in that clever satire of the Florida land-boom, *The New Klondyke;* or in *Conrad in Quest of His Youth*—or in any one of a dozen top Paramount films opposite such stars as Gloria Swanson and Leatrice Joy. One of his very best remembered roles was with Gloria Swanson and Lila Lee in *Male and Female,* DeMille's pleasant (if considerably revamped) version of James M. Barrie's *The Admirable Crichton.* Meigham did particularly well in a role ideally suited to his personality—the ultra-capable but undemonstrative English butler, played on somewhat more jovial lines by Kenneth More in the recent re-make.

Sadly, Meighan is never referred to by the critics or the historians of the film. He is remembered only by the millions of moviegoers who made him a star.

At the height of his popularity, in *The Alaskan* (1924).

Tom Mix. A characteristic pose from *The Untamed*.

Tom Mix

Of all the cowboy stars who have ridden across the Hollywood sagebrush since movies began, there has never been much doubt that the greatest were Bill Hart and Tom Mix. Hart brought authenticity and a kind of stark poetry to the western; Mix brought it pep, escapism, and above all, showmanship. And in the process he developed a popularity and a box office value equalled by no other star, perhaps not even by Hart himself.

A rugged adventurer, Mix had been a soldier, bronc-buster for the British during the Boer War, western marshal, and rodeo performer long before the movies called him. His first movies were early one-, two- and three-reelers, done for Selig, and they were a strange group. Mix often wrote and directed them too, and quantity rather than quality was Selig's aim. Some of these early Mix films had moments of real hell-for-leather action. Others were folksy comedies in the Will Rogers vein. It wasn't until Mix joined Fox in 1917 that he really began to hit his stride. And by 1920, when Hart (who was no youngster when he started in films) was beginning to show his age a little, and when his pattern of austerity plus sentiment was beginning to lose its vogue, Mix was riding high as the

Shooting *Eyes of the Forest*. By the camera is ace photographer Dan Clark, while peering through the tripod, cigarette in mouth, is Lambert Hillyer, director of some of the best Mix and Bill Hart westerns.

Tom in his pre-movie days. During the Spanish-American war in Cuba, he was a personal courier for Major General Wheeler, a fighting veteran of the Civil War.

Tom astride his famous horse Tony; a scene from *Soft-Boiled*.

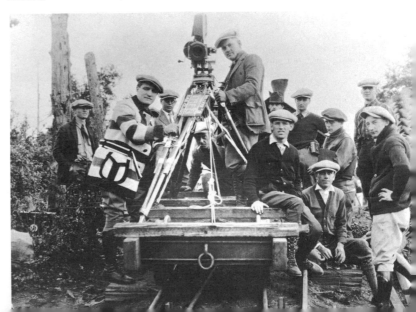

A leap to Tony's back in *The Rough Diamond*.

biggest western star of them all. His pictures literally "made" Fox during the 20's, just as the Gene Autry westerns in the 30's enabled Republic to grow and expand.

Mix's westerns were all pep and energy, and had the same spirit of boyish fun as the early Doug Fairbanks westerns. Unlike Hart, Mix made no great virtue of authenticity or realism. Being a tough-as-nails westerner himself, his performance naturally carried authority, but otherwise his films were breezy, cheerful, streamlined, aimed at a wide audience, careful not to contain elements that might disturb children,

Tom liked to bring modern touches into his westerns—like auto-racing, in *The Road Demon*.

and free of serious romantic entanglements. Mix's screen hero never drank, smoke or cursed, and eschewed unnecessary violence. Action there was in plenty, but never of a vicious nature. Tom would never shoot a villain if he could subdue him by other means—and since these "other means" usually entailed fancy work with a lariat, or a helter-skelter chase climaxed by a fistic fracas, nobody missed the blood. Today's sadistic and blood-splattered westerns might take note of Tom's healthy approach to it all—and remember at the same time that no other western star has since duplicated Tom's appeal.

Most of Mix's films were made far away from the studios, on choice locations. He made a point of using the scenic beauties of the National Parks in his movies, and had an especial fondness for the Grand Canyon. These picturesque locations were flawlessly photographed by Dan Clark, Mix's favorite cameraman—an adventurous individual with a rugged pre-movie background similar to Mix's own. Sharp, well-framed shots, fine panoramics and crystal clear focus were all a matter of course with Clark. He was one of the best cameramen in the business, and his contribution to the success of Tom's pictures was a major one.

All in all, Mix made over 60 films for Fox, including a few non-western adventures like *Dick Turpin* and *Tom Mix in Arabia*. All were good, and all made money. Tom never let his public—or his studio—down. Some of his best films were *Just Tony*, designed as a tribute to his handsome black horse, the most famous of all movie horses, and two exceptionally good Zane Grey adventures, *The Lone Star Ranger* and *The Rainbow Trail*. For fast, furious stunting *The Great K. & L. Train Robbery* and *Sky High* are unbeatable. Mix certainly used a double less than any western star, and since most of his stunts were photographed relatively close up, there can be no doubt about it. *Sky High*, which had aerial stunting, too (Tom liked to use fast cars, airplanes, anything that would add *speed* to his movies) was a real thriller, photographed in the Grand Canyon, with some amazing shots of Tom performing tricky action on the very rim of the canyon itself. Occasionally, as in *Riders of the Purple Sage* (too heavy a Zane Grey story for the sprightly Tom) his pace would slacken a little, but even a second-rate Mix was still a first-rate western. Off-screen as well as on, Tom remained a colorful personality, living in an enormous mansion at a rate of fantastic extravagance, wearing western clothes that resembled uniforms more than practical rangeland outfits, doing everything with color, dash, and speed.

Tom probably never quite realized what good films he was making, movies that would retain their appeal and merit long after films hailed as great at the time, would be forgotten. All Tom Mix wanted to do was to put on a darned good show—and he always did.

A striking contrast in styles—a contrast that eloquently sums up the "emancipation" of the screen heroine: As a wide-eyed innocent while playing for Triangle-Fine Arts in 1916.

Colleen Moore

Twelve years later, a very different Colleen as the flapper heroine of *Synthetic Sin*.

In 1925, the same year she made *Sally* from Ziegfeld's stage hit, Colleen switched to a heavy dramatic role as the heroine of *So Big*. John Bowers is with her in this scene; others in the strong cast included Ben Lyon, Wallace Beery, Jean Hersholt, Ford Sterling, and Phyllis Haver.

Although her pictures were often misleadingly titled (*That's a Bad Girl, Flirting With Love, Naughty But Nice,* and *Her Wild Oat* are typical) to give the impression that they were spiced with sex and sin, there was little of the typical flapper about Colleen Moore, although the bulk of her pictures were made in the flapper era and, not surprisingly, reflected a good deal of the spirit of those times. While Colleen copied nobody, perhaps it wouldn't be stretching things too far to suggest that she was really something of a latter-day Mary Pickford. Though Mary favored the sentimentality of the earlier, pre-1920 period, and Colleen was a little more hardboiled, there were definite similarities in their screen characters. Colleen, for example, was frequently the small town girl caught up in big city business and society—and coming out on top through sticking to her principles. She was slow to think ill of anyone, quick to extend a helping hand. There was less melodrama in her movies than in Mary's, but that, after all, was because she was essentially a comedienne.

Essentially—not exclusively. Films like *So Big* proved that she could be a fine dramatic actress, too. Colleen was not a beautiful girl in the accepted sense; indeed, with her severe haircut she deliberately played down glamor in the interests of creating a more down-to-earth type. But the beauty was there, when she chose to use it. In one sequence in *Ella Cinders*, for example, Colleen was supposed to strike a pose reminiscent of Lillian Gish. As a gag it fell quite flat, be-cause Colleen looked extraordinarily lovely in that shot!

Her pictures were lively, full of fun, and must have made a fortune for First National. Even the least of them, like *Ella Cinders*, were thoroughly enjoyable. And the best of them, such as *Orchids and Ermine* (a fine comedy with Jack Mulhall as the leading man and a diminutive Mickey Rooney in his first role—playing an adult midget in grand style) and *Irene*, were just wonderful. *Irene* had some wonderful comedy routines and a spectacular fashion show climax, filmed in pleasing early Technicolor. Colleen started out (as did so many others listed in this book) under Griffith. In fact, she was an extra in *Intolerance*. She played opposite Robert Harron in *The Bad Boy*, had the lead in Selig's *Little Orphan Annie*, and starred in two-reel comedies like *A Roman Scandal*. But it was in the 20's, beginning with a film called *Flaming Youth*, that she really came into her own. From lively farce such as Christie's *So Long Letty*, to the captivating charm and quiet humor of that excellent Sam Goldwyn film, *Come On Over*, Colleen went on to a lengthy series of hits for First National, in which she combined her talents of actress and comedienne in films which were basically light and frothy, but which had far more substance and "sock" entertainment values than the flapper comedies everybody seemed to be making at that time.

Colleen was one of the greatest little stars of them all.

Mae Murray

When Mae Murray was shown *Sunset Boulevard*, that fine 1950 film in which Gloria Swanson played an age-ing movie queen, she applauded the film as a film, but was more than a little skeptical about the realism of the Norma Desmond character. "None of us floozies were *that* nuts!" was her now classic comment.

In one respect, though, *Sunset Boulevard*'s Norma Desmond *did* resemble Mae Murray. That film's celebrated line, "We didn't need voices; we had *faces* then!" is particularly applicable to Mae. She was never a great actress and never pretended to be. But she was a vibrant personality; she had a face that millions of moviegoers knew and loved. Too many of today's star-lets, attractive though they may be individually, col-lectively seem cut from an identical mold—all with the same hair, same face, same measurements. That wasn't the way in the 20's. Whether it was a star of the magni-tude of Mae Murray, or a lesser light like Arline Pretty, there was no mixing up the face with someone's else's!

Mae was a movie star all the way. She lived lavishly and expected to be treated like a star. And when she wasn't, temperament flashed—although the only serious display of that temperament was when she worked for Erich von Stroheim in *The Merry Widow*. However much she may have disliked the ultra-demanding Stro-heim, she gave of her best for him, and her perform-ance in that film was not only the best of her career, but gave her a profitable new sideline—touring the country giving exhibitions of the "Merry Widow" waltz. (Mae had been a "Ziegfeld Follies" girl before entering the movies, and was an accomplished dancer.)

In *Circe the Enchantress*—an adaptation of an Ibáñez novel, made for Metro by Miss Murray's husband, Robert Z. Leonard.

At one time married to director Robert Z. Leonard, Mae made some interesting films for him—including an unusual melodrama, *The Mormon Maid*, which de-picted the Mormons' secret vigilante force, the Seeing Eyes. Mae hasn't made a movie since the early 30's, when her singing voice was put to good use in one or two movies, such as a re-make of her old success *Pea-cock Alley*. But even though she's been off the screen for so long, she still remembers that she was a movie queen of the 20's, and acts accordingly. Occasionally I see her striding down 42nd Street in New York, be-jewelled, richly dressed, disdainfully avoiding even a glance at the clusters of movie houses all playing films starring actresses who talk and talk—but few of whom have "faces."

One of the sterner moments from *The Merry Widow*, wherein there was more Stroheim than Lehar! The wed-ding night—her husband, an old and crippled nobleman (Tully Marshall) collapses and dies of a heart attack.

Alla Nazimova

Elsewhere in this book, I have written about Greta Garbo and the inadvisability of her returning to the screen as a character actress. Nazimova found herself in a similar position, and *did* return to the screen with a character performance in the 40's. Although it was a good performance, the image was shattered, and the legend that was Nazimova is no more. I'd be sorry to see the same thing happen to Garbo.

Nazimova's position in the silent period was even loftier than Garbo's. She never had the same enormous mass appeal that Garbo had, and neither demanded nor expected it. Consciously or otherwise, there was a goddess-like quality to Nazimova; she was respected from afar, held in awe, but never really loved by her subjects. The Russian actress had definite ideas about the art of the cinema, and they were very specialized ideas.

Once she was powerful and rich enough to produce her own movies, she began to put these ideas into practice. Audiences were bowled over by her sumptuous sets and costumes, by her own bizarre and stylized acting, and by the strange ballet-like atmosphere she brought to films like *Salome*—which was more than a little influenced by that German expressionist classic, *The Cabinet of Dr. Caligari*. They were bowled over— but they weren't too entertained. The fiery but still human Nazimova of old, the Nazimova that stood against the Hun in such propaganda melodramas as *War Brides*, they had liked; but this new Nazimova was a little too much for them. Respect for her grew— and receipts from her movies dwindled. Like Garbo, she made a legend of herself; unlike Garbo, it was not a *living* legend. To audiences, it was as remote as the legends of the ancient Greeks—and as unattractive to them.

In 1925, she made an attempt to swing back into popular approval with more down-to-earth romantic dramas. But it was too late. One year later, the arrival of Greta Garbo from Sweden erased any chances Nazimova had of regaining her former throne. Still she left quite an impression on Hollywood, this unique, fascinating, idealistic woman, who made movies that were both beautiful and grotesque and who, in her own way, loved the movies, saw their potentialities, and tried so hard to raise their standards.

As Camille.

In her most famous film—the near-surrealistic *Salome* (1922), based on the Oscar Wilde play.

Pola Negri

Pola Negri

In the 20's, Hollywood suddenly got "culture-conscious," coming to the conclusion (based on a few European films, most of which don't hold up too well today) that the film in Europe was Art with a capital "A". Certainly, a few great European films *were* being made, but more good pictures were being made here in the good old U.S.A. But Hollywood eyed Europe, and principally Germany, and the game of luring the big names from UFA and other European companies to Hollywood began. At that, some pretty impressive talent came over—Ernst Lubitsch for one. And with him came his star, Pola Negri, who had caused something of a sensation over here playing the fiery heroines of *Gypsy Blood* (Carmen) and *Passion* (Madame du Barry).

Pola caused the same sort of sensation when she began appearing in Hollywood movies, too, and her penchant for front-page publicity (such as her romance with Valentino) made her name a household word in no time. Negri devotees were fanatical and loyal,

One of her most famous roles, *The Cheat*.

The Cheat again, with Jack Holt.

A dramatic pose from *A Woman of the World*.

Reunited with her German director, Ernst Lubitsch, she made a delightful satire, *Forbidden Paradise*, with Rod La Rocque. Both Lubitsch and Pola developed a subtler and less heavy handed style as they became acclimatized to Hollywood.

and remain so until this day. For them, Pola could do no wrong. It was just as well, because she made quite a few clinkers at first—like *Bella Donna*, and the magnificently opulent, but quite dull, *The Spanish Dancer*.

Looking at Pola's old movies today, one ponders a bit: just what was all the fuss about? She was a good actress, but not a great one, and there were lots of good actresses around. She wasn't an exceptional beauty in an era that also boasted Lillian Gish, Billie Dove, and Norma Shearer! Handsome might be a better word for her. But what she had was something that was quite rare in the American cinema of the 20's (though commoner in Europe, where Asta Nielsen and others were cast much in the Negri mould). It was a kind of down-to-earth animal magnetism—the same kind of magnetism with which Anna Magnani caused such a furor when *Open City* first hit American screens after World War II. Pola projected passion, but with

a kind of world-weary cynicism; she played no dewy-eyed heroines, but somewhat shop-soiled women who had *lived*. With her decidedly off-beat screen character neatly surrounded by plots that reflected a pseudo-European cultural flavor, she appealed both to the intellectuals, and to the youngsters who wanted something a little more substantial than Mary Pickford and Charles Ray. Pola's best American films were her later ones, particularly *Hotel Imperial* and *Barbed Wire*. Actually, comparatively few of her films are remembered well, even by her most devoted followers. But her name—and what an exotic, movie-queenish name it is—has come to be one of the few great ones that symbolize a glamorous age of the movies now departed—an age that will never be forgotten.

Mabel Normand

That old movie plot about the clown who made millions laugh but never achieved happiness himself has a striking real-life parallel in the career of Mabel Normand. Perhaps it would be an exaggeration to say that Mabel was never happy; she lived life to the fullest, considering only the present, and having a wonderful time doing it. But her life was such a determined pursuit of a lasting happiness that somehow always eluded her, with tragedy stalking both her private life and her public career, that it seemed almost a mockery of the carefree spright that she played on the screen.

Mabel was a lovely girl. "As beautiful as a Spring morning" is the way Mack Sennett once described her. And though she specialized in comedy—both violent slapstick, and gentler Cinderella whimsies—she had exceptional dramatic ability too. Many thought she could have been one of the screen's finest dramatic actresses had she been given the chance. Even in her comedies, there were often moments of pathos or drama that showed there were good foundations for

this belief. Indeed, Mabel had started out under Griffith at Biograph as a straight actress. An athletic young lady, and something of a daredevil, she enjoyed doing roles that required a little more strenuous effort than usual. And Griffith, glad to oblige, cast her in films like *The Squaw's Love*, in which, as an Indian girl, she had to struggle with a rival atop some high rocks, dive into the river below, and swim under water to wreck the canoes of the her Indian pursuers.

While at Biograph, Mabel met Mack Sennett, then struggling along as a writer and actor, but with definite ideas of his own about making films—comedy films. Mabel and Mack were attracted to each other, and for a time it seemed that they would get married. Indeed, it seemed so on and off during the ensuing years— but unconsciously Mabel's restless nature seemed to rebel at the idea of settling down to marriage. Two wedding dates were set; both were called off. But when Sennett left Biograph to set up his own company, Mabel Normand came along with him as his leading star.

In the Keystone comedies that followed, Mabel worked like the proverbial horse. If it was for a laugh, nothing was too much trouble. She was manhandled and tied to the railroad tracks in *Barney Oldfield's Race for Life*; dragged through a muddy lake by the Keystone Cops in *A Mud Bath*, and frequently plastered with goo of one kind or another by Ford Sterling or some other Keystone comedian. Occasionally, in films like *Mabel's Stratagem*, in which she had an amusing sequence masquerading as a man and flirting with the boss's wife, she had an opportunity for a subtler kind of comedy, and when she began to be co-starred in Charlie Chaplin films she started to feel that she was worthy of something better than two-reelers. Mack Sennett agreed, and in 1917 put her into a charming seven-reeler called *Mickey*. It was a delightful combination of slapstick, whimsical comedy and pathos; Mabel had a glorious role as a tomboy from the mountains loosed on society, and the film had a jim-dandy melodramatic climax with Mabel fighting off the villain (Lew Cody), and clambering over the roof of a crumbling old mansion until rescued by the hero (Wheeler Oakman), who gave the villain his come-uppance in a terrific fistic set-to.

Mickey was a wonderful picture, but somehow nobody seemed to want it. It lay on the shelf for over a year, and Mabel drifted away from Sennett, doing features elsewhere. She seemed bored with life, yet determined to find pleasure in every waking moment. She was an ice-cream-for-breakfast girl—and her parties went on late into the night. Rest and relaxation just weren't allowed for on her schedule. Then, suddenly, *Mickey* was released and was a tremendous hit.

It made a small fortune for Triangle, and Sennett, sure he had found the right formula for Mabel, asked her to come back. But she was vague and evasive; it was to be some time before she was to make another feature for Mack.

And now stories of Mabel's wild living began to circulate around Hollywood. She was late turning up at the studio, sometimes disappeared for days at a time. Once she even took off unannounced for Europe. There were hints of scandals, but never anything more than rumors and hearsay. Then, suddenly, came the murder (still unsolved) of beloved and respected director William Desmond Taylor. Since the question of dope came up in the proceedings, the newspapers, still full of the Fatty Arbuckle-Virginia Rappe case, had a field-day. Mabel was involved—deeply—and though she was proved innocent of any connection with the murder, the damage done by yellow journalism was serious. Courageously, she fought back and continued with her work. Just as it seemed that she had risen above it all, she was involved in another scandal in which a prominent Hollywood personality was shot. She was tired and dispirited. And an appearance in a play in New York, for which she was rapped mercilessly by the critics, didn't serve to bolster her sagging spirits.

During all this time, she had been busy making movies. She had made a group for Sam Goldwyn, and had returned to Sennett for some good films—*Susanna, Molly O* and *The Extra Girl*. In the latter she had had some great material, including a still very funny scene where she leads a lion around the studio, fondly imagining that it is merely Teddy, the studio dog, in makeup. It was an unusual Cinderella story in which the small-town-girl *doesn't* make good in Hollywood, and was one of her best pictures since *Mickey*.

But the pace was beginning to tell on Mabel. It was known that she had turned to drugs, and her health was suffering badly. She put on a brave front, but she often looked tired and ill—and the camera eye is perceptive. Her popularity began to wane a little. She no longer felt up to doing features and the studios were unwilling to risk starring her until she was herself again. Almost overnight, she descended from the top rung of stardom and was back where she started. Her last films were two-reel slapstick comedies made not for Sennett but for his rival, Hal Roach. In a last, desperate measure to attain some kind of contentment, she married Lew Cody, an old friend. It was a curious marriage that puzzled all their friends, and it was an unhappy and a tragic one. Both stars were dying—Cody from a heart ailment, news of which he gallantly kept from his wife.

Like a meteor which burns itself out by the very

With Mack Sennett (left) and Ford Sterling in *Barney Oldfield's Race For Life* (1913).

In the title role of Sam Goldwyn's *Peck's Bad Girl*.

speed which gives it light, Mabel Normand had burned herself out. In 1930, she entered a health retreat, suffering from a tubercular condition accelerated by her exhausting and reckless living over the past thirteen years. There, a few months later at the age of 32, she died—just as the silent screen, of which she had been one of the brightest and most beloved stars, was dying too.

Ramon Novarro

With Alice Terry in *Where the Pavement Ends* (1923).

Ramon Novarro

"The noblest Roman of them all"—Novarro as Ben-Hur.

Mexican-born Ramon Novarro, one of the big romantic idols of the 20's, and object of many a teen-age crush, might well have been an even bigger star if his arrival in Hollywood had been a little more opportune. He rose to fame overnight as the lovable scoundrel, Rupert of Hentzau, in *The Prisoner of Zenda* (1923). But two years earlier, Valentino, who owed his sudden fame to the same director, Rex Ingram, had created a sensation as a new type of Latin lover. Rudy was still riding the crest of his fame when Ramon came along and, illogically but not too surprisingly, Novarro found himself being sold as "a second Valentino."

This he certainly wasn't. In fact, the only thing that the two really had in common was a Latin background. But it was going to take time—and good pictures—to prove this. Via films like *Scaramouche*, Novarro set out to prove it—and then, suddenly, a new bombshell hit! After years of struggling along in only gradually more rewarding roles, John Gilbert, at M-G-M, became the principal threat to Valentino. The two stars represented extremes in romantic idols—one the sleek Latin lover, exotic in his appeal; the other, Gilbert, a "classical" lover, the noble romantic of literature and history. Each had his own loyal, fanatically devoted following.

Ramon Novarro, with some of the qualities of both stars, found himself somewhat in the middle, attracting moviegoers who found him a little more virile and down-to-earth than either of the reigning kings, yet unquestionably in third place in terms of popularity. M-G-M wisely decided that he shouldn't compete with Rudolph and John on their own ground, and switched him more and more to modern roles with adventurous backgrounds. It is interesting, however, that in the long run Novarro fared better in talkies than did Gilbert. Because his pedestal was less lofty, Novarro had a shorter distance to fall when the lush romantic films of the 20's died, and accordingly he found it easier to adjust. A fine singing voice gave him an added advantage in the early days of sound. Later on, in character roles, he proved to be a finer and subtler actor than many had given him credit for in earlier days.

Of course, it was as the romantic lover and swashbuckling hero of the 20's, that Ramon Novarro exercised his greatest appeal. An early stint with Mack Sennett, playing a burlesque gladiator in *Small Town Idol* (1921), was discreetly overlooked in the studio biographies, which refused to admit any roles earlier than *The Prisoner of Zenda*! Of the many hits that followed, my own two favorites are *Ben Hur* (naturally), Ramon's finest role—one to which he did full justice —and that lovely, underrated Lubitsch film, *The Student Prince*, in which Ramon's love scenes with Norma Shearer are among the most touching and eloquent I have ever seen.

A particularly lovely portrait of "America's Sweetheart."

A slightly more mature Mary, only a year or two later.

Mary Pickford

To far too many people, the name Mary Pickford conjures up the traditional "America's Sweetheart" image of a dimpled darling with golden curls—a slightly more mature forerunner of Shirley Temple.

Such an image not only distorts movie history, but also does a distinct injustice to Miss Pickford herself. Her films were sentimental, true, and they played, shrewdly, on the emotions of the masses and the tempo of the times, but there was nothing wishy-washy or cloyingly sentimental about Miss Pickford's pictures. In her prime, between 1914 and 1919, she was a radiantly beautiful creature, more than a girl yet not quite a woman. She was warm, lovely, and had a spontaneity to her work that inevitably lessened as she grew older and had to *act* the screen character she had evolved instead of actually *being* it. Most current audiences tend to judge Mary solely by *Little Lord Fauntleroy*, for the simple reason that it is the only one of her feature pictures that has been available for study to the general public through the Museum of Modern Art in New York, and at film societies and museums throughout the country. Actually *Little Lord Fauntleroy* is not only one of the weakest (and most overly-sentimental) of all the Pickford vehicles, but it is also one of the least typical.

Mary started out, as did so many stars, with D. W. Griffith at the Biograph Studios in New York. Lillian and Dorothy Gish, Blanche Sweet and Mae Marsh were Mary's contemporaries, although Mary started to work for D. W. a little before they did, her first films having been made in 1909. Mary soon developed very definite ideas of her own about how films should be made, and in time became quite particular about the films she appeared in—all still one-reelers, of course. Apparently her judgment, even at that early stage, was quite sound, because her pictures turned out to be among the most enduring of all the Biograph films. *The New York Hat*, opposite Lionel Barrymore, was a good one. So was *The Mender of Nets*, a beautifully directed (Griffith) and photographed (Billy Bitzer) dramatic romance filmed against lovely sea-scapes on the California coast. Griffith recognized Mary's worth, but was unwilling to let the star dominate the director and story. So he groomed Mae Marsh to replace Mary, and Mary went her own way —first to the stage, and then to Famous Players, First National, and ultimately, as a partner, to United Artists.

During the period in which she came to be perhaps the best-loved of all movie stars from any era, Mary made an astonishingly large number of movies. And yet there was no assembly-line, rubber-stamp look to them. She switched from whimsy and comedy to high

Mary in one of her most famous roles, *Tess of the Storm Country*. This scene is from Mary's 1922 re-make of her earlier success.

In *Scraps*.

In *Through the Back Door;* note the larger-than-life stools, designed to make Mary look even more petite.

drama and western heroics quite effortlessly; her basic stock-in-trade was in playing the tomboy who yet manages to remain essentially feminine. A neat trick if you can do it—and Mary did, in picture after picture. But even here there was no standardization, and for every *Pollyanna* there was a far more serious *Stella Maris* for contrast. Playing no small part in Mary's success was her great cameraman Charles Rosher, who enhanced her already lovely features with just the right amount of back-lighting here, and just the right filter there. To heighten the illusion of the child-character Mary invariably played, her sets were always built a little out of scale, furniture, doors, windows, etc., all being made a trifle larger than life so that by comparison, Mary appeared even more diminutive than she was. As for Mary's directors, they were among the best in the business—ranging from Maurice Tourneur to Cecil B. DeMille—but one suspects that

Mary did more than a little directing herself!

What delightful memories the titles of her pictures bring back—the calculated heart-throbs of *Tess of the Storm Country*, the pictorial beauty of *Pride of the Clan*, the melodramatic thrills of *Heart of the Hills* (John Gilbert was her leading man in this, an exciting Ku Klux Klan thriller), the pathos of *Through the Back Door*, the robust adventure of *Romance of the Redwoods* and *The Little American*. Mary's later pictures were all good—even those in which she realized that her "little girl" appeal was gone, and tried instead to climb aboard the jazz-age band wagon in films like *Kiki*—but it is the pre-1922 vehicles that show Mary at her loveliest and best. With her grace and beauty, a never-ending flow of good pictures, and a happy marriage to Hollywood's undisputed "king," Douglas Fairbanks, how could she be anything *but* "America's Sweetheart"?

With Lloyd Hughes in *Tess of the Storm Country*. Despite its tear-jerking qualities, *Tess* had some really rugged melodrama—and good comedy too.

From one of the last of Mary's "tomboy" pictures, *Little Annie Rooney*.

With Richard Dix in *The Lucky Devil*, a popular auto racing romance of the mid-20's.

Esther Ralston

I don't know what some of the leading ladies of the 20's had, but I know quite a few stars of later decades who wish *they* had it. Esther Ralston was one of the most beautiful heroines ever to grace the screen. When I chatted with her on my show in 1958, there she was —thirty years later—looking just as lovely, with that same combination of graceful charm and vigorous determination that had made her such a popular Paramount star. She now has a pretty daughter (whose singing career Esther manages), who should inherit much of her mother's popularity in the not-too-distant future.

Esther started out as a serial queen at Universal in 1923—with twelve thrilling chapters of *The Phantom Fortune*. (Incidentally, Esther returned to cliff-hangers in the sound period.) But it wasn't long before she was under contract to Paramount, and all the top directors there—James Cruze, Herbert Brenon, Sidney Olcott, Josef von Sternberg—were clamoring to have her in their pictures. I doubt if many Paramount players appeared in more films than Miss Ralston at this time. She was cast as Wendy's mother in *Peter Pan* (a lovely, graceful performance), the good fairy in *A Kiss for Cinderella*, Richard Dix's fiery girl friend in *Lucky Devil*, a lady-almost-permanently-in-distress in *Old Ironsides*, about Steven Decatur and the Tripoli

In *The Sawdust Parade* (1928).

pirates. Established stars like Neil Hamilton and Louise Brooks shared top billing with her; up and coming youngsters such as Gary Cooper and Boris Karloff played in support.

Nobody took the time to establish Esther Ralston as a "great actress," except possibly Josef von Sternberg in *The Case of Lena Smith*—and Miss Ralston more than showed that his faith was justified. For the most part, however, she was handed parts that didn't pose any enormous acting problems, but did make considerable demands on her beauty, sensitivity and general ability. She answered those demands admirably—on into the sound period, too—but that's material for another book.

An interesting shot taken between scenes of *Figures Don't Lie* (1927). Miss Ralston's companion is swimming star Johnny Weissmuller, his "Tarzan" roles still several years in the future.

Charles Ray in *The Barnstormer* (1922).

Charles Ray

It's rather difficult to pin-point the secret of Charlie Ray's success—doubly so because there is no contemporary equivalent to whom one can point and say "*That's* what Charles Ray had too."

Charlie's forte was the small-town boy who made

In *Bill Henry* (1919), a Thomas Ince production.

good—the lanky youth with the battered straw hat, open-neck shirt, and a fishing rod slung over his shoulder—a more mature and less mischievous Tom Sawyer, perhaps. He was too decent a fellow to be considered a bumpkin—but not quite determined enough to stop others from pushing him around. Until the last reel, of course—then he'd prove his worth with a vengeance, turn on his tormentors, and win the girl. He came along at just the right time, reaching his peak right after World War I, and riding the crest of his popularity until audiences grew a little tired of his style—and other old-fashioned things—with the coming of the roaring jazz age.

He might have lasted a little longer had he varied his screen character a bit—if he'd invested it with some of the get-up-and-go that Mary Pickford had. But he thought that being "a nice boy" was enough, and he became so determinedly "nice" in his pictures, even to being something of a whining milksop at times, that his pictures took on a uniformity that Mary Pickford's never had.

Sure that his approach was right, and being unwilling to listen to the sage advice of others, he watched his popularity wane until it was almost too late. Then, belatedly deciding it was time for a change, he went all the way, sinking a small fortune into a costume drama of Pilgrim days, *The Courtship of Miles Standish*. It was a colossal flop, and just about wiped Ray out. He continued in films, but no longer

A different Charles Ray in *The Garden of Eden* (1928). This time it was leading lady Corinne Griffith who played the country innocent and Ray was the city slicker. Lewis Milestone directed.

as the country kid. In fact, he went to quite the other extreme, playing men about town and society playboys in such films as *Vanity* and *The Garden of Eden*.

But his boyish mannerisms were hard to shake, and the new "sophisticated" Ray didn't jell. He was through as a name of importance. Like Harry Langdon, he had failed because he hadn't the ability to see himself objectively and wouldn't admit the possibility that others might know more than he about what was best for him.

But like Langdon, he left a handful of really fine films—not great, in the way that Langdon's were, but delightful, often moving, and usually authentic slices of Americana. Most of all, they reflect so much of the spirit of those "innocent years" between the first World War and the topsy-turvy late 20's.

The best of the Ray films were *The Old Swimmin' Hole* and *The Girl I Love*—and the weakest were the rather repetitive and obvious *The Pinch Hitter* and *The Clod Hopper*. But the good ones far outweighed the disappointing ones, and his average standard was quite high. *The Busher* (in which up-and-coming stars John Gilbert and Colleen Moore supported Ray) and *Sweet Adeline* (with Gertrude Olmstead) are two that even today retain much of their charm. Since I'm often asked my opinions on contemporary equivalents of the silent greats, I'll go out on a limb and say that if there is a parallel to Ray today, it's in Pat Boone. But it's a parallel of personalities primarily, since they are miles apart in their types of entertainment.

The Courtship of Miles Standish, the film that wrecked Ray as an independent producer-star.

Wallace Reid, with Gloria Swanson in *The Affairs of Anatol,* directed by Cecil B. DeMille.

Wallace Reid

Wallace Reid's sudden death in the early 1920's, at the height of his fame, brought Hollywood its first major scandal with the revelation that Reid's death had come about primarily through addiction to narcotics. This came as doubly shocking news because

The Dictator (1922), with Lila Lee. One of Reid's last films, it was directed by James Cruze.

Reid had always specialized in playing clean-cut American youths, possessed of all the virtues and none of the vices. Moreover, he looked the part: a strapping, handsome fellow, always cheerful, and with an air of contentment and optimism that was one of the main reasons for his popularity not only with fans, but with his co-workers.

His end was one of the major Hollywood tragedies. Almost as tragic in its own way, however, is the fact that this tremendously popular star had almost no really important films to his credit. Big money-makers, yes; great films, no. Reid had scored a big success as Jeff, the fighting blacksmith, in *The Birth of a Nation.* And he'd had a couple of scenes in *Intolerance.* These were great films, but they were not exactly Wallace Reid vehicles. In his earlier days, Reid made some really good little one- and two-reel dramas at Majestic, under Griffith's supervision. This was in 1914, and the films were fine little shorts such an *At Dawn* (one of Reid's few villain roles) and *His Mother's Influence.*

Reid was extremely fortunate in that he possessed acting ability, youth, good looks and a fine physique— four assets that were very rarely found in the same person, especially in those days when the best acting talent was usually centered in more mature players who had been brought to the movies from the stage. Reid joined Famous Players, forerunner of Paramount, and was quickly raised to star status. Unfortunately, the company's policy at that time was to turn out quantity rather than quality for the most part. Seeing that they had a goldmine in Reid, they rushed him from one picture to another. Some were quite good, but most were cheaply made, hurriedly made, and practically bereft of plot. It was enough that there was a situation—Reid as a go-getting young salesman, Reid as a society playboy who makes good, Reid as a daredevil racing driver—this latter being perhaps his most popular screen guise. *Excuse My Dust* and *The Dancing Fool* were so bare of substance that only a top personality could have carried them.

That Reid did carry the load, and merely added to his popularity in the process, is a tremendous tribute to the esteem in which his admirers held him. Had he been put into really worthwhile pictures, he might well have been the worldwide sensation that Valentino was to become. But even with a few good pictures like *Forever* (an early version of *Peter Ibbetson*) and a whole string of pictures turned out as though from a frozen custard machine (Jesse Lasky's own description, in his autobiography), Reid earned himself a fantastic following, on a par with the other big names of the period—Chaplin, Pickford and Fairbanks.

Wallace Reid was just thirty when he died. Valentino passed on three years later at thirty-one.

Rin Tin Tin

Symbolic of the transition from old stars to new in the hectic period when sound came to the screen is this off screen shot at Warners'. Rin Tin Tin, one of the studio's top names in the silent period, greets Al Jolson, herald of a new era of all-talking movies.

In case you think I'm writing this page with my tongue in cheek, let me assure you that I'm *not*. Rin Tin Tin was one of the big box office names of the silent era; indeed, his pictures often saved the day for Warner Brothers, bringing home the bacon in sufficient quantity to pay off the losses on the costly prestige pictures with John Barrymore! And even if box office value weren't enough, Rinty was a good actor too. Moreover, he improved as he went along. In some of his early films, like *Where the North Begins,* you can see him looking to his trainer for direction. He'll go through some action, cock his head around for further signals, and obediently carry on. But in his later films, Rinty was much more sure of himself, going through long and complicated takes without a single fluff.

If you don't think that Rinty could really act, then you haven't seen films like *The Night Cry,* in which he is really put through an emotional wringer. Playing dead or listening at keyholes were elementary to Rinty; in *The Night Cry* he plays one whole scene in full closeup, literally registering hope and sorrow by a drooping of his ears and a moistening of his eyes. The heroine, in the same scene, has to express similar emotions, and Rinty acts her right off the screen. (The lady in question was June Marlowe—a very competent actress otherwise, but no match for her canine co-star!)

Rinty's films were often, admittedly, naive. In *Clash of the Wolves* for instance, he played a dog suspected of being a wolf. To "disguise" him, the hero cleverly fits him up with a false beard! Walking through the mining town, the bearded Rinty is taken for granted. Nobody spots him, or even pays attention, but ultimately the beard drops off, and then immediately—recognition, and a lynch mob hot on his heels. And this, believe me, was written and played straight and not for laughs!

But for the most part the Rin Tin Tin films were exceedingly well done, full of sure-fire mixtures of action, comedy, and sentiment. Although cheaply made, they were often given production treatment of a high order, with exceedingly fine photographic quality and excellent handling of animal material. Chester Franklin, who worked on the famous *Sequoia* and *The Yearling,* staged many of the animal scenes, and directors included such top-liners as Mal St. Clair and Herman Raymaker. One of the writers most frequently employed was Darryl F. Zanuck! But no matter who the writer was, the basic idea was to give Rinty as many *human* dilemmas as possible. He had to make decisions—whether to rescue his doggie lady-friend or the heroine was a typical one—and he had to think his way out of situations as well as be something of a canine acrobat!

Rinty was a beautiful animal and looked most docile, except to villains. Actually he wasn't docile, and was apt to take a bite at his co-star—whether it be husky John Harron or little Davey Lee—unless his owner and trainer, Lee Duncan, was around. Duncan, who rescued Rinty from an untimely end in World War I, raised him from a pup and had the dog's undying love and devotion. Nobody but Lee could handle Rinty. The canine star had no difficulty adjusting to the coming of sound, and barked far more dramatically than any of his many imitators. (Strongheart was Rinty's No. 1 rival. Other competitors, like Peter the Great, Napoleon Bonaparte, Dynamite and Lightning, weren't even in the running.)

However, Rinty was near the retirement age when sound came in, and he died, still in harness, shortly after finishing a serial for Mascot. Other Rin Tin Tins followed—all, like the current Rinty, trained by Lee Duncan—but not a one of them were a patch on their ancestor! Rinty never once let his audience down. He was a great star and a grand trouper.

Norma Shearer

Thanks mainly to such spectacular sound films as *Marie Antoinette* and *Romeo and Juliet,* Norma Shearer is regarded primarily as a talkie star. It's usually forgotten that she was in silents for as long a period as she was in sound films, and played opposite such great stars as Lon Chaney and Ramon Novarro. It's also usually forgotten that she also played Juliet *before* the 1936 film version, the previous occasion being for a sequence in M-G-M's early sound extravaganza, *The Hollywood Review of 1929*—in which she enacted one of Juliet's love scenes to a Romeo played by John Gilbert.

Canadian-born Norma made no secret of her desire to be a movie star, and as soon as she arrived in the United States, she set out to achieve that end the hard way, via an endless series of bit roles. By the close of 1920 she had stood around in crowd scenes in such films as *The Flapper* (a charming story of life at a

After Midnight (1927)

Her first really important role, opposite Lon Chaney in *He Who Gets Slapped* (1924).

girl's school, with Norma's open smile and stately beauty an immediate standout among the groups of schoolgirls) and Griffith's *Way Down East*.

At this period, the sweet, simple heroines were slowly being transformed into the more lively flappers. The stress was still very much on the former, but it was obvious that a change was coming. Norma, a calm, sophisticated type, fitted into neither category. Not yet more than a passable actress, her deficiencies in that direction were more than offset by her unusual beauty and her seeming maturity. Bigger roles, taking advantage of her ability to look older than she really was, came her way surprisingly quickly—such as one of the leads with Monte Blue and Irene Rich in *Lucrezia Lombard*. Norma worked hard towards being a star—and towards being an actress. While she never became a great actress, she did become a very good one, and a constantly improving one. Her expressive eyes and mouth stood her in particularly good stead in emotional scenes, and she was able to express deep emotion strongly and movingly by simple yet effective changes of expression. It wasn't quite acting, yet it was more than pantomime. Whatever it was, it paid off well, and continued to pay off, bolstered, of course, by acting refinements gathered during the years, in films as late as 1936's *Romeo and Juliet*.

When Norma married M-G-M production head Irving Thalberg, more than a few choice plums fell her way, and she made the most of them. Even when one of her films turned out badly, *she* was always worth watching. She was a picture of grace and gentility, good in straight romantic drama, but best in romantic "schmaltz" where a surface emotionalism mattered far more than an inner fire.

As an example of Norma Shearer's talents deployed to their very best advantage, I would point to Lubitsch's production of *The Student Prince* (1927). A silent, it had a music all its own, and one didn't miss the Lehar lyrics at all. It was "hoke," "schmaltz," Viennese fairy tale, all done with sugar and apple blossoms, complete with a glorious love scene in a (studio) field of waving grasses and daisy-studded hillocks. And how well it was done! Norma played enchantingly as the tragic Kathi, beloved by a prince (Ramon Novarro), and unable to marry him because of his own pre-arranged "marriage of state." She undoubtedly gave better dramatic performances in more demanding roles (who could not be moved by her guillotine sequence in *Marie Antoinette*?), but I cannot recall Norma Shearer ever being more delightfully appealing than as the barmaid-heroine of this lovely film. It is the one film that instantly springs to mind when Miss Shearer's name is mentioned—and I'm sure I'm not alone in so admiring the film and her performance in it.

Milton Sills

I'll go out on a limb and risk offending the admirers of both by categorizing Milton Sills as something of a popular John Barrymore. By that I don't mean to imply that Barrymore was *un*popular, but his name had an aura of "tone," "culture," and "dignity" that often caused his films to die the death of a dog in the Midwest, in lumber and mining towns and other areas where the demand was for "entertainment" rather than "art." (Of course, "art" is often surprisingly entertaining too, and John's films were often of a more rough-and-tumble nature than might be supposed!) Milton Sills didn't have Barrymore's grace or wit (for that matter, who did?) but he had a fine range, and good judgment. When he made a costume film, it was a sure-fire swashbuckler like *The Sea Hawk*, and not a stage adaptation like *Beau Brummel*. In fact, he played in everything that a "popular" actor should, from westerns to comedies, from roaring melodramas like *Valley of the Giants* to charming domestic trifles like *Miss Lulu Bett*—just like a contemporary equivalent, Gregory Peck.

Sills had had a thorough stage training, was a fine actor, and had good, rugged, determined features. He was enormously popular all through the 20's, and his fans have not forgotten him. A surprising number of requests come in to my office each week for "old Milton Sills pictures," and I'm only sorry that none seems to be available at present.

Sills, incidentally, was married to another popular star, Doris Kenyon, and they often appeared together on the screen. Like Lon Chaney, he had a good speaking voice, was at his peak as an actor when sound came in, and seemed set for a long career as a star of talkies. But, also like Lon Chaney, he died in 1930, after starring in only one sound film, that ever-reliable Jack London thriller, *The Sea Wolf*. Those who worked with him—and many are still active today—will tell you that Milton Sills was a fine actor, and an even finer gentleman.

Milton Sills with Betty Bronson in *Paradise,* an unusual bit of whimsy from the late 20's. It was filmed entirely in New York—even the tropical island sequences!

In his early days at the World studios in Fort Lee, New Jersey. This is a scene from *The Rack* (1915), with Alice Brady, who was the studio's top star and, incidentally, daughter of producer William A. Brady.

Madonna of the Streets, a First National drama of the 20's.

Lewis Stone in *The Lady Who Lied.*

The Private Life of Helen of Troy (1927). Helen is Maria Corda, wife of director Alexander Korda. The interloper in the middle is Gordon Elliott, in later years better known to western fans as "Wild Bill" Elliott.

Lewis Stone

I don't suppose Lewis Stone was ever considered one of the really top box office names—but where would movies have been without him? One of the best of the small group of "gentleman-heroes," he lacked the dash and devil-may-care style of Ronald Colman, but was the foremost proponent of the gallant, loyal, sportsmanlike hero. Often, this gallantry did him little good in the romantic department, and in films like *The Lost World* he stood aside, concealing his own true feelings, and leaving the heroine to a younger man—in that particular case, Lloyd Hughes. The ending of *The Lost World* couldn't have been more typical; impeccably dressed, keeping the proverbial stiff upper lip, Stone stands alone in the London fog as the girl he loves goes off with the man *she* loves. For no apparent reason, one passerby points him out to another with the (subtitled) explanation, "That's Sir John Roxton—Sportsman."

Not that Lewis always fared thus. In Rex Ingram's silent version of *The Prisoner of Zenda*, he played the dual role of Rudolf Rassendyll and the King, and won the heroine at the climax. And in *The Girl from Montmartre*, the last silent made by Barbara LaMarr before her tragic death, he had a more satisfying solution, romantically.

Stone never considered himself the romantic hero, however, and in effect played character roles, including occasional villains, from the beginning. He was a sturdy, versatile, ever-dependable actor, perhaps more at home in the drawing room than in a Civil War uniform (somehow his innate dignity didn't seem to suggest a man of action), but always first-class. He had a fine, well-modulated voice too, and made a thoroughly successful changeover to sound films, where he remained consistently active right through to the nineteen-fifties, when, among other films, he played a supporting role in his old starring success *Scaramouche*.

His end was particularly tragic. Juvenile delinquents invaded his meticulously-kept garden and Stone ran out to prevent damage, and to ask them to leave. The exertion proved too much for the gallant old man, and he collapsed with a heart attack, dying within a few minutes.

Today on television, his familiar "Judge Hardy" role in the M-G-M "Hardy Family" series of the 30's and 40's is winning him new admirers. Let's hope that some of his fine performances of the *silent* screen will also be available to televiewers in the not-too-distant future.

In the Rex Ingram production of *Trifling Women.*

Erich von Stroheim

When Erich von Stroheim died in Paris on May 12, 1957, the list of surviving directorial giants of the silent screen grew pitifully small. Indeed, with Griffith, Eisenstein, Pudovkin and Murnau having already passed on, only two were left—Carl Theodor Dreyer, and Charles Chaplin. Yet ironically, to the majority of moviegoers, Stroheim was "The Man You Love To Hate," a villain more associated with sound movies than with the silents in which he had actually been such a tremendous force.

Never a great actor, he was often a very good one, and as a director he was perhaps the most controversial of them all—maligned and accused out of all proportion to his "crimes" by his denigrators, and praised equally out of proportion to his accomplishments by his supporters.

From the very beginning, the Austrian emigré turned actor proved to be a difficult customer to handle. Even as an actor in a bit part, he was an egotist with an unusually individual talent. Often he was right, but he alienated a great many people in proving it. Stroheim was not a man for patience or biding his time, nor was he a man for compromise. If he had been, he might have "gotten along" better, made more friends—and made more pictures. But he didn't, and his record is one of a few successful pictures, one masterpiece (*Greed*, discussed elsewhere in this book), and endless frustrations as pictures were taken away from him half-completed and given to others, or savagely re-cut after

he had finished work on them. Stroheim's talent was often variable, and in looking at decidedly weak films like *The Merry Widow*, one wonders why there is so much clamour about his genius and his ruined masterpieces. Then one turns to *Greed*, and decides anew that this man was a giant among film men, after all!

Stroheim worked initially with Griffith, both as an

Stroheim wrote, directed and starred in *Foolish Wives*, playing an amoral and lecherous scoundrel living by his wits on the Riviera. This attempted seduction of Miss Dupont (a Universal star who billed herself just that way) was foiled by the accidental but timely arrival of a priest.

An early (and typically unpleasant) role with Lucille Young in *Farewell to Thee*.

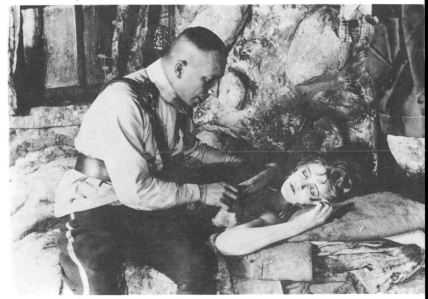

Another *Foolish Wives* scene, with Mae Busch on the receiving end of some Stroheim sadism.

The last film in which director Stroheim had actor Stroheim as the star. It was *The Wedding March*, with Erich as the sympathetic hero, and Zasu Pitts, from *Greed*, in another fine dramatic portrayal, up and coming Fay Wray was the heroine. (1928)

actor in such films as *Intolerance* and *Old Heidelberg*, and also as an assistant director. "Von" idolized "D. W." and often went on record as saying that all he knew about film he learned from Griffith. Oddly, there was little similarity in their films, and if Stroheim learned the mechanics and grammar of film-making from Griffith, he shared little of Griffith's philosophy. Whereas Griffith liked, as in *Broken Blossoms*, to find amid settings of squalor and poverty situations of love and beauty, Stroheim conversely would take elegance, luxury and royal society, and in such surroundings find only ugliness and depravity. He had a strange fascination for the old Austro-Hungarian Hapsburg era, and several of his films were built around that period. Stroheim was a past master at creating the most decadent and debauched of orgies on the screen—but, alas, relatively little of such material ever appeared on the screen!

Stroheim once wrote:

"If you live in France and you have written one good book, or painted one good picture, or directed one outstanding film, fifty years ago, and nothing ever since, you are still recognized as an artist, and honored accordingly. People take their hats off and call you *maître*. They do not forget. In Hollywood—in Hollywood, you're as good as your last picture. If you didn't have one in production in the last three months, you're forgotten, no matter what you have achieved ere this. It is that terrific, unfortunately necessary, egotism in the makeup of the people who make the cinema, it is the continuous endeavor for recognition, that continuous struggle for survival and supremacy, among the newcomers, that relegates the old-timers to the ash-can."

Even apart from Stroheim's other good directorial work, and often very fine dramatic performances, if it takes only one film to merit the title "maître," Stroheim has it—for *Greed*.

Stroheim's biggest box office success was *The Merry Widow*, in which he directed John Gilbert and Mae Murray.

A courtly bow for the Emperor Franz Josef—a familiar figure in Stroheim's films and his novel *Paprika*. In this case, the Emperor is actor Anton Vaverka, being prepared for a scene in *Merry Go Round*.

With Bobby Vernon in an early Sennett-Keystone comedy, *The Danger Girl.*

Gloria Swanson

The very epitome of the traditional "movie queen," Gloria Swanson—like Joan Crawford—has worked at being a star all her life. It's significant that both Joan and Gloria are still names to conjure with, while other stars, to whom the hard grind of publicity was just too much bother, have faded away completely.

Once Gloria was on her way, there was no stopping her. A trip to Europe was something for newsreels and newspapers to play up to the hilt, and Gloria gave them every cooperation, staging touching displays of emotion at her welcome, shedding a tear here, clasping a flower there. Artificial? Phony? An act? If you like. I prefer to call it darned good showmanship. The public loved their stars in the silent era, and the stars, most of them at least, reacted accordingly. Today we still have movie idols of course—but that warmth and love emanating from the audience of movie fans has gone. Fame is a more transient thing now; the accolades are louder and more hysterical, but they are less sincerely felt, and burn out quickly—as soon, in fact, as another idol comes along.

In *The Sultan's Wife,* a 1917 Mack Sennett comedy. Bobby Vernon is the boy in the white uniform.

Opposite Thomas Meighan in Paramount's *Why Change Your Wife?* (1920). DeMille directed.

With John Elliott in *Prodigal Daughters.*

Gloria started out at the Essanay Studios in Chicago, but got nowhere until she moved to Hollywood and the Triangle Studios. Appreciating her good (but strikingly out-of-the-ordinary) looks and sense of fun, Mack Sennett put her to work in Keystone comedies like *The Danger Girl.* In *Teddy at the Throttle,* a fine satire of the old theatrical melodramas, Gloria wound up being tied to the railroad tracks by the villain of the piece, Wallace Beery, who was also Gloria's first husband.

Gloria was a big hit in comedies, but soon moved on to better things—mainly tear-jerkers like *Shifting Sands.* Ultimately this was to be her real forte, but first came a period with Cecil B. DeMille at Paramount, where Gloria went through her expert comedy paces in a series of slick farces and bedroom comedies, most of which worked in some tantalizing and discreetly staged sequences in the most elaborate (and impractical) of bathrooms. *Don't Change Your Husband, For Better or Worse, Why Change Your Wife, The Affairs of Anatol, Male and Female,* and *Bluebeard's Eighth Wife* are some of her better films in this category. Another one of her good ones was *Manhandled,* opposite

Tom Moore. In it Gloria played a saleslady in Manhattan, and the film opened with a gem of a comedy sequence as Gloria, worn out, her arms laden with packages, and a particularly feminine hat perched on her head, braves the terrors of the subway—jammed in between the most unchivalrous group of rush-hour "gentlemen" that Paramount could assemble. It's still a wonderful and hilarious sequence, and a welcome reminder of what an able comedienne Gloria was.

But like most clowns, Gloria yearned most for drama —and as soon as she left Paramount and started on her own, she made up for lost time! Her favorite theme turned out to be an old-fashioned one, a throw-back to the days of *Shifting Sands.* She was the poor, virtuous, and basically decent girl who gets caught in a romantic morass, emphasizing differences in social strata. She was the lowly secretary who became the mistress of a big business tycoon. She was the white collar worker who marries a society playboy, whose parents force an annulment—with Gloria too proud, of course, to try to hold him by telling of the baby that was on the way! In films like *The Love of Sunya* and

The Wages of Virtue (1924).

Swanson and Valentino in *Beyond the Rocks,* a film neither star liked very much.

226

Gloria bravely faces a grim future; a pose almost symbolic of all the later Swanson roles. From *The Trespasser* (1929).

Bluebeard's Eighth Wife (1923), directed by Sam Wood.

The Trespasser Gloria ran the gamut of feminine emotions, throwing herself into the outdated stories so wholeheartedly that even today they still have a robust vigor which transcends their unadulterated corn.

Gloria threw this same energy into *Sadie Thompson* (with Lionel Barrymore as the Rev. Davidson, and director Raoul Walsh as the marine hero) and *Queen Kelly*—that ill-fated extravaganza directed by Von Stroheim, which cost a small fortune (largely Gloria's!) and was never shown in this country because it was abandoned when sound came in. (A version, hastily completed by Gloria, *was* released in Europe.)

It must be admitted that few, if any, of Gloria's films were exactly works of art. They were too flamboyant, too determined to be "sock" attractions for that. And they do tend to date a bit. Gloria's acting, often stirringly dramatic and sometimes surprisingly tender, *was* prone to theatrics and mannerisms of gesture and expression. When Gloria was at the reins, no mere director could control her, and if she was going to give a performance it would be a performance all the way. When sound came in, Gloria exploited it to the full. She had a good singing voice, and whether the plot demanded it or not, sooner or later she'd find herself seated at a piano, toying with the keys, and then bursting into glorious song on the flimsiest of excuses—or even without one!

But—that was Swanson. A movie queen through thick and thin. And when you were watching her, you knew damned well it was Gloria Swanson—in capital letters. No poking around in the mind, no turning over of a halfdozen names before remembering who *this* star was.

And there aren't too many people you can say that for today.

Seena Owen, as the mad Queen, whips Kitty Kelly (Gloria Swanson) from her palace. Gloria never did become "Queen Kelly" in the film of that name, for no more than seven or eight reels were shot before the picture was abandoned.

In *The Ragamuffin* (1916), directed by William DeMille, Cecil's talented brother.

Blanche Sweet

Although Blanche Sweet (that was her real name, by the way) had a long career that included one or two dramatic "comebacks" and extended into the talkie period, she was perhaps at her best in her very earliest films—the one-reel films that she made for D. W. Griffith in the 1909-1913 period, both at the Biograph New York studios on 14th Street and in the early westerns that Griffith made in California. Blanche was a strikingly handsome woman (for that matter, she still is), and also an unusual type for those early movies. Griffith (and other producers) tended to favor the sweet, winsome and helpless-looking heroines, exemplified best by Lillian Gish and Mae Marsh. Blanche was far from that. Husky and well-built, she had a determined look about her.

Griffith made the most of that determined look, frequently casting her as a hardy frontier woman (in short westerns like *The Last Drop of Water* and *The Goddess of Sagebrush Gulch*) or as a plucky heroine who saves the day with only a mild assist from the hero. Typical of the latter is *The Lonedale Operator*, possibly the outstanding American film of 1911, and the film in which Griffith's revolutionary cutting techniques were seen at their most advanced up to that time. Blanche was seen as a courageous telegraph operator who holds payroll bandits at bay until help arrives. The short film gave her opportunities for playful romantics with her boy friend, and high-flown dramatics as she fights off the robbers. Her fine features were well photographed by cameraman Billy Bitzer in

Another scene from *In the Palace of the King*, with that grand old veteran, Hobart Bosworth.

Opposite Edmund Lowe in Sam Goldwyn's *In the Palace of the King* (1923).

several excellent closeups. Incidentally, it's interesting that Griffith chose Blanche to star opposite Henry B. Walthall in his first feature, *Judith of Bethulia*, in which Mae Marsh and Lillian and Dorothy Gish had much smaller roles. Blanche went on to such big films as *Tess of the D'Urbervilles*, *Anna Christie* (for Tom Ince), and *The Woman in White* (made for Herbert Wilcox in England in the 20's), but it's as the windblown and pleasantly plump telegraph girl in *The Lonedale Operator* that she's remembered best of all!

Constance Talmadge

Brooklyn-born Constance Talmadge (sister of Norma and Natalie) almost upset the apple-cart by being too good in her first important role—as the Mountain Girl in the Babylonian sequence of D. W. Griffith's 1916 classic, *Intolerance*. A born comedienne, she played the role's comparatively slight comedy moments for all they were worth, and as the part was a colorful one anyway—a tomboyish girl who fights with Belshazzar's armies against the hordes of Cyrus the Persian—Constance walked away with that sequence.

Indeed, since most of the other characters were historical figures, and thus tended to be a trifle stiff and unreal, she emerged as the most human and lovable person in that whole monumental story. Audiences were captivated by her wit and charm—and sorry that her role called for a tragic death scene. (When Griffith later released the Babylonian story separately under the title *The Fall of Babylon*, much additional footage was incorporated—including, wisely, a happy ending for Constance!) Incidentally, Constance also appeared briefly as Marguerite de Valois in the French episode of the four-storied *Intolerance*—but when she made such a big hit as the Mountain Girl, a new and fictitious name was created for her as Marguerite, so that audiences wouldn't be confused by seeing their new favorite in two roles within the same picture!

Constance was not beautiful in the classic sense, but she was an unusually pretty girl, and she exuded pep and personality. She was at her best in completely civilized and sophisticated surroundings—as the wife who wants to teach an erring husband a lesson or as the wife who is *taught* a lesson by a loving husband. Her marital farces had surprising polish and sophistication for the late teens and early 20's, and films like *A Pair of Silk Stockings* and *The Primitive Lover* (one of her best) foreshadowed by several years the slick and subtle society comedies of Ernest Lubitsch.

After a period with Griffith and Selznick, Constance switched to First National in the early 20's, and remained with that company until the end of the silent era, turning out hit after hit . . . *A Virtuous Vamp, The Perfect Woman, Dulcy, Her Night of Romance* and so many others that tipped off their contents by titles that told Talmadge fans exactly what they wanted to know —that their favorite was back again in a frothy and sparkling comedy.

I'd have no hesitation at all in labelling Connie one of the screen's finest natural comediennes.

Connie in action in a typical comedy; Ronald Colman is on the receiving end in 1925's *Her Sister From Paris*—directed, like many of her best films, by Sidney Franklin.

Movie life wasn't all champagne bubbles for Constance and occasionally straight drama would take over from comedy. Here her makeup is being adjusted for her role as Ming Toy in another Sidney Franklin production, *East Is West* (1922).

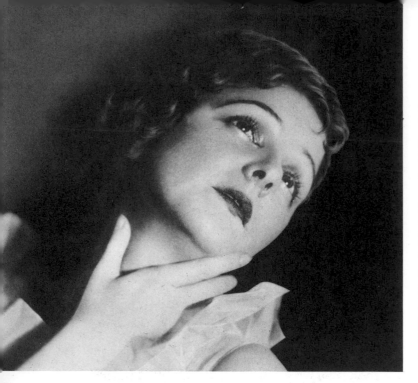

Norma Talmadge

In the late 30's and 40's, there were two stars of "women's pictures" who just about cornered the market on high-class soap-operas and tear-jerkers: Bette Davis and Greer Garson. And, of course, they had their equivalents in the pre-talkie era. Pauline Frederick was the counterpart of Bette Davis. And in less neurotic, and more flamboyant and exotic romances was Norma Talmadge—a rough equivalent to Greer Garson, but a bigger star by far than either Garson or Davis at their peaks. Norma suffered nobly in anything and everything from ill-fated East-West romances to modern triangle dramas, from the great lovers

of history (*DuBarry*) to the great lovers of literature (*Camille*). Not that Norma was limited to weepy roles. She played in a great many comedies in her early Vitagraph days (where she started, in Brooklyn, at the age of 14), and later on as well, at Triangle, Selznick, Select, and ultimately First National, for whom she made the bulk of her pictures.

But it was as the sorely beset heroine, smiling through her tears, defiantly pitting herself against the world (if need be) for the sake of love, that her fans liked her best. And fans in those days usually got what they wanted. The type-casting of really popular stars is almost a thing of the past now, with perhaps a few holdouts like Joan Crawford and John Wayne. But in the 20's, star "vehicles" cut to a pre-determined pattern were a matter of studio policy. And in most cases that policy paid off big dividends—spectacularly so where Norma Talmadge was concerned.

Norma Talmadge made only a couple of talkies, and they weren't too successful. She was beginning to age a bit by then, and was too big a star to want to continue in character roles. So she retired gracefully, devoting herself to her happy marriage to film executive Joseph M. Schenck, who produced many of her top pictures. She died in 1958.

All told, Norma Talmadge made over 250 movies. Some of the best were *A Tale of Two Cities* (she first attracted serious attention in this Maurice Costello version), *The Sacrifice of Kathleen, Children in the House* (a very nicely done drama, made under Griffith's supervision), *The Forbidden City* (opposite Thomas Meighan in a "Madame Butterfly" type of role), and a whole flock of expertly made emotional "specials" at First National—films with titles that still sound "big" and enticing— *The Woman Gives, The Branded Woman, Love's Redemption, Smilin' Through, The Eternal Flame, Ashes of Vengeance, Song of Love* and many others.

With Conway Tearle in *The Eternal Flame*.

1927, and a modern version of *Camille*, with newcomer Gilbert Roland. Fred Niblo directed.

Alice Terry

Alice Terry is a name one hardly hears mentioned when silent movies are discussed nowadays. It's a pity, because she was a graceful and lovely star, and a very good actress. I suppose it's because most of her films were critical rather than box office successes—and when she did have a "sock" commercial attraction to her credit, the thunder was always stolen by the new male star it introduced. *The Four Horseman of the Apocalypse,* for example, introduced Rudolph Valentino as a romantic idol; *The Prisoner of Zenda* did the same thing for Ramon Novarro.

Nobody thought of Alice as anything but a pretty young leading lady when she was at Triangle, appearing with William Desmond and Bessie Barriscale in pleasant but minor trifles like *Not My Sister* (1916). But her career took a sudden upswing when she met, and married, director Rex Ingram. They made an exceedingly handsome couple. Ingram himself would have made an enormously popular leading man, and was better-looking than almost any of the other romantic stars of the day.

Ingram was a dreamer, and sometimes his pictures did not quiet measure up to those dreams. Because he was such a meticulous director—refusing to rush through a film, disregarding schedules and budgets—he was not a popular director around the studios. He was not hated, as was Stroheim, by the front office men, but they couldn't understand his preoccupation with basically uncommercial properties—and especially with the mystical romances of Spanish novelist Vicente Blasco Ibáñez. *The Four Horsemen of the Apocalypse* was a surprise success, partially because of Valentino.

But *Mare Nostrum*—another Ibáñez story of World War I, with another tragic and mystical ending—was a complete flop at the box office.

Since she worked mainly in her husband's pictures, pictures that often had lengthy delays between them, Miss Terry's name never became synonymous with success. *The Four Horsemen* apart, the only real blockbuster they had was *The Prisoner of Zenda*—always a sure-fire subject, yet ironically enough, one of Ingram's lesser pictures. Alice made a lovely and serene Princess Flavia. It's interesting that the sound star most like Alice Terry in appearance, and in the type of heroine she portrayed, was Madeleine Carroll—and it was Miss Carroll who played Princess Flavia in the sound remake of *The Prisoner of Zenda*.

The Magician was based, after a fashion, on a W. Somerset Maugham story. The great German star Paul Wegener was a mad scientist who needed the blood of a pure girl (Miss Terry, of course) to complete his diabolical experiments. Considered a tasteless "misfire" in those days before the horror film cycle, it might be worth re-viewing today.

With Rudolph Valentino in *The Four Horsemen of the Apocalypse*. They were re-teamed by Rex Ingram in *The Conquering Power* shortly afterwards.

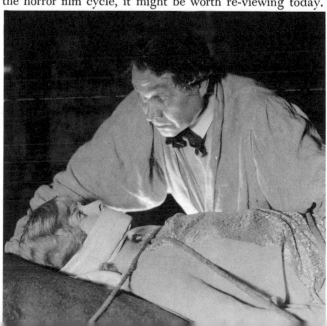

Fred Thomson

Next to Bill Hart and Tom Mix, Fred Thomson was the most popular western star on the silent screen, and like them, his popularity transcended a following by "horse-opera" fans alone. Fred was a star very much in the Mix mould, and was the very antithesis of Bill Hart,

That's a dummy substituting for the leading lady, but there is no double for Fred in this tricky stunt.

making the type of westerns that old Bill thoroughly despised. They were slick, streamlined and showy, specialized in action for its own sake, and presented the customary superficial and glamorized picture of the West. Thomson's clothing had a dude-like appearance too. But Thomson himself was far from a phony; he had a pleasant personality and was a fine athlete. Most of the tricky stunts in his films he performed without a double. And his effortless acrobatics were often introduced in the interests of comedy; in this his films bore more than a casual resemblance to the early westerns of Doug Fairbanks.

Fred was understandably a big favorite, and his religious background (he had trained for the ministry) and thoroughly "clean" and moral code of living earned him the respect and support not only of youngsters, but also of pressure groups at a time when Hollywood was having a great deal of trouble with filmland scandals exaggerated by the press. He was happily married to one of the top screen-writers, Frances Marion.

From straight supporting roles in bigger pictures (he had been Mary Pickford's husband in *The Love Light,* but it was a small role and had him killed off before the film was a third over), he became a western star in the early 20's for FBO. This company, Film Booking Offices, was an outgrowth of the old Robertson-Cole outfit, and later become RKO-Radio. They made some of the best little westerns on the market—fast, slick, full of action, and marked by top production techniques. Photographically, the FBO westerns were a joy to behold. Buzz Barton, Tom Tyler and Bob Steele were other FBO stars, and Tom Mix made a few for them, too, at the end of the 20's.

Fred and his handsome white horse, Silver King, rode through a score of top-notch horse operas for FBO, Fred's popularity growing all the time.

Ultimately, a larger studio beckoned. Fred signed with Paramount, which had come to a parting of the ways with Bill Hart and needed a more "modern" cowboy hero to take his place. Fred's pictures under his new contract were big and good. *Jesse James* was a particularly exciting one, starting off with some spectacular Civil War scenes, and bringing in some thrilling train hold-up scenes in the later episodes. Of course, it whitewashed old Jesse even more than the later Tyrone Power version was to do!

Fred's career came to an unexpected and tragic end, however. Taken suddenly ill, he died at the end of the silent era. There was a typical Hollywood mystery surrounding his death, his ghost having supposedly appeared shortly afterwards! Sadly, another top-line silent western hero, Art Acord, died not too long after, by his own hand. With their death, and Hart's retirement, Tom Mix remained the undisputed King of the Cowboys—but even he was aging, his star on the wane.

The old guard—Ken Maynard, Hoot Gibson, Buck Jones, Tim McCoy, et al—were to hold the line for a while, but within a few years the movies were to introduce an entirely new kind of western star via yodelling cowboy Gene Autry. And when the musical westerns took over, even the exaggerated adventures of Tom Mix and Fred Thomson looked like austere westerns of the old school!

Fred Thomson's personality—and his westerns themselves—stand up remarkably well today.

A scene from 1928's *Pioneer Scout,* one of his deluxe westerns for Paramount.

Ben Turpin

Most of the great comics of the silent screen had, or developed, film personalities that matched their visual appearances. Keaton's apparent gloom was paralleled by adventures in which nothing went according to plan; Harold Lloyd's perennial optimism was backed up by a smiling face that always reflected extreme self-confidence. Not Ben Turpin. No sir!

Ben was a little man with cross-eyes, a small moustache, and a general appearance that gave the impression of a confused, bumbling hen-pecked husband. Nevertheless he got his laughs not by exploiting what was already an amusing image, but by outrageous contrast. He'd play the dashing lover, the daredevil athlete, the suave man-about-town, the international playboy. He'd be sophisticated, alert, brave and always in supreme command of the situation. Film analysts might say that Ben was trying to champion the cause of the little man, the nonentity in whom hidden nobil-

One of Ben's best starring features for Sennett was *A Small Town Idol*. Ben's gallantry towards pretty Marie Prevost results in a nasty fall for Billy Bevan.

ity lurks, but I doubt that. Ben simply realized the laugh potential of such absurdity—and every so often, as he'd just wriggled smoothly out of some sticky predicament, he'd look directly at the camera, shrug his shoulders and grin, almost as if telling the audience, "Thank heavens this is a movie, or I'd never get away with it!"

Ben made many comedies, starting out under G. M. Anderson (Broncho Billy) in the old Essanay days. Too many of the early ones merely used him as a straight slapstick comic, and gave him far too little opportunity to establish a screen character of his own. But under Sennett, first at Keystone, and later at Pathé in the 20's, Ben had much better luck. Mack had the wit to leave Ben pretty much alone, and some real gems of comedy were the result. Ben had an especial fondness for lampooning serious movie hits, and his especial target was Erich Von Stroheim. At that time, Stroheim's reputation hung on his exotic studies in depravity—films like *Foolish Wives* and *The Merry Widow*. (*Greed* was too much of a masterpiece for Ben to want to kid it.) And so in films like *The Pride of Pikeville* and *When a Man's a Prince*, Ben copied the villainous and spectacularly lecherous foreign count that Stroheim had played in *Foolish Wives*. His uniform was an exact duplicate of Erich's, and so were his amatory adventures—but in a much lighter vein of course, and with less serious consequences. The sight of this funny little man, bedecked in officer's uniform and monocle, suddenly confronted by an irate husband and brazening his way out of it by a display of cool courage and European nonchalance, qualities quite foreign to those wildly popping eyes and tiny stature, always paid off in big laughs.

Perhaps Ben was partially letting off steam in these escapades. He never felt too secure in his stardom, and invested money in all sorts of side ventures in the event that he failed in pictures. He may have seen in these deliberately exaggerated heroics the chance to compensate for some of his doubts about himself, although I'm sure that was not the main reason for Ben's creation of such a unique comedy character.

Ben's films were rich in wild and wacky slapstick, but, as in films like *The Daredevil* (lampooning movie stuntmen) it was always slapstick with a sturdy inner lining of satire.

In talkies, Ben's appeal was less. There was nothing wrong with his voice but it *was* the voice of a hen-pecked husband. It was just enough to upset the balance of contrast, and Ben's former characterization was no longer possible. But he contributed innumerable comedy cameos to features, and was now too rich a man to worry about stardom having gone with the silents. He died in the 30's, in happy and wealthy retirement.

Rudy at the age of seventeen, before he left Italy.

Rudolph Valentino

When moviegoers, actors, and writers call to mind the great lovers of the screen, certain names inevitably come to the fore: John Barrymore . . . Greta Garbo . . . John Gilbert. . . . But it is the name of Rudolph Valentino that always heads the list. Perhaps because he specialized in exotic romantic roles even more than they did; perhaps because, unlike them, he never appeared in a talking picture, he remained the symbol of glamor and romance on the silent screen, just as Chaplin represented laughter, and Fairbanks adventure.

To me it has always seemed unfair that because Rudy was not a *great* actor, and didn't profess to be, the fact that he was a *good* actor has been somewhat obscured. The critics tended to see him only as a personality, and in their reviews would often overlook the fact that his performances were often surprisingly perceptive, even in roles which really gave him no opportunity at all. It's a fact that there are probably more *bad* Valentino films than good ones. But Rudy himself was the first to recognize this, and absented himself from the screen for a full two years at one point, at great financial hardship, in order not to have to make the

assembly-line programmers that his studio was turning out.

Actually, Rudy, or to give him his full Italian name, Rodolfo Alfonzo Raffaelo Pierre Filibert Guglielmi di Valentino d'Antonguolla, initially had no acting plans at all, and when he arrived in New York in 1913 at the age of eighteen, he drifted aimlessly, like many immigrants, from job to job, with gardening proving his most successful venture. But loving dancing, he frequented the casinos, and was soon a good enough dancer to be invited to be a performer rather than a customer at the famous Maxim's. For one tour, he was booked to replace Clifton Webb, and while on this tour, came to Hollywood. Friends there, such as actor Norman Kerry and director Emmett Flynn, urged him to try his luck at the movies, and he did.

There was no overnight stardom for Valentino, however, and several years in minor roles followed. One critic did tag him as "A good-looking hero the girls will think just grand," but for the most part Rudy's distinguished Italian features were, if anything, a liability. That was the peak era of the homespun American boy, of Charlie Ray and "Doug." Rudy, who looked anything but "Main Street, USA," was typed as a villain, a gigolo, and an apache, with sympathetic roles few and far between.

One of his typical unsympathetic roles was with

The famous tango scene from *The Four Horsemen of the Apocalypse.*

With Vilma Banky in *Son of the Sheik.*

Clara Kimball Young in *Eyes of Youth.* To Rudy it was just another picture, but it turned out to be far more than that. Two years later an M-G-M writer recalled how good he had been in it, and insisted that he would be perfect for the lead in *The Four Horsemen of the Apocalypse.* And perfect he was, in that adaptation of Ibáñez' novel of a carefree South American aristocrat who goes to fight for France in the first World War. Although the film had sincerity and a great deal of merit, it was not a great film, and it surely owed much of its popular success to the interest in it created by the new star.

Star? Well, not yet. Stardom really had to be earned in those days. Despite the 1921 furor over *The Four Horsemen of the Apocalypse,* Rudy didn't rate star billing for quite a while. Metro rushed him into three more pictures right away, but refused to pay him more than the small figure he had been getting as a featured player.

Dissatisfied, and with reason, Valentino left Metro and went to Paramount, at a salary of $500 a week. This was still a modest sum for a player of Rudy's magnitude, but it was a big improvement over his Metro stipend. Paramount promptly put him (but still without star status) into *The Sheik.* It was frankly a poor, over-melodramatic film, and Valentino's performance was not one of his best. He always hated the film. But it made him the hottest star on the screen, as

His death scene from *Blood and Sand.*

Opposite Gloria Swanson in *Be-yond the Rocks*—a dynamic team wasted on a trite picture.

His next-to-last role, as Dubrovski, in *The Eagle.*

With Bebe Daniels in *Monsieur Beaucaire*, the film that marked Rudy's return to the screen after a two-year absence.

well as introducing the word "sheik" into the teenagers' vocabulary.

Smoldering sex appeal was of course Rudy's stock in trade, and his producers made the most of it. But he had so many other qualities that were exploited too little; a gentleness, a sense of humor, and an athletic ability that came to the fore only in an occasional riding foray or duel scene. Most of all, despite all the clamor and fanatic devotion that he inspired, he impressed people most of all as being a "nice fellow"— the sort of fellow who would be a good, reliable friend. Of course, that's the sort of person that Rudy *was*— and it shows through today in his screen portrayals.

Valentino had bad films, tiltings with envious writers who attacked him in print, pans from critics, but he never lost the adoration of his public. *Cobra . . . Be-yond the Rocks . . . Blood and Sand . . . Moran of the Lady Letty . . . Monsieur Beaucaire . . .* the fans saw them avidly, again and again.

One can't help wondering, if Rudy's career had been longer . . . if he'd lived . . . how he'd have fared. He'd be in his sixties today. Would he, like John Barrymore, have been forced into lampoons of himself? Would he, like John Gilbert, have declined just because his vogue was over? Would he, like Ramon Novarro, have applied himself to character roles and directing? Or

A virile role combining romance with fast action. One of Valentino's best pictures, and his last, 1926's *Son of the Shiek.*

237

Valentino's tragic death was one of the big newspaper stories of all time. Foul play was hinted for a while, but this idea was quickly dropped.

would he, like Garbo, have retired—leaving the legend intact? I like to think he'd have done that—retired gracefully. Sweeping aside all the ballyhoo and publicity, the legend remains—and looking at the best of his films again today, particularly *Son of the Sheik*, one cannot dispute that his magic and eternal appeal remain, too.

Rudy was in New York making personal appearances for *Son of the Sheik* when tragedy struck, and he was rushed to Polyclinic Hospital for a gallstone operation. At first, it seemed that he was recovering quickly . . . his strength was returning, and he was in good spirits. . . . A world waited and held its breath.

But on August 23, 1926, at 12:10 P. M., the event that millions were praying would not happen, *did* happen, and Mark Hellinger wrote: "Rudolph Valentino, the man who brought happiness to the hearts of millions, is dead. The Great Director, who plays no favorites in screening the scenario of life, took him away at 12:10 P. M. yesterday."

The reaction from the whole nation—not just New York and Hollywood—was staggering; grief, hysteria, and an unbounded sorrow that moviegoers shared the world over. America put a black band around its sleeve and wiped away a tear. The Great Lover was gone. We have never seen his like since, and I doubt that we ever will.

Florence Vidor

Texas-born beauty Florence Vidor (she was married for a number of years to director King Vidor, hence her surname) was never one of the top stars of the silent screen—but she was among the most reliable and versatile. She started off at Vitagraph in minor roles, and began to attract attention at Fox in *A Tale of Two Cities* (1915) and in Sessue Hayakawa vehicles at Paramount. But it was in the 20's that she really came into her own as one of the most consistently active of all leading ladies.

There was a maturity and elegance to Florence Vidor that made her most appealing. Had she not decided on acting as a career, she would probably have made a top fashion model. The titles of some of her films—*Old Wives for New* (DeMille), *Lying Lips* (Ince) *The Patriot* (Lubitsch) and *Chinatown Nights*—of themselves indicate some of her range. At her best·in light comedy, she made two delightful pieces of frou-frou for Mal St. Clair, *Are Parents People?* (playing the mother of teenager Betty Bronson and the wife of Adolphe Menjou) and *The Grand Duchess and the Waiter*, again opposite Menjou, playing the most regal of Russian princesses!

She looked so lovely in period costumes that she was a natural for historical romances. In Frank Lloyd's *Eagle of the Sea*, an early essay on buccaneer Jean Lafitte, she made a most fetching heroine. And when Thomas H. Ince decided to film that old stage play about the Civil War, *Barbara Frietchie*, he selected Miss Vidor to play the heroine immortalized in poem and prose. Historically, there *was* a Barbara Frietchie, but she was a cranky, white-haired old lady whom nobody took too seriously. She certainly looked nothing like Miss Vidor, but that didn't stop Tom Ince's publicity department from issuing the following press statement, which I quote verbatim: "Florence Vidor, who stars in the title role of this epoch-making drama, was chosen to portray the great heroine because she possesses in superlative degree that innate charm and beauty typical of the best of American womanhood. Visually and histrionically, Miss Vidor is the ideal Barbara, and her interpretation of the role places it among the greatest characterizations in the history of the photodrama."

Having seen *Barbara Frietchie* recently, I don't entirely subscribe to the final statement, and I'm sure that neither Mr. Ince nor Miss Vidor really did either, back in 1924. But with Ince's enthusiasm for Florence Vidor I'm in full accord—a lovely woman and a most talented actress.

She was most at home in light comedy—and one of her best was *Are Parents People?*, with Adolphe Menjou and Betty Bronson.

in *Broken Ways,* for example) when stock company acting, rather than movie acting, predominated, but they were infrequent moments, and under Griffith's guidance soon disappeared entirely.

Walthall's acting was memorable, particularly in those early years when there was so much broad pantomime on the screen, for its restraint and sensitive underplaying. And it was an underplaying that was far more genuine and sincerely conceived than the phony "naturalness" and pseudo-sincerity of the post-Brando and Dean period. With a downward glance of those sad yet angry eyes, with an almost imperceptible shrug of the shoulder, Walthall could convey far more meaning and emotion than most current screen actors can with a full page of dialogue. Never a romantic leading man in the accepted sense, Walthall nevertheless cut a dashing figure in top hat and tails. In films like *Change of Heart,* an early Biograph film in which he played a Raffles-type character, he showed that he could have easily become a handsome hero had he chosen. But Walthall, like Barrymore in later years, was happier with stronger and more bizarre roles. If he had a "mad scene," as he had in many Biographs and in later important silents like *Ghosts* and *The Raven* in which he played the tortured genius Edgar Allan Poe, he was really in his element!

Walthall's performance in *The Birth of a Nation,* giving him opportunities for pathos, heroics, tender

Henry B. Walthall

Henry B. Walthall, born in the South on March 16, 1878, is both one of the finest, and one of the most neglected, of silent screen stars. After studying law in Alabama, he came to New York and entered the theatrical profession instead, achieving no little distinction and appearing for several seasons with Henry Miller and Margaret Anglin. When D. W. Griffith persuaded Walthall to enter films in 1909, the actor devoted himself wholeheartedly to the new medium, making occasional returns to the theatre (especially in his later periods of filmic ill-fortune), but concentrating on the screen.

He adjusted himself to the movie set rather than the theatre stage with remarkable ease. There were a few moments in his early years (the over-done death scene

Walthall's greatest role, the "Little Colonel" in *The Birth of a Nation.*

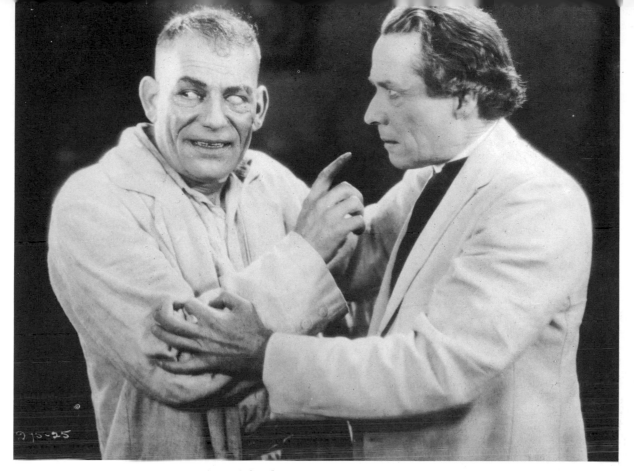

As Lon Chaney's brother in *The Road to Mandalay* (1926).

romantic scenes and solid dramatics, remains one of the great performances of the screen, silent or sound. The tragedy is that after its release, Walthall left Griffith to strike out on his own. His career, which undoubtedly would have developed along the spectacular lines of those of Lillian Gish, Mae Marsh and Richard Barthelmess, came to a sudden standstill, and he wasted a decade in interesting but minor films quite unworthy of him. Towards the end of the twenties he made a number of important films for M-G-M, among them *The Barrier* and *The Scarlet Letter*, but his prime was past, and the break came too late to be of real use to him.

With the coming of sound, however, Walthall suddenly found himself very much in demand. As with John Barrymore, one of his greatest assets was his voice —rich, moving, beautifully modulated. He played supporting roles in major productions and leads in minor films, and as the 30's wore on, he began to receive more and more choice roles. Death came to him while he was acting in *China Clipper*—playing a craftsman so devoted to his work that he kept at it, even knowing that the strain would mean his death. Ironically, his screen death-scene had to take place off-screen; Walthall himself had died before the scene could be shot.

Pearl White

I must confess that I could never get too enthusiastic about the serials of Pearl White. I recognize their importance in setting the style for so many other serials, but somehow they seemed to lack the speed and zip of the Ruth Roland serials, or the later ones of Allene Ray and Walter Miller.

But Pearl herself—that's a different story! I can't think of any other player in 1914 who had more sheer *personality* than Pearl. There were better actresses around, and more beautiful girls, but Pearl had that indefinable something that made her "special." For one thing, she seemed to be enjoying everything she did—and she was able to convey that enjoyment to the audience. Then too, she was a lovely girl in a healthy, open-air, big-sister fashion.

The prevailing standards of beauty for heroines at that time demanded a girlish innocence, a *little* sister look, if you like. Pearl's laughing face wasn't the kind to inspire romantic sighs from the boys—but it wasn't the kind to suggest that she needed kindness and protection either. Pearl could take care of herself—and the boy-friend too. As such, she was at least a generation ahead of her time, and her good looks and bouncing personality were insufficiently appreciated at the time. Moreover, her off-screen self matched the screen image perfectly; she would shake your hand vigorously, like a man, and lovely as she looked in all her finery, there was always the feeling that she'd be more comfortable in slacks and open-necked shirt.

Pearl's serials (contrary to the Hollywood background given to them in Paramount's biography, *The Perils of Pauline*) were all made largely in Ithaca, in upstate New York, or in and around Fort Lee, New Jersey. Since she concentrated on mystery stories rather than out-and-out adventures, her serials tended to be a little slower-paced than most of her contemporaries— but her own personality made up the difference, and she was always the most popular of all the serial queens. She had several flings in straight dramatics too, including a lively adventure made in France. She often employed doubles for her daredevil stunts, but after all, discounting all the publicity releases, what star hasn't?

People who have never seen Pearl White tend to laugh condescendingly when her name is mentioned, as though her name in itself is synonymous with an ultra-simple, ridiculous period of film-making. These people

A tense moment from episode 4 of *The Black Secret.*

Pearl in action—a typically hectic moment from *Plunder,* one of her best-known serials.

From episode 9 of *The Black Secret*—this time with Pearl dishing it out instead of taking it!

One of Pearl's features for Fox—*A Virgin Paradise* (1921).

just don't know their movies. They don't know that there *was* no "ridiculous" period in film history, any more than there was a "ridiculous" period in literature or in music. But most of all, they don't know Pearl White—and I guarantee they'd be more than a little surprised to find out how very little Pearl has dated since 1914. She still comes across as a beautiful woman, but most notable of all, her natural and unforced acting and her infectious gaiety put to shame the work at that time of many an actress who is regarded in far more reverential a manner.

Why none of the writers on film have ever discovered this is beyond me. Is it because none of them have ever seen Pearl White? Is it because they consider her serials and features "beneath" them? If so, a lot of books on film history, and especially on film personalities, are going to have to be re-written one of these days!

Clara Kimball Young

Clara Kimball Young—active in films until the 40's—was one of the most popular, and the most valued, of all the early Vitagraph players. She had a good sense of satire, and so was most useful in several of the Sidney Drew short comedies. At the same time, she was young and winsomely pretty, ideally suited for ingenue roles. Far from least, she looked elegant and fetching in costume, and frequently added distinction to period melodramas. She made an especially effective Trilby in an early Vitagraph adaptation of that Du Maurier classic.

Clara in her early days at Vitagraph—in 1914's *Goodness Gracious,* a smart little satire of movie melodramas, opposite Sidney Drew.

"THE MARCH OF THE MOVIES"

While Clara was never hard to get along with, and certainly not temperamental, she knew what she was worth to the studio, and used that as a lever to get better opportunities (and more money!) for her husband, actor-director James Young. Their marriage didn't endure, but after they split, each went their individual successful ways, with Clara, a good business-woman as well as a popular actress, achieving the greater fame.

Like Pauline Frederick, she specialized in heavy emotional roles—in later years, she seemed to be the wronged-wife in every other picture! One of her best roles, however, was as the much sought-after heroine in *Eyes of Youth*—in which she envisions her future with a number of different men, one offering love, another fame, a third position, and so on. It was the same story that Gloria Swanson later re-made as *The Loves of Sunya*—but Clara's version had a slight edge in that one of the romantically-inclined young men in the film was played by still-unknown Rudolph Valentino.

Clara Kimball Young's name never stood for smash box office success, but it did stand for steady, reliable, well-made entertainment. Exhibitors knew that a Young film would always make them a neat little profit —and audiences knew equally well what to expect in terms of solid dramatic entertainment. Clara never let either the exhibitors or her public down.

In the late 20's—opposite Conway Tearle in *The Forbidden Woman.*

Part Three
APPENDIX

The author chats with Buster Keaton on "Memory Lane."

Questions and Answers

Every week, a large percentage of the letters that come in to my office ask questions about the silent films—*who* did this, or *why* that. Interest in the silent photoplay seems to be enormous and constantly growing. So I've sorted through my files and picked out thirty of these questions—the ones that are asked the most frequently, and the ones that seem to me to be of the most general interest. So here goes:

1. Q. Was John Gilbert's voice really so bad that he had to quit talkies because of it?

A. Definitely not; this is the sort of story that grows and grows because the first time it appeared nobody bothered to refute it. Gilbert's voice wasn't great. But it was good. And it was improving with every picture. He made more talkies than most people realize. As I've explained in my section on Gilbert in this book, he failed only because talkies were no longer making the *type* of pictures that that he had specialized in.

2. Q. Who would you nominate as the silent movies' best villain?

A. I don't see how I could pick just *one*. Noah Beery, Walter Long, Montague Love, Sam de Grasse, Warner Oland and Brandon Hurst were all great.

3. Q. What was the first feature film? I keep reading that it was *The Squaw Man.* Is that right?

A. Definitely not. Neither I nor anyone else in his right mind would hazard a guess as to the first anything in movies. There are too many gaps in the record. But there were certainly features made before *The Squaw Man*; to give just two examples, Griffith's *Judith of Bethulia,* and Helen Gardner's *Cleopatra.*

4. Q. Is it true that *A Star is Born* was suggested by the life of John Gilbert?

A. No. For one thing, Gilbert didn't commit suicide. *A Star is Born* was *actually* suggested by the career of John Bowers, who was married to Marguerite de la Motte, and *did* end his life by walking into the sea. However, the film romanticized a bit, as neither Bowers nor Marguerite were as big as the stars depicted in the two versions of *A Star is Born.*

5. Q. Who would you nominate as the greatest director of all?

A. Usually I hedge about coming out with flat statements like that. Too much is a matter of opinion. But in this particular case, there's no doubt at all. D.W. Griffith. Everything that you see in films today traces back to him, as Alfred Hitchcock, DeMille and other directors have frequently acknowledged.

6. Q. I have read in interviews that Marlene Dietrich claims *The Blue Angel* to be her first film. But didn't she make others before that?

A. The lady is strangely sensitive about it. I don't know why—she looked lovely, and her acting was good. She made a good half-dozen German silents like *Manon Lescaut* before *The Blue Angel* came along.

7. Q. Was DeMille's *Ten Commandments* ever remade in the early 30's? I could have sworn I saw it then, but now I can find no reviews or other records of it.

A. No, there was no remake—until the current one of course. But in the early days of sound Paramount brought out a feature called *Modern Commandments* which used the big battle scenes and other highlights from the silent DeMille film. Maybe this is what you're thinking of.

8. Q. Why do silent films move so fast? How could audiences of those days have enjoyed them at that speed?

A. So many people are under this misapprehension. Silent films moved no faster than today's, and the action was perfectly normal. But they were photographed at a different speed, and required a different speed of projection. When sound came in, that speed had to be changed because of the mechanical problems involved in putting a sound track on the film. Most of today's projection machines (at least, those in theatres and on television) are equipped for sound speed projection only, and that's how the silents have to be shown. It's almost twice as fast as they were originally shown.

So be patient next time, and don't blame the speed on the apparent crudity of the day. Silents achieved an astonishingly high degree of technical perfection.

9. Q. Why are silent films so often blurred and flickery?
   A. This question is a logical follow-up to number 8. Again, they weren't. Photography as far back as 1898 was often crystal clear; there are films playing on Broadway now with worse photography than some old Biographs of 1909! But just as a newspaper gets wrinkled with age, so does a film pick up scratches and tears. Also, many of the silents you see may have been copied four or five times, and are several generations away from the original. Imagine taking a snapshot, making a photograph of it, then another photo of the copy, and so on down the line. That happens with certain films too, and a lot of quality is lost each time the process is repeated.

10. Q. Did any of the stars who really needed their voices —singers for instance—ever make a go of it in silent films?
    A. You'd be surprised how many *did*, even though of course all of them achieved greater picture fame when sound came in. Jolson made a silent; Eddie Cantor made very successful silent comedies like *Special Delivery* and *Kid Boots* and so did W.C. Fields. Will Rogers made a whole flock of shorts and features in the 20's, and even a sophisticated comedian like Clifton Webb made a batch of silents—long before the movies officially "discovered" him in *Laura*.

11. Q. Did Mary Pickford and Douglas Fairbanks ever make a picture together?
    A. Two. They co-starred in a lively adaptation of Shakespeare's *The Taming of the Shrew*, which came out in both silent and sound versions. And Mary made a sort of "guest" appearance in Doug's *The Gaucho*.

12. Q. Which period of the movies produced the most beautiful leading ladies—in your opinion?
    A. Beauty, like fashions, is not only a matter of personal taste, but also of national—even international—taste. Heroines of the pre-1920 era tried for that simple, innocent, old-Valentine type of beauty. In the 20's, they were either the gay flappers or the serene, classic beauties. Today, sex-appeal seems to have taken on more importance than facial beauty. I think most of us tend to look backwards for our ideals. I look back to the Norma Shearers and Billie Doves with a nostaligic sigh, just as in twenty years, my son Brad (now two) will turn away from 1980's movie queen with a sneer and say, "Now in Marilyn Monroe's day, they really *had* something."

13. Q. Often, when looking through old souvenir programs from the silent days, I come across references to "prologues." What were they, special shorts, or long trailers, to introduce the films?
    A. No, they were stage presentations—and as such usually limited to the first-run engagements of really important films in key cities. Often they were extremely elaborate affairs, staged on a scale that no movie theatre could afford today. When *What Price Glory?* opened at the Roxy, it was preceded by a fantastically spectacular stage prologue, which wound up with bombings, machine gun fire, and flying debris. Just as the audience expected the Roxy to collapse in a mass of rubble, the main titles were flashed on the screen, and the din slowly subsided to permit the orchestra to be heard. Movie showmanship was really showmanship in those days!

14. Q. What percentage of silents have been re-made as talkies?
    A. In hard figures, I don't know. But a lot—an awful lot. Not only most of the big hits—*The Sea Hawk, Ben-Hur, Quo Vadis?, The Squaw Man*—but an amazing number of smaller pictures too. For example, the old Milton Sills picture *The Making of O'Malley* was re-made as *The Great O'Malley* with Pat O'Brien. Even a little "B" western like *Death Valley* was re-made twenty years later—same plot exactly, even the same title! More movie stories than you could possibly imagine have been re-made—officially and unofficially—during the years.

15. Q. What story (i.e., an adaptation of a book or play) has been re-made the most number of times by the movies?
    A. A good guess would be Victor Hugo's *Les Miserables*. There must be thirteen or fourteen versions of that. And *The Count of Monte Cristo* can't be too far behind. *Crime and Punishment* is another popular one, and *The Spoilers* has first place among the westerns, with five versions to date.

16. Q. Apart from Jackie Coogan, you never hear much about silent day child stars. What happened to them?
    A. As with talkie child stars, most of them graduated to adult roles. Dawn O'Day became Ann Shirley, Virginia Grey, who was Little Eva in *Uncle Tom's Cabin*, turned into a very slim and lovely actress and is still going strong. Madge Evans had a big talkie career, and Phillipe de Lacy, who played Greta Garbo's son in a couple of movies, is now directing. He made one of the Cinerama movies. One of the Edison child stars grew up to have a spectacular career in quite another field—Claire Booth Luce!

17. Q. I read in a newspaper interview recently that Donald Crisp really directed the battle scenes in Griffith's *The Birth of a Nation*; is there any truth in this?
    A. Not a word. Now that Griffith is no longer around, a lot of people are all too anxious to claim

credit for work that was his. Griffith had a whole corps of assistants on *The Birth of a Nation,* chief of whom was George Siegmann, who also had a big part in the film. Crisp may or may not have been one of the minor assistants. He had only a few scenes in the film otherwise, as General Grant. I think the answer can be seen for itself in Griffith's films—and in Crisp's. The battle scenes in all the other big Griffith spectacles are obviously the work of the same man. Crisp is a fine actor, but his directorial talent has always been slight.

18. Q. I have a great deal of respect for silent movies, but I'm always surprised at their carelessness in one respect, namely that scenes that are supposed to take place at night are always obviously done in broad daylight. Why such slipshod methods?

    A. No carelessness and no slipshod methods. Night scenes are usually shot in the daytime. Nowadays they use special filters which give the illusion of darkness. In the silent days, they shot night scenes in the normal way in daytime—but in release prints, these scenes were always tinted blue. The results were both convincing and beautiful. A lot of these original prints are still around. But new prints, made up from the old negatives, are all in black and white since tinted film stock isn't available anymore. You've probably seen only these new prints; believe me, the men who made the films would have been horrified if they knew that prints would one day be made up without regard to their tinting requirements.

19. Q. Was there any attempt to make a sound film before *The Jazz Singer?*

    A. Plenty of them, right from the beginning. Edison made a whole group of sound films between 1906 and 1915, and so did other producers. We had three-dimensional films, color films and sound films —all long before these things became commonplace. Some of the old Edison "soundies" weren't bad either; in fact I've heard worse sound tracks on the Late Late Show!

20. Q. The Thomas Edison studios made *The Great Train Robbery* and were apparently important movie pioneers. How come they never became really important studios in later years?

    A. Films to Edison were just merchandise, to be turned out like so many electric lights. Once an invention was perfected, Edison lost interest, and left it to run itself. There was no attempt at progress within the Edison film set-up, and no effort to develop stars or directors. The films stood still while those of other companies forged ahead. Without a man at the helm who really cared about, and believed in, the movies as an art rather than as a product, there wasn't that necessary spark of stimulation. The Edison company continued to make shorts and occasional features until 1917 or '18, and then dropped them. They made some interest-ing things, including a 1906 version of *Franken-stein,* but I think that *The Great Train Robbery* was really their only important contribution to movie history.

21. Q. Do you think silent comedies were funnier than talkies?

    A. For the most part, yes. Too many sound comedies have been influenced by dialogue-requirements of comedians who came from radio. The pantomimic, or sight-gag comedy, which was so great in the hands of masters like Keaton, Lloyd and Chaplin, became a thing of the past. However, sound comedies *did* bring a lot of new laughter to the screen too. Laurel & Hardy successfully coupled silent-type sight gags with dialogue. And of course, the screwball comedy of the *Nothing Sacred* type, and the insanity of W.C. Fields and the Marx Brothers, wouldn't have been as effective in the silent film.

22. Q. Do you think there ever was, or will be, another Valentino?

    A. I doubt it. Gable came closest, and even then there was a big difference. Gable was a more down-to-earth hero; young swains in the audience could kid themselves (if not their girlfriends) that they were just like him. But no youngster in the 20's ever had the temerity to assume that he had Rudy's appeal; he just sat back, sighed, and *wished* he had it!

23. Q. Is it true that there were no closeups in movies before Griffith invented the device?

    A. No. And he didn't invent the closeup. There had been closeups back in 1900. But usually they were closeups for convenience, because it was easier to see a given object, or look at a famous face, from as close as possible. Griffith was the first to realize the dramatic possibility of the closeup, and to use it creatively. It is amazing how many potentially good little films before Griffith (and for some time after his arrival on the scene) were spoiled because their directors didn't realize what added punch closeups could give to their scenes. The same applies to moving the camera, and developing fast editing, two more elements of film grammar exploited by Griffith.

24. Q. I haven't seen silent films; do the titles explaining action or giving dialogue seem strange and old-fashioned today?

    A. Not really. Of course, when you see a lot of them you come to accept them as naturally as you accept spoken dialogue. Bad titles *do* date, especially the anything-for-a-wisecrack policy in some of the cheaper comedies. The forced puns and strained jokes really have to be seen to be believed. But title writing was a fine art, and many really beauti-fully composed titles can be found in the best silents, accompanied by impressive art back-grounds. And some of the titles in comedies had all the slick punch and immediate laugh response of a cartoon in *The New Yorker.*

25. Q. Of the silent films you've missed, which are the five you'd most like to see—

A. *Hollywood; Mare Nostrum; One Exciting Night; A Woman of Paris; The Bat.* Great films all of them, I'm sure. I know where there's a print of *A Woman of Paris,* but the rest seem to have vanished from the face of the earth; there'll be a handsome fee to anyone who can locate a print of any of them for me!

26. Q. Who would you consider more important; the columnists or the critics?

A. That's a tough question to answer. In a historical sense, as keepers of records, the critics must be rated first. Their views are of lasting value. Films themselves are often of a transient quality; what is good when it is new may seem obvious and dated ten years later. Or it may have been so much ahead of its time, that it can only be fully appreciated much later on. Further, national feelings, philosophies and moralities change so much that films can be interpreted in completely different lights at different periods. The critics' opinions, given at the time of the film's release, are of far more significance and historical value than we may all imagine. The columnist, with rare exceptions, does not editorialize however, and merely passes on facts —facts which are of no significance a year, let alone ten years, later. However, the columnist has a tremendous value commercially in that he or she is often read far more avidly than are the critics; a casual plug from a nationally syndicated columnist can often do more for a film than a rave review from a specific critic. The columnist is a liaison between the studio and the public; to the studios he is invaluable—a publicity outlet without the stigma of publicity. To the movie fan, he's a direct link with the glamor of filmland.

Many of the columnists have of course appeared in films at one time or another. Hedda Hopper, for example, was a top leading lady—and a good actress to boot—in the silent period. Others, like Walter Winchell, Ed Sullivan, Leonard Lyons, Sidney Skolsky, Jimmy Fidler, etc., have all appeared in films at one time or another. They carry tremendous weight with their public. Sometimes I feel that this weight is a little abused, and occasionally the *opinion* of the columnist is considered by him or her to be of more importance than the story or fact being commented on. This results in very one-sided reporting, against which there is no comeback. But luckily, the good work done by the columnist usually outweighs by far the harm done by temporarily inflated egoes. I have isolated specific instances in mind, not any one columnist, so to name names would be unfair and pointless.

27. Q. We've had such a lengthy cycle of horror movies this time, that I can't help wondering—did the silent cinema ever have such a cycle?

A. In horror movies, no. The horror film, as a general classification, didn't get its boost until the arrival of *Frankenstein* and *Dracula* in 1931. The closest thing to a silent horror cycle was the fantasy period in Germany in the 20's. Many films in that group were basically horror films—they made a version of *Dracula,* for example—but the basic intent and design was fantasy, and there were as many psychological studies as there were out-and-out "scare" pictures. *The Cabinet of Dr. Caligari* of 1919 was, of course, the instigator of this particular cycle. In America and elsewhere, horror films were made occasionally (*The Bat, The Phantom of the Opera*) but they were not related in any way, and were far less prevalent than the cycles in mystery films, or in biblical spectacles.

28. Q. Quite often in very old silents, I've noticed letters and trademarks stuck to the walls in scenes. Was this because in the days before the star system, a company trademark had box office value?

A. No, it was a purely precautionary procedure. In the early days, prints of films were not registered for copyright—only odd scenes from those films. There was no legal comeback if some illegal operator made a copy of a film, and put it out under his own trademark. So Biograph, Edison, Vitagraph and the others took to inserting their trademarks quite plainly into the key scenes of their films— scenes that would *have* to be used if anyone wanted to use the film. Their presence would thus prove beyond any shadow of a doubt that the footage had been stolen. This practice died out after 1912, when the copyright laws were revised and provided more protection.

29. Q. Since double-features came in mainly with sound, weren't there any "B" films in the silent period at all?

A. Oh yes—and some of the silent "B"s were real shockers, made in a few days for peanuts. However, that of course applies to sound films too. There have always been "B" films and, as you know, some of them have been little gems. And they've been used to provide valuable training ground for up and coming stars and directors. They definitely have a place in the film field, and I was sorry to see them begin to go in the mid-50's. Comparatively few are made now. In the silent days of course, the short subject was of much more importance than it is now. What we would term a "B" picture of only five reels could still form the bulk of a really fine little show, backed by a newsreel, a serial episode, and a great two-reel comedy.

30. Q. Every so often I read how some great star of the silent screen has just died in conditions of poverty. How many of them really saved the fabulous money they made?

A. I'd hate to hazard a guess, except to say that

there's no reason to suppose that it's any different in the movie business than in any other business. Because the personalities involved are world-famous, it's always a bit of a shock to hear that one of our old favorites has wound up in poverty, but we wouldn't think twice about it if a similarly prominent politician or financier came to the same end. Newspapers know that tragedy like that always makes a good story; thus we hear of *all* the unfortunate cases, and not as often of the other side of the picture. Stars like Lillian Gish, Harold Lloyd, Richard Barthelmess and Mary Pickford made fabulous fortunes in those days of limited taxes, invested wisely, and have remained wealthy. Norma Talmadge left millions. Other stars turned businessmen, and were less successful in handling themselves than they thought; Douglas Fairbanks, for example, lost a good deal of money in some of his sound picture ventures. In other cases, the losses were occasioned by deliberate, courageous integrity. D. W. Griffith made a fortune from *The Birth of a Nation*, but poured it all into *Intolerance* because it was the only way to get the film made. Then, when it proved a financial failure, he had to use the profits from subsequent pictures to pay off additional debts that it incurred. Back on his feet again with *Way Down East*, he used the profits from that to pay for other films of artistic integrity but little box office attraction. We can be thankful that he did, and while he left but a small estate in a monetary sense, he *did* leave a fabulous heritage of great motion pictures—which he wholly owned.

And, of course, not all stars were as fabulously paid as you might assume. Some of the stars now most in the doldrums are the popular western personalities of the twenties and early thirties. They were enormously popular, and made lots of movies —but their renumeration was surprisingly small when contrasted with their fame and box office pull. There is just no way of generalizing. Accustomed to being treated almost like royalty, many former greats will not accept any kind of charity, and *prefer* to live in poverty rather than by the generosity of others. There is a wonderful home for motion picture veterans in Hollywood—private, luxurious, out of reach of sightseers—yet I know of several old-timers who, on being urged to retire to its spacious grounds, have preferred to live on in loneliness in little rooms, keeping their independence to the last.

Casts of Films

In this section are listed the complete casts of 47 of the 50 films discussed in this book. No cast listing was available for *The Great Train Robbery*, and the documentaries *Nanook of the North* and *Tabu* of course had no professional casts.

BEAU GESTE (Paramount) Director: Herbert Brenon
Ronald Colman (*Michael Geste*); Neil Hamilton (*Digby Geste*); Ralph Forbes (*John Geste*); Alice Joyce (*Lady Patricia Brandon*); Mary Brian (*Isobel*); Noah Beery (*Sergeant Lejaune*); William Powell (*Boldini*); Norman Trevor (*Major de Beaujolais*); Victor McLaglen (*Hank*); Donald Stuart (*Buddy*).

BEN-HUR (M-G-M) Director: Fred Niblo
Ramon Novarro (*Ben-Hur*); Francis X. Bushman (*Messala*); May McAvoy (*Esther*); Betty Bronson (*Madonna*); Claire McDowell (*mother of Hur*); Kathleen Key (*Tirzah*); Carmel Myers (*Iras*); Nigel de Brulier (*Simonides*); Mitchell Lewis (*Sheik Ilderim*); Leo White (*Sanballat*); Frank Currier (*Arrius*); Charles Belcher (*Balthasar*); Dale Fuller (*Amrah*); Winter Hall (*Joseph*).

THE BIG PARADE (M-G-M) Director: King Vidor
John Gilbert (*James Apperson*); Renee Adoree (*Melisande*); Hobart Bosworth (*Mr. Apperson*); Claire McDowell (*Mrs. Apperson*); Claire Adams (*Justyn Reed*); Robert Ober (*Harry*); Tom O'Brien (*Bull*); Karl Dane (*Slim*); Rosita Marstini (*French mother*).

THE BIRTH OF A NATION (Epoch Producing Co.) Director: D.W. Griffith
Henry B. Walthall (*Ben Cameron*); Lillian Gish (*Elsie Stoneman*); Mae Marsh (*Flora Cameron*); Violet Wilkey (*Flora as a child*); Miriam Cooper (*Margaret*); Josephine Crowell (*Mrs. Cameron*); Spottiswood Aitken (*Dr. Cameron*); Andre Beranger (*Wade Cameron*); Maxfield Stanley (*Duke Cameron*); Ralph Lewis (*Austin Stoneman*); Elmer Clifton (*Phil Stoneman*); Robert Harron (*Ted Stoneman*); Mary Alden (*Lydia Brown*); Sam de Grasse (*Senator Sumner*); George Siegmann (*Silas Lynch*); Walter Long (*Gus*); Elmo Lincoln (*White Arm Joe*); Wallace Reid (*Jeff the blacksmith*); Joseph Henaberry (*Abraham Lincoln*); Donald Crisp (*General U. S. Grant*); Howard Gaye (*General Robert E. Lee*); William Freeman (*sentry*); Olga Grey (*Laura Keene*); Raoul Walsh (*John Wilkes Booth*); Tom Wilson (*Stoneman's servant*); Eugene Pallette (*Union soldier*); William de Vaull (*Jake*); Jennie Lee (*Cindy*); Erich von Stroheim (*man who falls from roof*).

THE BLACK PIRATE (United Artists) Director: Albert Parker
Douglas Fairbanks (*the Black Pirate*); Billie Dove (*the Princess*); Anders Randolf (*pirate leader*); Sam de Grasse (*his lieutenant*); Donald Crisp (*McTavish*); Mrs. Piggolt (*Duenna*); Charles Stevens (*powder man*).

BROKEN BLOSSOMS (Griffith-United Artists) Director: D.W. Griffith
Lillian Gish (*the girl*); Richard Barthelmess (*the chinaman*); Donald Crisp (*Battling Burrows*); Arthur Howard (*his manager*); Edward Piel (*Evil Eye*); Kid McCoy (*a prizefighter*); George Beranger (*the spying one*).

THE CAT AND THE CANARY (Universal) Director: Paul Leni
Laura La Plante (*Annabelle West*); Creighton Hale (*Paul Jones*); Forrest Stanley (*Charles Wilder*); Tully Marshall (*Lawyer Crosby*); Gertrude Astor (*Cecily*); Arthur Edmund Carewe (*Harry*); George Siegmann (*Hendricks*); Flora Finch (*Susan*); Lucien Littlefield (*the doctor*); Martha Mattox (*Mammy Pleasant*); Joe Murphy (*milkman*); Billie Engel (*taxi driver*).

THE CROWD (M-G-M) Director: King Vidor
Eleanor Boardman (*Mary*); James Murray (*John*); Bert Roach (*Bert*); Daniel G. Tomlinson (*Jim*); Lucy Beaumont (*Mother*); Dell Henderson (*Dick*); Freddie Burke Frederick (*Junior*); Alice Mildred Puter (*daughter*).

CITY LIGHTS (Chaplin-United Artists) Director: Charles Chaplin
Charlie Chaplin (*the tramp*); Virginia Cherrill (*the blind girl*); Florence Lee (*her grandmother*); Harry Myers (*an eccentric millionaire*); Allan Garcia (*his butler*); Hank Mann (*a prizefighter*); Albert Austin (*street-cleaner*); John Rand (*tramp*); Henry Bergman (*janitor*).

THE COVERED WAGON (Paramount) Director: James Cruze
J. Warren Kerrigan (*Will Banion*); Lois Wilson (*Molly Wingate*); Alan Hale (*Sam Woodhull*); Ernest Torrence (*Jackson*); Charles Ogle (*Mr. Wingate*); Ethel Wales (*Mrs. Wingate*); Tully Marshall (*Jim Bridger*); Guy Oliver (*Dunston*); Johnny Fox (*Jed Wingate*).

DR. JEKYLL AND MR. HYDE (Paramount) Director: John S. Robertson
John Barrymore (*Henry Jekyll*); Millicent Carewe (*Martha Mansfield*); Brandon Hurst (*Sir George Carewe*); Nita Naldi (*Miss Gina*); Charles Lane (*Dr. Lanyon*); Louis Wolheim (*music hall proprietor*).

DON JUAN (Warner Bros.) Director: Alan Crosland
John Barrymore (*Don Juan*); Mary Astor (*Adriana*); Willard Louis (*Pedrillo*); Estelle Taylor (*Lucretia Borgia*); Warner Oland (*Cesare Borgia*); Montague Love (*Count Donati*); Helene Costello (*Rena*); Jane Winton (*Beatrice*); Myrna Loy (*Maia*); John Roche (*Leandro*); June Marlowe (*Trusia*); Yvonne Day (*Don Juan, age five*); Phillipe de Lacy (*Don Juan, age ten*); John George (*hunchback*); Gustav von Seyffertitz (*Nehri*); Helene D'Algy (*a murderess*); Josef Swickard (*Duke Della Varnese*); Lionel Braham (*Duke Margoni*); Phyllis Haver (*Imperia*); Nigel de Brulier (*Marquis*

Rinaldo); Hedda Hopper (*Marquise Rinaldo*).

FLESH AND THE DEVIL (M-G-M) Director: Clarence Brown

John Gilbert (*Leo Von Harden*); Greta Garbo (*Felicitas*); Lars Hanson (*Ulrich von Eltz*); Barbara Kent (*Hertha*); William Orlamond (*Uncle Kutowski*); George Fawcett (*Pastor Voss*); Eugenie Besserer (*Leo's mother*); Marc McDermott (*Count von Rhaden*); Marcelle Corday (*Minna*).

THE GENERAL (United Artists) Directors: Buster Keaton and Clyde Bruckman

Buster Keaton (*Johnnie Gray*); Marion Mack (*Annabelle Lee*); Charles Smith (*her father*); Frank Barnes (*her brother*); Glenn Cavender (*Captain Anderson*); Jim Farley (*General Thatcher*); Frank Hagney (*recruiting officer*); Joe Keaton (*Confederate officer*).

THE GOLD RUSH (United Artists) Director: Charles Chaplin

Charlie Chaplin (*the Lone Prospector*); Mack Swain (*Big Jim*); Tom Murray (*Black Larson*); Georgia Hale (*Georgia*); Henry Bergman (*Hank Curtis*).

GREED (Metro-Goldwyn) Director: Erich von Stroheim

Gibson Gowland (*McTeague*); ZaSu Pitts (*Trina*); Jean Hersholt (*Marcus Schuler*); Chester Conklin (*Mr. Sieppe*); Sylvia Ashton (*Mrs. Sieppe*); Dale Fuller (*Maria*); Joan Standing (*Selina*); Austin Jewell (*August Sieppe*); Oscar Gottell, Otto Gottell (*the Sieppe twins*); Tempe Piggott (*McTeague's mother*).

HELL'S HINGES (Ince-Triangle) Director: William S. Hart

William S. Hart (*Blaze Tracey*); Clara Williams (*Faith Henly*); Jack Standing (*Rev. Robert Henly*), Alfred Hollingsworth (*Silk Miller*); Robert McKim (*clergyman*); Louise Glaum (*Dolly*); J. Frank Burke (*Zeb Taylor*); Robert Kortman (*henchman*); Jean Hersholt, John Gilbert (*townspeople*).

THE HUNCHBACK OF NOTRE DAME (Universal) Director: Wallace Worsley

Lon Chaney (*Quasimodo*); Patsy Ruth Miller (*Esmerelda*); Norman Kelly (*Phoebus*); Ernest Torrence (*Clopin*); Kate Lester (*Mme. de Gondelaurier*); Brandon Hurst (*Jehan*); Raymond Hatton (*Gringoire*); Tully Marshall (*Louis XI*); Nigel de Brulier (*Dom Claude*); Edwin Wallack (*King's chamberlain*); John Cossar (*Justice of the Court*); Harry L. Van Meter (*Monsieur Neufchatel*); Gladys Brockwell (*Godule*); Eulalie Jensen (*Marie*); Winifred Bryson (*Fleur de Lys*); Nick de Ruiz (*Monsieur le Torteru*); W. Ray Meyers (*Charmolu's assistant*); William Parke, Sr. (*Josephus*).

INTOLERANCE (Wark Producing Co.) Director: D.W. Griffith

THE MODERN STORY:
Mae Marsh (*the Dear One*); Robert Harron (*the Boy*); Fred Turner (*the girl's father*); Sam de Grasse (*Jenkins*); Vera Lewis (*Mary Jenkins*); Mary Alden, Eleanor Washington, Pearl Elmore, Lucille Brown, Mrs. Arthur Mackley ("*uplifters*" *and reformers*); Miriam Cooper (*the Friendless One*); Walter Long (*the Musketeer of the Slums*); Tom Wilson (*the kindly policeman*); Ralph Lewis (*the Governor*); Lloyd Ingraham (*the Judge*); Rev. A. W. McClure (*Father Fathley*); J. P. McCarthy (*prison guard*); Dore Davidson (*the friendly neighbor*); Monte Blue (*strike leader*); Marguerite Marsh (*debutante*); Tod Browning (*a crook*); Edward Dillon (*a crook*); Billy Quirk (*bartender*).

THE JUDEAN STORY:
Howard Gaye (*the Nazarene*); Lillian Langdon (*Mary*); Olga Grey (*Mary Magdalene*); Gunther von Ritzau (*first Pharisee*); Erich von Stroheim (*second Pharisee*); Bessie Love (*bride of Cana*); William Brown (*the bride's father*); George Walsh (*bridegroom*); W. S. Van Dyke (*a wedding guest*).

THE FRENCH STORY:
Margery Wilson (*Brown Eyes*); Eugene Pallette (*Prosper Latour*); Spottiswoode Aitken (*Brown Eyes' father*); Ruth Handford (*her mother*); A. D. Sears (*the mercenary*); Frank Bennett (*Charles IX*); Maxfield Stanley (*Duc d'Anjou*); Josephine Crowell (*Catherine de Medici*); Constance Talmadge (*Marguerite de Valois*); W. E. Lawrence (*Henry of Navarre*); Joseph Henabery (*Admiral Coligny*); Chandler House (*a page*).

THE BABYLONIAN STORY:
Constance Talmadge (*the Mountain Girl*); Elmer Clifton (*the Rhapsode*); Alfred Paget (*Prince Belshazzar*); Seena Owen (*the Princess Beloved*); Carl Stockdale (*King Nabonidus*); Tully Marshall (*High Priest of Bel*); George Siegmann (*Cyrus the Persian*); Elmo Lincoln (*the Mighty Man of Valor*); Gino Corrado (*the runner*); Wallace Reid (*a boy killed in the fighting*); Ted Duncan (*Captain of the Gate*); Ted Duncan and Felix Modjeska (*bodyguards to the Princess*); George Fawcett and Robert Lawlor (*judges*); Kate Bruce (*old Babylonian woman*); Ruth St. Denis (*solo dancer*); Alma Rubens, Pauline Starke, Mildred Harris, Eve Southern, Natalie Talmadge, Colleen Moore, Winifred Westover, Carol Dempster, Ethel Terry, Jewel Carmen, Daisy Robinson, Anna Mae Walthall (*slave girls, dancers and handmaidens*); the Denishawn Dancers; *and as extras*: Owen Moore, Wilfred Lucasm, Douglas Fairbanks, Sir Herbert Beerbohm Tree, Frank Campeau, DeWolfe Hopper, Nigel de Brulier, Donald Crisp, Tammany Young.

LINKING THE STORIES:
Lillian Gish (*the woman who rocks the cradle*).

THE IRON HORSE (Fox) Director: John Ford

George O'Brien (*Davy Brandon*); Madge Bellamy (*Mariam*); Fred Kohler (*Deroux*); Charles Edward Bull (*Abraham Lincoln*); Gladys Hulette (*Ruby*); Francis Powers (*Sergeant Slattery*); James Welch (*Private Schultz*); Jack O'Brien (*Dinny*); J. Farrell MacDonald (*Corporal Casey*); George Wagner (*Colonel Cody*); Cyril Chadwick (*Peter Jesson*); Charles O'Malley (*Major North*); Delbert Mann (*Charles Crocker*); Thomas Durant (*Jack Ganzhorn*); Chief White Spear (*Sioux chief*); James Marcus (*Judge Haller*); Stanhope Wheatcroft (*John Hay*); Will Walling (*Thomas Marsh*); Colin Chase (*Tony*); Walter Rogers (*General Dodge*); John Padjan (*Wild Bill Hickok*); Charles Newton (*Collis P. Harrington*); John Padjan (*General Stanford*); Chief Big Tree (*Cheyenne chief*); Frances Teague (*Polka Dot*); Edward Piel (*Old Chinaman*); Winton Miller (*Davy as a child*); Peggy Cartwright (*Mariam as a child*); James Gordon (*David Brandon, Sr.*).

A KISS FOR CINDERELLA (Paramount) Director: Herbert Brenon

Betty Bronson (*Cinderella*); Tom Moore (*policeman*); Esther Ralston (*Fairy Godmother*); Henry Vibart (*Richard Bodie*); Dorothy Cumming (*Queen*); Ivan Simpson (*Mr. Cutaway*); Dorothy Walters (*Mrs. Maloney*); Flora Finch (*second customer*); Juliet Brenon (*third customer*); Marilyn McLaine (*Gladys*); Patty Coakley (*Marie-Therese*); Mary Christian (*Sally*); Edna Hagen (*Gretchen*).

LAST OF THE MOHICANS (Associated Producers) Directors: Maurice Tourneur and Clarence Brown

Albert Roscoe (*Uncas*); Wallace Beery (*Magua*); Barbara Bedford (*Cora Monroe*); Lillian Hall (*Alice Monroe*); Harry Lorraine (*Major Heyward*); James Gordon (*Hawkeye*).

THE LOST WORLD (First National) Director: Harry Hoyt

Bessie Love (*Paula White*); Lewis Stone (*Sir John Roxton*); Wallace Beery (*Professor Challenger*); Lloyd Hughes (*Edward Malone*); Arthur Hoyt (*Professor Summerlee*); Alma Bennett (*Gladys Hungerford*); Virginia Brown Faire (*Marquette*); Bull Montana (*Ape Man*); Finch Smiles (*Austin*); Jules Cowles (*Zambo*); Margaret McWade (*Mrs. Challenger*); Charles Wellesley (*Major Hibbard*); George Bunny (*Colin McArdle*).

THE MARK OF ZORRO (United Artists) Director: Fred Niblo

Douglas Fairbanks (*Don Diego Vega* and *Señor Zorro*); Noah Beery (*Sergeant Pedro*); Charles H. Mailes (*Don Carlos*);

Claire McDowell (*his wife*); Marguerite de la Motte (*Lolita*); Robert McKim (*Captain Ramon*); George Periolat (*Governor Alvarado*); Walt Whitman (*Frey Felipe*); Sydney De Grey (*Don Alejandro*); Charles Stevens (*peon*).

ORPHANS OF THE STORM (Griffith-United Artists) Director: D.W. Griffith

Lillian Gish (*Henriette Girard*); Dorothy Gish (*Louise*); Joseph Schildkraut (*Chevalier de Vaudrey*); Monte Blue (*Danton*); Frank Losee (*Count de Linieres*); Catherine Emmett (*Countess de Linieres*); Morgan Wallace (*Marquis de Praille*); Lucille la Verne (*Mother Frochard*); Sheldon Lewis (*Jacques Frochard*); Frank Puglia (*Pierre Frochard*); Creighton Hale (*Picard*); Leslie King (*Jacques Forget-Not*); Sidney Herbert (*Robespierre*); Leo Kolmer (*King Louis XVI*); Adolphe Lestina (*the doctor*); Kate Bruce (*Sister Genevieve*); Flora Finch (*starving peasant*); Louis Wolheim (*executioner*); Kenny Delmar (*the Chevalier as a boy*).

OUR DANCING DAUGHTERS (M-G-M) Director: Harry Beaumont

Joan Crawford (*Diana*); John Mack Brown (*Ben Black*); Dorothy Sebastian (*Beatrice*); Anita Page (*Ann*); Kathlyn Williams (*Ann's mother*); Nils Asther (*Norman*); Eddie Nugent (*Freddie*); Dorothy Cummings (*Diana's mother*); Huntley Gordon (*Diana's father*); Evelyn Hall (*Freddie's mother*); Sam de Grasse (*Freddie's father*).

THE PERILS OF PAULINE (Eclectic) Director: Louis Gasnier

Pearl White (*Pauline Harvin*); Crane Wilbur (*Harry Marvin*); Paul Panzer (*Koerner*).

PETER PAN (Paramount) Director: Herbert Brenon

Betty Bronson (*Peter Pan*); Ernest Torrence (*Captain Hook*); Esther Ralston (*Mrs. Darling*); Mary Brian (*Wendy*); Cyril Chadwick (*Mr. Darling*); Virginia Brown Faire (*Tinker Bell*); George Ali (*Nana, the dog*); Anna May Wong (*Tiger Lily*); Phillipe de Lacy (*Michael*); Jack Murphy (*John*).

THE PHANTOM OF THE OPERA (Universal) Director: Rupert Julian

Lon Chaney (*Erik, the Phantom*); Mary Philbin (*Christine Daae*); Norman Kerry (*Raoul' de Chagny*); Snitz Edwards (*Florine Papillon*); Gibson Gowland (*Simon*); John St. Polis (*Philippe de Chagny*); Virginia Pearson (*Carlotta*); Arthur Edmund Carewe (*the Persian*); Edith Yorke (*Mamma Valerius*); Anton Vaverka (*the Prompter*); Bernard Siegel (*Joseph Buquet*); Olive Ann Alcorn (*La Sorelli*); Edward Cecil (*Faust*); Alexander Bevani (*Mephisto*); John Miljan (*Valentine*); Grace Marvin (*Martha*); George B. William (*M. Richard, mana-

ger*); Bruce Covington (*M. Monacharmin*); Cesar Gravina (*retiring manager*).

SAFETY LAST (Pathé) Director: Sam Taylor

Harold Lloyd (*the Boy*); Mildred Davis (*the Girl*); Bill Strother (*the Pal*); Noah Young (*the Law*); Westcott B. Clarke (*the Floorwalker*); Mickey Daniels (*the Kid*); Anna Townsend (*the Grandma*).

THE SCARLET LETTER (M-G-M) Director: Victor Seastrom

Lillian Gish (*Hester Prynne*); Lars Hanson (*Rev. Dimmesdale*); Henry B. Walthall (*Roger Prynne*); Karl Dane (*Giles*); William H. Tooker (*governor*); Marcel Corday (*Mistress Hibbins*); Fred Herzog (*jailer*); Jules Cowles (*beadle*); Mary Hawes (*Patience*); Joyce Coad (*Pearl*); James A. Marcus (*French sea captain*); Chief Yowlachie (*Indian*); Polly Moran (*townswoman*).

SEVENTH HEAVEN (Fox) Director: Frank Borzage

Janet Gaynor (*Diane*); Charles Farrell (*Chico*); Ben Bard (*Brissac*); David Butler (*Gobin*); Albert Gran (*Boul*); Gladys Brockwell (*Nana*); Emile Chautard (*Pére Chevillon*); George Stone (*Sewer Rat*); Jessie Haslett (*Aunt Valent*); Lillian West (*Arlette*); Marie Mosquini (*Mrs. Gobin*).

SHERLOCK JR. (Metro) Director: Buster Keaton

Buster Keaton (*the boy*); Kathryn McGuire (*the girl*); Joe Keaton (*her father*); Ward Crane (*the villain*); Erwin Connelly (*his henchman*).

SON OF THE SHEIK (United Artists) Director: George Fitzmaurice

Rudolph Valentino (*Ahmed, and his father, Ahmed Ben Hassan*); Vilma Banky (*Yasmin*); George Fawcett (*André*); Montague Love (*Ghaba*); Karl Dane (*Ramadan*); William Donovan (*S'rir*); Agnes Ayres (*Diana*); Bull Montana (*Albi*); Erwin Connelly (*the Zouave*); Bynunsky Hyman (*the Pincher*); Charles Requa (*Pierre*).

SPARROWS (United Artists) Director: William Beaudine

Mary Pickford (*Mama Mollie*); Gustav von Seyffertitz (*Grimes*); Roy Stewart (*Richard Wayne*); Mary Louise Miller (*Doris Wayne*); Charlotte Mineau (*Mrs. Grimes*); Specs O'Donnell (*Ambrose Grimes*); Lloyd Whitlock (*Bailey*); A. L. Schaeffer (*his associate*); Mark Hamilton (*hog buyer*); Monty O'Grady (*Splutters*).

THE SPOILERS (Selig) Director: Colin Campbell

William Farnum (*Roy Glennister*); Tom Santschi (*MacNamara*); Kathlyn Williams (*Cherry Malotte*); Wheeler Oakman (*Broncho*); Bessie Eyton (*the City Girl*); Frank Clark (*Old-Timer*).

STELLA DALLAS (United Artists) Director: Henry King

Ronald Colman (*Stephen Dallas*); Belle Bennett (*Stella Dallas*); Alice Joyce (*Helen Morrison*); Jean Hersholt (*Ed Munn*); Lois Moran (*Laurel Dallas*); Douglas Fairbanks, Jr. (*Richard Grosvenor*); Vera Lewis (*Mrs. Tibbits*); Beatrice Pryor (*Mrs. Grosvenor*).

THE STRONG MAN (First National) Director: Frank Capra

Harry Langdon (*Paul Bergot*); Priscilla Bonner (*Mary Brown*); William V. Mong (*Parson Brown*); Robert McKim (*Roy McDervitt*); Gertrude Astor (*Gold Tooth*); Arthur Thalasso (*Zandow the Great*); Brooks Benedict (*passenger on bus*).

SUNRISE (Fox) Director: F. W. Murnau

George O'Brien (*the man*); Janet Gaynor (*the wife*); Margaret Livingston (*the woman from the city*); Bodil Rosing (*the maid*); J. Farrell MacDonald (*the photographer*); Ralph Sipperly (*the barber*); Jane Winton (*the manicurist*); Arthur Housman (*the obtrusive gentleman*); Eddie Boland (*the obliging gentleman*); and Barry Norton, Robert Kortman, Gino Corrado and Sally Eilers.

THE TEN COMMANDMENTS (Paramount) Director: Cecil B. DeMille

Part I: Theodore Roberts (*Moses*); Charles de Roche (*Rameses*); Estelle Taylor (*Miriam*); Julia Faye (*wife of Pharaoh*); Terrence Moore (*son of Pharaoh*); James Neill (*Aaron*); Lawson Butt (*Dathn*); Clarence Burton (*the Taskmaster*); Noble Johnson (*the Bronze Man*); Gino Corrado (*Joshua*).

Part II: Richard Dix (*John McTavish*); Rod La Rocque (*Dan McTavish*); Leatrice Joe (*Mary Leigh*); Nita Naldi (*Sally Lung*); Edythe Chapman (*Martha McTavish*); Robert Edeson (*Redding*); Charles Ogle (*the Doctor*); Agnes Ayres (*the Outcast*).

TILL THE CLOUDS ROLL BY (United Artists) Director: Victor Fleming

Douglas Fairbanks (*the young man*); Kathleen Clifford (*his fiancée*); Ralph Lewis (*his uncle*); Frank Campeau (*the jilted villain*); Bull Montana (*the man in the nightmare*).

TOL'ABLE DAVID (Inspiration-First National) Director: Henry King

Richard Barthelmess (*David Kinemon*); Warner Richmond (*Allen Kinemon*); Ernest Torrence (*Luke Hatburn*); Gladys Hulette (*Esther Hatburn*); Edmund Gurney (*Hunter Kinemon*); Lawrence Eddinger (*Senator Gault*); Forrest Robinson (*Grandpa Hatburn*); Walter P. Lewis (*Iscar Hatburn*); Ralph Yearsley (*Saul Hatburn*); Harry Hallam (*the Doctor*); Marion Abbott (*Mother Kinemon*); Patterson Dial (*Rose Kinemon*); Lassie, the dog (*Racket*).

WAY DOWN EAST (Griffith-United Artists) Director: D.W. Griffith
Lillian Gish (*Anna Moore*); Richard Barthelmess (*David Bartlett*); Lowell Sherman (*Lennox Sanderson*); Burr McIntosh (*Squire Bartlett*); Kate Bruce (*Mother Bartlett*); Mary Hay (*Kate*); Creighton Hale (*the Professor*); Emily Fitzroy (*Maria Poole*); Porter Strong (*Seth Holcomb*); George Neville (*constable*); Edgar Nelson (*Hi Holler*).

WHAT PRICE GLORY? (Fox) Director: Raoul Walsh
Victor McLaglen (*Captain Flagg*); Edmund Lowe (*Sergeant Quirt*); Dolores del Rio (*Charmaine*); William V. Mong (*Cognac Pete*); Phyllis Haver (*Shanghai Mabel*); Elena Jurado (*Carmen*); Leslie Fenton (*Lieutenant Moore*); Barry Norton (*Private Lewisohn*); Sammy Cohen (*Private Pipinsky*); Ted McNamara (*Private Kiper*); August Tollaire (*French mayor*); Jack Pennick (*a private*).

WHITE GOLD (Prod. Dist. Corp.) Director: William K. Howard
Jetta Goudal (*Dolores Carson*); Kenneth Thompson (*Alec Carson*); George Bancroft (*Sam Randall*); George Nichols (*Alec's father*); Robert Perry (*Bucky O'Neil*); Clyde Cook (*Homer*).

WHITE SHADOWS IN THE SOUTH SEAS (M-G-M) Director: W. S. Van Dyke
Monte Blue (*Dr. Matthew Lloyd*); Racquel Torres (*Fayaway*); Robert Anderson (*Sebastian*); Renee Bush (*Lucy*).

WINGS (Paramount) Director: William A. Wellman
Clara Bow (*Mary Preston*); Charles "Buddy" Rogers (*John Powell*); Richard Arlen (*David Armstrong*); El Brendel (*August Schmidt*); Jobyna Ralston (*Sylvia Lewis*); Richard Tucker (*Air Commander*); Gary Cooper (*Cadet White*); Gunboat Smith (*sergeant*); Henry B. Walthall (*Mr. Armstrong*); Julia Swayne Gordon (*Mrs. Armstrong*); Arlette Marchal (*Celeste*); George Irving (*Mr. Powell*); Hedda Hopper (*Mrs. Powell*); Nigel de Brulier (*Peasant*).